'GOODBYE, GREAT BRITAIN'

'GOODBYE, GREAT BRITAIN'

The 1976 IMF Crisis

KATHLEEN BURK & ALEC CAIRNCROSS

YALE UNIVERSITY PRESS

NEW HAVEN & LONDON · 1992

Set in 11/12½ Bembo by SX Composing Ltd, Essex, England
Printed and bound in Great Britain by The Bath Press, Avon

Library of Congress Cataloging-in-Publication Data

Burk, Kathleen.
    Good-bye, Great Britain : the 1976 IMF crisis / Kathleen Burk &
Alec Cairncross.
        p.   cm.
    Includes bibliographical references and index.
    ISBN 0–300–05728–8
    1. Monetary policy—Great Britain.   2. Great Britain—Economic
policy—1945–   3. Great Britain—Politics and
government—1964–1979.   4. International Monetary Fund—Great
Britain.   I. Cairncross, Alec, Sir, 1911-   .   II. Title.
HG939.5.B87   1992
332.4′941—dc20
                                                            91–42929
                                                               CIP

CONTENTS

LIST OF FIGURES

LIST OF TABLES

PREFACE AND ACKNOWLEDGEMENTS

This book was conceived and executed as a joint effort. Nevertheless, readers will probably wish to know that Kathleen Burk was responsible for Part I and Alec Cairncross responsible for Part II.

Kathleen Burk wishes to thank the British Academy for a grant which enabled her to carry out research for the book in the United States. She is grateful for access to the material in the Ford Presidential Library, Ann Arbor, Michigan, and for the help given by the staff. She also wishes to thank Tony Benn for allowing her unrestricted access to his unpublished diaries, and for looking over two of the chapters; Ruth Winstone, the Editor of the published version of the Benn Diaries, was also extremely helpful, giving endless advice on the content and personalities found in Benn's text, and reading two of the chapters. Edmund Dell very kindly allowed her to read his book, *A Hard Pounding: Politics and Economic Crisis 1974–76* (Oxford 1991) in manuscript, and likewise took the time to read and comment on two of the chapters of the current work. She wishes to thank the following for agreeing to be interviewed and, in several cases, for commenting on chapters which drew on their interviews: Stephen Axilrod, Fred Bergsten, David Finch, Andrew Graham, Lord Lever, Sir Kit McMahon, Sir Derek Mitchell, Scott Pardee, Sir Leo Pliatzky, Dr Karl-Otto Pöhl, Dr Wolfgang Rieke, Sir William Ryrie, Sir Alan Whittome, Jeremy Wormell and an American Anonymous.

Alec Cairncross wishes to thank David Worswick for commenting on his chapters; the Bank of England and particularly Peter Bull for assistance in interpreting balance of payments statistics; and the Central Statistical Office and particularly E. A. Doggett for providing up-to-date estimates of the PSBR and PSFD. He is also grateful to Sir Douglas Henley and Harold Copeman for guidance on the development of cash limits. Both authors thank Sir Bryan Hopkin for commenting on selected chapters, and Jeremy Wormell for taking the time to read and comment extensively – and most helpfully – on the entire manuscript. They also wish to thank Stephen Fay, Hugo Young and *The Sunday Times* for permission to quote from three articles which appeared in that newspaper in May 1978, and the Controller of Her Majesty's Stationery Office for permission to reproduce as an Appendix the letter of the Chancellor of the Exchequer of 15 December 1976.

Harwell and Oxford
November 1991

INTRODUCTION

'Goodbye, Great Britain'

The IMF crisis that hit Britain in 1976 had as its focus the request by the Labour government for a loan from the IMF and the negotiations that followed over conditions for such a loan. It was no ordinary crisis. There had been plenty of those over the thirty years after the war, usually associated with the balance of payments and hardly noticed by the mass of the population except when the pound was devalued or allowed to float. There had been a crisis of a different kind at the end of 1973 with a miners' strike and a three-day week, followed by an election fought by the Conservatives under Edward Heath on the issue 'Who Governs Britain?'. The election brought Labour to power without an overall majority and the strike was settled soon afterwards. That was indeed a crisis that came home to the public, just as did the winter of discontent in 1978–79, when strikes multiplied, inflation took hold again, and Labour lost office.

The events of 1976 were less traumatic but had a deeper and more lasting impact. The crisis was one of ideology and priorities. It was a watershed in postwar economic policy in which the postwar consensus on how the economy should be managed broke down, full employment ceased to be the overriding object of policy, and control of inflation became the abiding preoccupation of government. The 'searing experience' of the older generation had been unemployment; for the younger generation it had become inflation.[1]

Not only so, but the causes of inflation and the policies required for its control came to be seen by many in a way that, while not new, was very different from the one prevalent in postwar years. Inflation in those years had been attributed either to excess demand or to cost-push (that is, rising wage costs or raw material prices); now it was attributed by economists labelled 'monetarists' to an excess of money. Control of the money supply rather than control of demand was the remedy for inflation, and monetary policy, rather than budgetary policy and government spending, was the instrument to be used. But since many people use the word 'money' to mean 'purchasing power' and identify too much money with too much demand or spending, this shift of emphasis was not always grasped.

The dispute between monetarists and Keynesian economists was partly over the priority to be attached to maintaining employment as against keeping prices stable and partly over the technique appropriate to securing either of those objectives. It was a dispute at the very heart of economic policy and extended far beyond the ranks of professional economists. Politicians, journalists, bankers and others all joined in, whether they understood the technicalities or not, asserting their views with all the more vehemence the less familiar they were with the literature on the subject.

The conflict of ideas between economists of the older, Keynesian, school and economists holding monetarist or quasi-monetarist views came to a head in the 1970s and was at its height in 1976. Keynesian economists were accused of having no adequate explanation of inflation and of treating it too lightly. It is true that they did not look to monetary policy as a cure for inflation although they agreed, as a rule, that it could contribute to keeping inflation under control. They thought of it as affecting the cost of borrowed funds rather than the stock of money and differed among themselves as to how soon, and how much, changes in the cost of borrowing would affect demand, and through demand, prices and employment. Monetarist ideas went back to the centuries-old quantity theory of money which made the value of money, like the value of other things, depend on how much there was of it. Neo-Keynesians, on the other hand, pointed out that governments had little direct influence on the stock of money and that interest rates, which they did influence, usually had a more powerful effect on the foreign exchanges than on domestic prices and activity, especially if exchange rates were fixed.

We discuss in Chapter 5 the shift in opinion that occurred in the 1970s. We deal briefly with the merits of the different views and explain why a decisive change occurred in 1976. It is no part of our argument that the truth prevailed and false doctrines were rejected. Indeed, whatever the limitations of the older ideas, we think the newer, monetarist, ideas to be largely mistaken. But the circumstances in 1976 were such that the government was obliged to take urgent action to reassure financial markets that the money supply was under control. For the first time ever, the government publicly announced a target for the money supply in July 1976: an increase of 12 per cent in the financial year 1976–77 in what was described as 'broad money' £M3.[2] This not only signalled that a new importance was attached to changes in the money supply but also circumscribed the government's freedom to finance public expenditure by borrowing from the banks.

The announcement of a monetary target was only one of a number of steps taken by the government in 1975–76 to counter inflation and satisfy financial markets that were increasingly imbued with monetarist ideas. Distrust in government policy, which was not confined to financial markets, arose from a sense that the economy was out of control. The balance of payments had been plunged into deficit by the sharp rise in import prices in 1973 followed by the fourfold increase in oil prices at the end of the year; the money supply (£M3) had been swollen by 50 per cent in the last two years of the Heath government; the Budget was in heavy and growing deficit; wages, by the spring of 1975, were rising at well over 30 per cent per annum. No wonder a chorus of dismay in the financial press greeted Denis Healey's fourth Budget on 15 April 1975, providing for a record public sector borrowing requirement (PSBR) of £9 billion or nearly 9 per cent of GDP at market prices. Commentators denounced borrowing on this scale as profligate and inflationary. Public spending (as measured at that time) would be just under 60 per cent of GDP in 1975–76 but 'by now,' *The Economist* declared on 19 April 1975, 'official estimates of public expenditure are regarded as works of fiction.'[3]

How was it, *The Economist* asked, that in spite of this outpouring of public money the economy was expected to slide deeper into recession in 1975–76? Instead of giving the obvious answer that, as in every industrial country, stocks were running down and would eventually cease to run down, *The Economist* put the blame on inflation. 'As the rate of inflation accelerates,' it argued, 'it is not sufficient that the public sector's expenditure should rise. The rate at which it increases must also go up if employment is not to come down' – an attractive but doubtful proposition since employment varies not with public expenditure but with the margin between expenditure and revenue (which also rises with inflation). 'If the government had to finance every increase in wages to defeat unemployment,' *The Economist* went on, 'the end-product would be hyperinflation' – a proposition implying that government spending went on raising wages rather than on more jobs.[4]

The views of *The Economist* were echoed in the *Wall Street Journal* on 29 April 1975 in a leading article entitled 'Goodbye, Great Britain'. This article, which made a great impression on British financial opinion, advised readers that 'the British government is now so clearly headed towards a policy of total confiscation that anyone who has any wealth left is discounting furiously [*sic*] at any chance to get it out of the country', adding that 'a Briton earning $24,000 this year will have to get a pay rise of $9,600 merely to maintain his purchasing power'. It was only 'by some mad twist of logic' that the Budget could be praised as 'brave', 'courageous' and 'mildly deflationary' when it 'imposed another $3 billion in taxes on an economy whose chief problem is that it is already strangling on taxes'. Britain had revealed 'the ultimate result of economic and social policies rapidly gaining ascendancy in the United States' – policies giving effect to 'the welfare state – manic-Keynesian syndrome'. In waving goodbye to a sinking economy, the United States, 'by following down the same road', could expect to meet it again later.[5]

Whatever the merits of the rhetoric, the article was not one to encourage lending to the United Kingdom, then in heavy external deficit. In the absence of such lending the country would be forced into extreme courses such as savage deflation or widespread import restrictions – both of them courses that were later urged on the government, the first by the Conservatives and the second by the left wing of the Labour Party. Neither *The Economist* nor the *Wall Street Journal* gave much prominence to monetary policy (no doubt because in the spring of 1975 the demand for bank funds was sluggish and the money supply rising relatively slowly). Stress on the money supply did, however, grow with the size of the government's borrowing requirement, as its efforts to borrow ran up against the hesitations of financial markets over the prospect of continuing inflation. As *The Economist* warned, 'enthusiasm for long-dated gilts [i.e. government bonds] is not going to revive until Mr Healey gives some clear indication that he intends to curb wage inflation or signs a letter of intent to the IMF, or both'.[6]

Other commentators after the 1975 Budget took a more robust view of the government's failure to check inflation. Why, asked *The Banker*, did the government persist in regarding the rise of oil prices as deflationary when it was plainly *inflationary* and had contributed powerfully to a rise in prices averaging 14 per cent in the OECD countries by the time of the IMF meeting in September 1974?[7] Other countries took 'the common sense view' that this must be reduced by deflation. Only the United Kingdom, in a 'uniquely eccentric' effort to sustain world demand, thought it necessary to set a good example by running a large Budget deficit – an allegation which, as we shall see, was quite untrue since there were large Budget deficits all over the world.

Comments such as these were expressive of deep distrust in government policy and it was essentially this distrust that brought on the crisis in 1976, forcing the government, against its will, to seek financial support from the IMF and in the process obtain an implied approval for the policies it was pursuing. We discuss in Chapters 6 and 7 how distrust persisted and how the government, in face of the distrust and an alarming rise in money wages, appeared unable to control public expenditure, the money supply or the exchange rate. There was no complete breakdown of control, but it was necessary to look abroad, in the end to the IMF, to overcome the government's difficulties. Once trust was re-established, at least for a year or two, the situation was transformed. The rate of exchange was stabilised, the Budget deficit fell, the money supply grew slightly faster than before, but largely because of a vast inflow of funds from abroad; and the increase in wages rates, which had already slowed down, continued at a relatively moderate rate until the spring of 1978.

In course of time many of the old problems returned, some of them intensified by the ending of the prolonged postwar boom. There was no lasting transformation in the performance of the economy. In the ten years from 1976 to 1986, as will be seen from Table 1, the national income grew in almost the same proportion as in the previous ten years, productivity in manufacturing a little more slowly, consumer prices at much the same rate. The stock of money rose faster – twice as fast if one takes narrow money (M1) but perceptibly faster also if one takes broad money (£M3). Unemployment continued to rise for nearly the whole of the ten years after 1976 and although the rate of growth in unemployment was actually less than it had been, the absolute increase by 2 million in the second period was more than twice the increase in the first. The rise in average weekly earnings slowed down with the reduction in labour's bargaining power as unemployment increased, and so also (since inflation changed little) did the rise in real wages.

The events of 1976 had more enduring effects on economic policy.

Table 1

*Changes in economic performance between
the decade before and the decade after 1976*

	Percentage increase 1966–76	Percentage increase 1976–86
Gross domestic product	19.7	20.1
Output per head in manufacturing	35.4	33.3
Consumer prices	151	146
Stock of money		
Broad money (£M3)	208	271
Narrow money (M1)	149	290
Unemployment		
(excl. school-leavers)	270	360
Weekly earnings	348	286

Source: National Institute *Economic Review*, various issues.

The lesson that inflation had to be brought under control and could not be disregarded in the interest of maintaining employment was absorbed by ministers and officials alike. It was accepted that there were limits to the public sector deficit that could be readily financed. Monetary targets continued to be announced and monetary policy veered towards monetarist precepts.

So much for the economic significance of 1976. The political aspects of the crisis have an interest of their own which is explored in Chapters 1 to 4. There was, first of all, a domestic aspect in the handling of the crisis by a minority government in danger of being torn apart by its own supporters. The policy pursued by the Labour government was strongly criticised by the Conservatives, who called for cuts in government expenditure on a scale well in excess of what was finally agreed with the IMF. But the Conservatives were closer in outlook to the government than was the left of the Labour Party. A large section of the Party was bitterly opposed to cuts in public expenditure. Many wanted import controls across the board. At the Party conference in Blackpool at the end of September 1976 – the conference to which the Chancellor turned back in alarm instead of joining other finance ministers at the IMF conference in Manila – Clive Jenkins, a leading trade unionist, denounced the government's 'ineffective' control over the outflow of capital, called for stricter control of prices, urged more speed in imposing selective import controls, and moved a resolution, which was carried, proposing that the government should make plans to direct investment into 'socially worthwhile and value-added [*sic*] enterprises'. Such views were widely shared, not confined to a small minority. More extreme re-solutions (which were rejected) called for the restoration of all cuts in public expenditure except those on defence and for 'immediate steps to control inflation by Socialist control of the economy'.[8]

Within the Cabinet itself there were divisions that might have proved fatal to its survival. Anthony Wedgwood Benn, the Secretary of State for Energy, was pushing for an enlarged role for the state in running British industry, opposing cuts and arguing for import con-trols and a siege economy as a solution to the country's problems. Anthony Crosland, the Secretary of State for Foreign Affairs, was also opposed to the cuts asked for by the IMF on the grounds that there was no need to release additional resources when unemploy-ment was so high. Denis Healey, the Chancellor of the Exchequer, did not know at the beginning of December, when negotiations with the IMF were coming to a head, whether he could count on the sup-port of the Prime Minister. James Callaghan, the Prime Minister, was chiefly concerned to find a solution to the sterling balances prob-lem – the danger of large-scale withdrawals of liquid funds from London by foreign monetary authorities – when the immediate and compelling problem was to find the necessary foreign exchange to pay back $1.6 billion on a short-term loan falling due in December.

The Prime Minister and his Cabinet were conscious of the danger of a repetition of the dramatic events of 1931 when the Labour Cabi-net (and Party) split and gave way to a National Government over the cuts in public spending needed in order to satisfy foreign bankers that the United Kingdom was creditworthy. It was recollection of that precedent, and the determination of the Prime Minister to do all in his power to avoid a similar outcome, that ultimately brought un-animous agreement to conditions that satisfied the IMF.

There was also, secondly, an international aspect to the crisis. The *Wall Street Journal* might wave goodbye to a Britain thought to be on the verge of disaster, but friendly governments could not take so detached a view. They disapproved of what they saw as excesses and had scruples about offering assistance if it merely encouraged more riotous behaviour. The drunkard must first be reformed and take the equivalent of the pledge by signing a letter of intent to the IMF. Britain's neighbours were quite willing to advance money in June 1976 for the period of six months normal under such conditions. But

they did so, well aware that repayment in December would be difficult without a change of policies and that in the absence of funds for
repayment the United Kingdom would have little option but to go
to the IMF and accept the IMF's conditions.

The story of the IMF crisis is thus also a case-study in international
relations. It throws light on the way in which the international financial problems of industrial countries are dealt with, how external
pressures impinge on the political and economic structure of a
country in difficulties, what machinery is brought into action, who
advises and who decides on the complex issues involved. Precisely
because it was a crisis, it is easier to obtain material that would otherwise remain secret, to examine in detail the sequence of events and to
pinpoint the forces that determined the outcome.

We begin, then, with a narrative and analysis of the political events
of the crisis. But we are acutely conscious – as were some participants at the time, although not all – that the events had their own
history, and that our account must set out this context. This is what
we do in Chapter 1. We look briefly at the importance of Britain in
the international system: after all, why was the condition of Britain
perceived by other countries, and particularly by the United States,
as so crucial? Secondly, if Britain had to be saved from herself, why
was the IMF the chosen instrument? Thirdly, it is important to remember that the 1976 crisis was merely the latest in a long line of
sterling crises; in particular the episode of the devaluation of 1967,
and its attendant agreement on the sterling balances, was in the
minds of many of the participants, who had been involved in the
earlier events. Lessons were drawn – although not always the same
lessons – and applied in the 1976 and 1977 negotiations. Finally, the
1976 crisis did not blow up out of a clear sky, but was the end result
of decisions taken, or not taken, during the previous six years. In
particular, this was not the first application to the IMF by the Labour
government: two had been made in late 1975. However, the earlier
events determined that the September 1976 application became the
crucial one.

With Chapters 2, 3 and 4 we concentrate largely on the narrative of
events. Beginning with the fall of sterling on 4 March 1974, we trace
in Chapter 2 the attempts of the British government to forestall
crisis, first by a stand-by credit and then by cuts in future public expenditure, until finally the Chancellor was driven to announce the
application for a loan to the IMF on 29 September. In Chapter 3 we
concentrate on the negotiations for a loan, ending with the debate in

the House of Commons on 21 December 1976. In Chapter 4 we focus on the negotiations over the sterling balances, for Callaghan the cause of Britain's economic problems. In this chapter we leave Britain and concentrate on negotiations in Washington and on the Continent, ending with the ambiguous nature of the outcome.

In Part II we move from the political to the economic aspects of the crisis. We deal in Chapter 5 with the climate of opinion, the changes in ideas and priorities, and the bearing of these changes on policy. In Chapter 6 we look at the pressures on the balance of payments to which it was necessary to respond: the fluctuating prospects of the current account; the withdrawals of sterling balances; the resulting external deficit and how it was financed; and the fall in the rate of exchange by nearly one-third within eight months. We then turn in Chapter 7 to the domestic economy and the limitations to the government's control over it, taking first public expenditure and the Budget deficit; then monetary policy and the introduction of a monetary target; and finally, endeavours to limit the rise of money wages. In the final chapter, before drawing conclusions we ask why the crisis should have occurred in 1976 and why other European countries, Italy excepted, escaped an exchange crisis when many of them faced problems similar to those of the United Kingdom.

Our conclusions are stark and simple. First of all, the visit of the IMF was absolutely necessary: governments that wish to borrow money need the confidence of lenders; the British government had lost this confidence, and the imprimatur of the IMF was required for its return. But secondly, the visit of the IMF mission and the agreement made no lasting change either in government or in followers, neither in expectations nor, in due course, in activities. Even the sterling balances refused to die.

PART I

The Politics

CHAPTER 1

What's Past is Prologue

The 1976 IMF crisis was that most quintessential of British events, a sterling crisis, but with a difference: many of those involved who were not British were determined that it was to be the last such, and were prepared to use whatever pressure was necessary to ensure this. Why they – in particular, the Americans – were thus prepared, even eager, is the question which this chapter sets out to answer. There are many themes. First of all, why should other countries care so much what happened to Britain and to sterling? What roles had they played, and perhaps were still playing? Here it is necessary to look briefly at Britain's role in the international system, and in the hearts and minds of the Americans, and at the role sterling played in the international monetary and trading systems. Secondly, what was the role of the International Monetary Fund? Again, it is necessary to look briefly at the early postwar years, when the Americans and then others increasingly looked to the Fund to play a mediating role when pressure had to be applied to sovereign states. Thirdly, and more specifically, attention should be paid to the 1967 devaluation of sterling and the 1968 Basle Arrangement on funding the sterling balances. Many of the same questions arose and, of equal importance, many of the same people were involved in both episodes, if in different positions. And fourthly, the 1976 crisis grew out of the decisions taken on both monetary and fiscal policy by the Conservative government of 1970–74 as well as by Labour governments since March 1974. These decisions were taken in the midst of an international economic crisis over which British governments had little influence and even less control.

First of all, then, why was the condition of Britain seen as so crucial to other states? There were obvious systemic reasons, in particular Britain's membership of NATO and other alliance systems and of the European Community. American officials such as Brent Scowcroft of the National Security Council were reported as fearing that Britain might crouch behind a siege economy and withdraw from NATO and Europe. The Germans, however, believed such fears to be groundless: a high official of the Deutsches Bundesbank was later quoted as saying 'I never accepted these views that the system would collapse. That's a naive view . . . I always asked them [the US] to spell out what they meant by collapse.'[1] Another, perhaps more reasonable, fear was that Britain might slap tighter exchange controls on the pound and, in particular, adopt import controls. As Edwin Yeo, then the Under-Secretary of the US Treasury for Monetary Affairs, later recalled, 'we feared that if a country like Britain blew up, defaulted on its loans, introduced foreign exchange controls and froze convertibility, we could have a real world depression.'[2] This would reverse the progress made towards the American-sponsored ideal of a multilateral, free-trading world fuelled by fully convertible currencies.

There were, however, a number of countries in NATO and in Europe: why did Britain affect Americans emotionally when other countries in difficulties at the same time, such as Portugal and Italy, did not? Here, for good or ill, and however one defines it, the special relationship came into play. There was the language, the common history, what appeared to be the common culture. In truth, the two countries are very different, particularly in vital aspects of their political cultures, and this frequently led even the knowledgeable astray. One example appears to have been the persistent belief that President Ford could 'help' Britain if he wanted to, when in fact the independent power of the American president is much less than that of a British prime minister. But because superficially the two countries appeared to have many traits in common, there was a fear of infection, a fear that it might be 'Goodbye America' as well, if the British disease were not cured at source.[3]

Secondly, other countries were concerned about what happened to Britain because of the role sterling played in the international economy. The end of the First World War had marked the end of the century-long reign of sterling as undisputed Top Currency (in Susan Strange's typology),[4] while in the 1920s London was increasingly supplanted by New York as the world's leading financial centre.[5]

Nevertheless, 1945 still saw the pound sterling an important currency, both for trading purposes (as a 'transaction currency') and for forming part of the official reserves of many countries. Unfortunately for Britain and for the holders of sterling, the thirty years after the war saw repeated sterling crises, frequently although not always stemming from balance of payments deficits. There was the convertibility crisis of July–August 1947, the devaluation of 1949, a crisis in 1951, 1955 and 1957, in 1964 when Labour came to power, again in 1965 and 1966, and then devaluation in 1967. In 1972 the UK joined the European monetary 'snake', only to be forced out less than two months later; in June 1975 the threat of another sterling crisis weakened objections to the adoption of tough 'voluntary' wage controls. In short, sterling crises were a repeated and tedious fact of life.

A substantial proportion of the total stock of sterling was owned outside the UK.[6] One form it took was the so-called sterling balances. The official sterling balances, those owned by other governments and central banks, had ballooned during the Second World War, when payments for war supplies were made in sterling which was retained on deposit in London. The sterling balances can be thought of as current account deposits, able to be withdrawn at any time – and 'withdrawn' would most likely mean sale into gold or other currencies, thereby threatening a sterling crisis. These balances were the source of much anxiety and conflict within Britain during the postwar period. Sometimes the Bank of England supported the retention, and even the building up, of the sterling balances: they were seen as coin with which foreigners could buy British exports, and an addition to the reserves. The reverse of this was that the Bank had to suport the retention of the balances for fear that running them down quickly and unexpectedly would put intolerable pressure on the exchange rate. Because of this threat, the Bank at other times agreed with those, both within the government and without, who perceived the balances primarily as a threat. For years many had seen the solution in 'funding' the balances, which essentially meant to come to an agreement with the holders to exchange them for bonds with a maturity of five to ten years, which would ensure that the sterling would not be unexpectedly dumped on the market.

One who increasingly saw the sterling balances as a threat was James Callaghan, Chancellor of the Exchequer during the sterling crisis in 1967 which had led to devaluation, and Prime Minister during the 1976 crisis. A decision on the sterling balances was tantamount to deciding whether or not Britain would continue to maintain sterling as a reserve currency, with the advantages (as well as the disadvantages) which that entailed. Deciding to maintain the balances meant taking steps to maintain the exchange rate of the pound. For those such as Callaghan whose priorities lay in domestic politics and policy, the price required to maintain the rate, and thereby lessen the threat of a precipitate withdrawal of the balances, was frequently too high. The UK's inflation undermined confidence, threatening to dislodge the balances, and the answer to this appeared to be deflation and higher unemployment. But the main point here is that Britain was a cause for concern because of the balances, since sterling was still an international trading and reserve currency, although one of declining importance.

In an earlier sterling crisis in 1931, rescue attempts were made and coordinated by central banks; after 1945 this task was meant to be taken over by the IMF. But the Fund is no more an independent power than is the Trade Union Congress, the activities of both being constrained by the wishes of their members. International organisations such as the IMF serve chiefly as the instruments for the co-ordination of policy amongst countries who have the main financial resources: 'they reflect power resources more than exercising a significant influence on outcomes'.[7] In the case of the IMF, predominant power was from the outset exercised by the US. She was the largest shareholder, i.e. contributor of funds, with over 33 per cent of the voting power in 1944 (Britain had just under 16 per cent), and even though the American proportion fell over the years, the US retained a veto over most important IMF decisions. Furthermore, geography is important: the headquarters of the Fund is in Washington.

Two important implications arise from this dominating position of the US: conditionality, and the use of the Fund as a surrogate. Conditionality refers to the terms to be imposed on the borrower of funds from or through the IMF. In the earliest years of the IMF most countries other than the US believed that shareholder countries had an automatic right to resources from the Fund in order to allow them to make payments consistent with the purposes of the Fund. The US, on the other hand, from the beginning wanted conditions attached to borrowing; by May 1947 the Executive Board of the Fund, had agreed to reject the idea that a country had an automatic right to draw funds (other than the gold tranche – see below) within the quantitative limitations specified in the Articles setting up the IMF. In 1952 the Board went further and bowed to the insistence of the US that the Fund specifically adopt the principle of conditionality; this was not because other members believed that the principle was vital to a functioning IMF, but because they needed the cooperation of the US as a source of credit.[8]

Each member has a 'quota' in the Fund, which is equal to the member's subscription to the Fund's resources. The subscription is payable partly in gold and partly in the member's own currency, normally 25 per cent in gold and 75 per cent in currency. A 'loan' from the IMF is not, strictly speaking, a loan: it is a transaction by which a member purchases gold and other currencies from the Fund by giving it the equivalent amount of its own currency. The amount a member can draw from the Fund depends on the member's quota, and drawings are divided into tranches. The first tranche, called the gold tranche, is equal to the member's net contribution to the Fund; drawings from the gold tranche are 'immune from challenge'. Tranches beyond the gold tranche are called 'credit tranches'. Ignoring certain special facilities, tranches are measured at intervals of 25 per cent of quota; therefore purchases by a member that increase the Fund's holdings of a member's currency from 100 per cent to 125 per cent of quota fall in the first credit tranche, while purchases which increase the Fund's holdings of said currency from 125 per cent to 150 per cent fall in the second credit tranche, and so on.[9]

Conditionality becomes fiercer as the amount of support required increases. In 1955 it was decided to differentiate between drawings on IMF funds in successive credit tranches. What is called first tranche conditionality has very few restrictions, but the larger the amount required in relation to the member's quota (that is, the amount the country subscribed to the total resources of the Fund), the stronger the justification required of the member in order to borrow.[10] This was to be the main point of conflict between the IMF and the Labour government in 1976: Britain's borrowings from the Fund in December 1975 had been on the basis of her gold tranche and of first credit tranche conditionality (see below), but she had thereby used up all that was available to her on easy terms; the fight in 1976 was over the harshness or otherwise of conditions to be required of Britain in exchange for the IMF loan.

It is the need to impose harsh conditions when countries want to borrow the higher tranches of their quotas that makes the role of the IMF as a surrogate for the richer industrial nations part of its remit. Certainly, since the 1950s, the US has consciously used the IMF to try to impose its will in the international monetary arena. The Fund's multilateral character enables it to make suggestions which, if coming directly from the US or other creditors, would be rejected as interference in the affairs of a sovereign state. The influence of the states working through the IMF is enhanced because countries do not turn to the IMF for conditional loans unless there are few alternatives. 'The fact that all credit then becomes unavailable without the IMF seal of approval in the form of an agreed domestic stabilization program aids the IMF in enforcing its conditions and prevents deficit countries from playing off one another.'[11] Therefore the way the US worked through the IMF to try to force Britain to adopt certain policies as a condition for a loan was traditional rather than innovatory; what was more unusual was that the pressure in this case was being put on a rich, industrialised country, and the US made no attempt to dissemble.

It should be noted that there is another way in which the term 'IMF loan' is not strictly correct, in that the IMF does not always have the necessary convertible currencies itself, and must then turn to the central banks and Treasuries of the richer industrial nations. In early 1962 the General Arrangement to Borrow was organised, under which ten countries (the later Group of Ten) agreed to stand ready, under certain conditions, to lend a total of $6 billion to the Fund. The deputies of the finance ministers of the ten countries met, exchanged information, decided whether or not to lend to the Fund, and apportioned the loan amongst themselves.[12] In 1976 the Fund had to borrow currencies from the so-called Group of Ten. Once agreement had been reached between the IMF and Britain in December 1976, it had to be presented to, and accepted by, the representatives of the Group for their acquiescence, and the Group apportioned the necessary sum amongst themselves (plus Switzerland).[13] The IMF has the formal right to call the Group together and to administer the borrowing arrangement, but the Group of Ten plus Switzerland frequently supply a substantial proportion of the money.

This group of richer nations – or more specifically, the governors and officials of their central banks and the finance ministers and their officials – has been of continuing importance in the postwar international political economic system. The constitution of the Group reflects the growth of the Eurocurrency markets from the late 1950s. Fuelled in particular by the Eurodollars flowing abroad through the workings of American foreign and military aid and the investments of multinational companies, this fostered huge and uncontrollable capital flows, as money searched restlessly for a profitable home (preferably one where restrictions were few). The upshot for cur-

rencies, and particularly for sterling and later the dollar, was speculative attacks joining the normal flows. To try and fend off attacks,
or simply to support a currency temporarily weak, the habit grew of
central banks' making stand-by credits available to each other. The
central banks set up a 'swap network' to enable them to issue short-
or medium-term credit lines to each other. A further actor must be
mentioned here, and this is the Bank for International Settlements,
the so-called central bankers' bank. The then president of the BIS, Dr
J. Zijlstra, was instrumental in helping to organise the stand-by (i.e.
short-term) credit extended to Britain in June 1976, while the meeting of the representatives of the Group of Ten who approved the
IMF agreement with Britain met at the BIS in Basle.

In short, then, focusing solely on the IMF as the single opponent
of the British government during the 1976 crisis misses part of the
point. Certainly the agreement with the IMF was vital: without it
there would have been no loan. But the IMF had to ensure that the
conditions upon which it insisted would satisfy its masters, for
equally, without the agreement of the Group of Ten to conditions of
that kind, they would not have funnelled their money through the
IMF into British coffers. The Prime Minister, as a former Chancellor, fully realised where the power lay, and he spent a great deal of
time and energy trying to persuade the German and US governments to influence the IMF to lessen the pressure on Britain. They
could have done so, but they did not to the extent that Callaghan
would have liked. Because it was the IMF imposing the pressure –
that is, a supposedly neutral, certainly multilateral, institution –
Britain was able to accept the interference in domestic political and
financial decision-making which she would not have entertained if
the pressure had been seen formally as coming directly from the US
and Germany.

Many of the same problems and pressures came together in the
episode of the 1967 devaluation of sterling. It is unnecessary to re-
count the events,[14] but in brief, after three years of repeated sterling
crises, which saw the increasing alienation of the Labour government's supporters as all effort appeared to be concentrated on the
support of the exchange rate, and in spite of strong pressure by the
US not to devalue, Britain finally did so in November 1967.

There are several ways in which a direct line runs from the crisis of
1967 to that of 1976. Not least is the fact that a number of the same
people were involved in both. Dr Zijlstra was President of the
Netherlands Central Bank and of the BIS in 1967 as well as 1976; Cal-

laghan, Chancellor of the Exchequer in 1967, was in the firing line
both times; a number of British Treasury officials were involved in
both, although Sir William Ryrie is perhaps unusual in having
changed sides, in a sense: in 1967 he was head of the Treasury's FG
Division, which dealt with foreign currency matters, and he took
part in the management of the 1967 devaluation; in 1976 he was in
Washington as the UK's Executive Director of the IMF. Christopher
McMahon of the Bank of England was involved in negotiations for
both the 1968 and the 1977 sterling balances agreements. Alan Whittome, Deputy Chief Cashier at the Bank of England, had left the
Bank and joined the Fund in 1964; in 1967 he took part in the negotiations for the standy-by credit from the Fund associated with the
devaluation, while in 1976 he led the IMF mission to London. A
number of the officials of the Federal Reserve in the US and in the
Bundesbank were career finance officials involved in both 1967 and
1976 and, indeed, in other sterling crises before and in between. One
American official, Scott Pardee, has emphasised that by 1976 many
on the American side had decided that Britain had to make some
fundamental changes, because they were sick of sterling crises.[15]

A second thread links the question of conditions to be imposed in
1967 and 1976. In November 1967, when the UK devalued, the Fund
approved a stand-by of $1.4 billion. This took the UK far beyond the
first credit tranche and into the uppermost reach of the fourth credit
tranche; accompanying it, in the ordinary course, should have been
stringent conditions. Indeed, from the point of view of some of the
British officials involved, the conditions were stringent. However,
from the point of view of the Fund, the stand-by was approved with
the minimum of conditions, with the result that several of the executive directors from developing countries objected that industrial
countries were getting off much lighter than developing countries;
they called for uniform treatment of members with regard to conditions in stand-by arrangements. Consequently, in September 1968
the Fund decided on policies and procedures which were to be common to all stand-by arrangements: members drawing from the Fund
would have to remain in consultation during the life of the stand-by;
and the borrower would not receive the loan all at once, but in in-
stalments, with certain criteria having to be met to be eligible for
each drawing. In short, all members, when in need, were to be
treated equally.[16]

This message stayed with Fund officials and dominated the
approach of the Fund to Britain. As Alan Whittome, the leader of the

1976 IMF mission to London, later remarked, 'as a result of 1967 the Fund had had to give the most solemn pledges that the Fund would treat all countries alike. Thus when 1976 came we were determined [with regard to] the UK above all that we'd treat her exactly the same as other countries, same credit ceilings, everything.'[17] It was this equality of treatment, which a number of ministers interpreted as the imposition of wrongheaded and shortsighted policies irrelevant to Britain's real problems (regarded as unemployment and the underuse of existing resources), that the British Cabinet objected to most robustly.

The third thread linking the two crises related to the sterling balances, in particular between the 1968 Second Basle Group Arrangement and the 1977 agreement. Even before the devaluation, a number of sterling area countries had begun to run down the sterling component in their official reserves, and this accelerated after November 1967. Again, a decision on what to do about sterling balances – if anything – depended on what part it was believed sterling should continue to play as a reserve currency. Feelings about this began to change in Britain, as a result of repeated exchange rate crises. By mid-1967, repeated criticism both in Britain and abroad had unsettled official opinion and put it on the defensive, the Chancellor, James Callaghan, stating that the world role of sterling was not a 'matter of prestige but a practical matter';[18] the Bank of England for example believed that the habit of 'invoicing in sterling' provided a major advantage for Britain. When moves out of sterling accelerated in 1968, the British government decided to come to agreements with other countries.[19]

The question was, should the role of sterling as a reserve currency be phased out? Should the balances be run down or stabilised? Although Roy Jenkins, then the Chancellor, was quoted as having told Labour MPs in May 1968 that he intended to phase out sterling as a reserve currency,[20] neither the Bank of England nor the Treasury nor the Foreign Office thought this was either necessary or desirable. Beyond the political implications of managing the decline of sterling, it would require that Britain take on substantial long-term debt.[21] So on 25 September 1968 it was announced that twelve central banks and the BIS had come to an agreement to facilitate the stabilisation of balances. The agreement fell into two parts: firstly, the UK guaranteed the dollar value of 90 per cent of each sterling area country's sterling reserves, in return for their undertaking to maintain an agreed minimum proportion of their reserves in sterling; and secondly, the BIS, backed by the twelve central banks, made available to the Bank of England a credit facility of $2 billion to protect the UK reserves from the effects of any decline in the sterling balances of the overseas sterling area below the agreed level. The agreement, which covered both official and private balances, was for three years, with provision for an extension to five.[22]

This agreement stabilised the balances, and the expectation was that by remaining stable against a background of world monetary growth, they would gradually lose their relative importance. The reality, however, was different, in that the agreement seems to have so reassured holders of sterling that the balances increased substantially. As Keegan and Pennant-Rea pointed out, 'the offer of an exchange rate guarantee and good rates of interest, when combined with the subsequent recovery in confidence, were too much: the sterling balances went up again between 1968 and 1972.'[23] The facility remained in force until September 1973, when it was replaced by a six-month unilateral guarantee by the UK on most of the sterling reserves held by the sterling area countries: they would be compensated if the pound should, on average over the six months, fall below $2.42, a costly arrangement for the UK.[24] By 1973 and especially 1974, oil producers in particular were banking their sterling in London – it had to go somewhere – and the government used the balances to help finance the growing balance of payments deficit (see Table 5, p. 171). By the spring of 1976 the official balances were over twice the size they had been in 1968 (£1.8 billion in September 1968, £4 billion in March 1976), and it was the coincidental selling of sterling (wild market rumours attributed it to the Nigerians)[25] on the same morning as the Bank of England sold pounds to buy dollars that triggered off the sterling crisis of 4 March 1976.

What might be called the long-term context of the 1976 crisis, then, included the historical roles both of Britain and of sterling, American perceptions of Britain, the role played by the IMF in international monetary affairs on behalf of the US in particular, and the 1967 devaluation and 1968 sterling balances agreements. Finally, the point must be made that the 1976 crisis did not blow up out of a clear sky: rather, it was the end result of trends in monetary, fiscal and wage policies which had been developing during Edward Heath's 1970–74 Conservative government as well as in the Labour governments of Harold Wilson and James Callaghan since March 1974. Equally important, Britain could not remain untouched by the economic gales blowing worldwide, when the quadrupling of the price of oil following the Yom Kippur war in October 1973 sparked off global stagflation. How Britain reacted to this economic crisis – and the fact that her reaction differed from that of most other industrial countries – was fundamental to the development of events.

The economic causes and effects of these trends are described in some detail in Chapters 6 and 7, with a look at the balance of payments, and at monetary, fiscal and incomes policies. The intention in this chapter is to give a brief outline of their political effects, and of one outcome in particular: the need to turn to the IMF. The application in September 1976 was the third application in less than a year; the end of 1975 saw the other two.

By March 1974, when the new Labour government took office, the oil price had quadrupled, and the international economy was, for a time, knocked into a spin. Countries differed in their approach: as Sir William Ryrie has said, 'we reacted to the crisis by saying, offset the recessionary effects of this tax which is being imposed on us, while others were saying, offset the inflationary effects of this price increase which is being imposed on us.'[26] Sir Douglas Wass, then Permanent Secretary to the Treasury, has set out the strategy the Treasury and the government followed: first of all, to try and persuade other countries that all should maintain aggregate demand and not regard the control of inflation as the primary target; secondly, to let the sterling exchange rate take the strain rather than deflate internally (the pound had been floating since June 1972); and thirdly, to sell gilt-edged stock (government stock) and preserve confidence. Monetary policy was, he has said, a 'cosmetic' instrument, supplementary to the other two.[27]

The main concern of the new Labour government, however, was not economics at all: rather, it was their relationship with the trade unions. There were two main reasons for this. Firstly, they believed that they had lost the 1970 general election partly because of a split between the party and the unions; in addition, they had 'won' the February 1974 general election partly because the public apparently believed that Labour could work with the unions in a way impossible for the Conservatives. Thus, to keep the painfully rebuilt trust between Labour government and unions, the government believed that it had to demonstrate that this time it would keep its manifesto commitments, no matter what the economic cost. The need to keep the support of trade unions and their members was especially acute in the months after the February election: since it was a minority government, a further general election was expected before the end of the year.

There was a darker thread in the relationship between Labour government and unions: fear. Tony Benn recorded in his diary on 21 January 1974 that Callaghan 'expressed his anxiety about the power of the trade unions . . . "They're much too powerful . . . . This is our problem"'. Benn returned to this theme on 5 December 1974, writing that 'Harold [Wilson] is beginning to emerge more strongly as an anti-union man. Jim [Callaghan], of course, has been anti-union for a long time, very frightened by their power.'[28] Andrew Graham, a member of the Prime Minister's Policy Unit in 1974 and 1975, has recalled that there was a real smell of fear in the air, with Labour people in Whitehall and Westminster asking each other which side of the barricades they would join – the miners' or the army's.[29] Thus, there was a confused mixture of motives, an attempt to placate the unions and to keep them under some semblance of control, by means of close consultation on government policies, high public spending and legislation thought to favour their interests, the so-called 'social contract'. Or as one dissident minister put it, through 'letting the buggers have exactly what they want'.[30]

One manifesto commitment had been to 'free collective bargaining', and in July 1974 statutory pay controls were removed. However, the government did more than that, as Gavyn Davies, at that time an economist in the Downing Street Policy Unit, recalled:

we . . . made what I think were two very stupid early mistakes from an economic point of view but which were probably essential politically. The first one was that we honoured the Heath thresholds [in which pay increases were linked automatically to the cost of living] . . . I don't think the thresholds would have ever been thought of had the government then known that the oil prices and commodity prices would sky-rocket. The Labour government came to office pledged to honour them and decided very quickly thereafter to honour them. That, I think, gave a tremendous twist to the inflationary spiral . . . . Secondly, we either honoured comparability agreements in the public services or added to them between the two 1974 elections as a vote-winning or vote-preserving idea which greatly increased public service pay . . . [It] seems to me that those two decisions by the Labour government added to the inflation rate between 5 and 10% points during 1974 to take it to its peak of 27%.[31]

Certain members of the Labour Cabinet, such as Barbara Castle, Secretary of State for Health and Social Security, cultivated the concept of the 'social wage'. This term encompassed spending on personal public goods – pensions, food subsidies, the National Health Service – and the intention was that the working classes would consider this spending as part of their wage packets and thus restrain their own wage demands. Barbara Castle had a phenomenally high success rate in Cabinet in winning agreement to her spending bids – aided by a Chancellor, Denis Healey, who described himself as the most political Chancellor a Labour government had ever had[32] – and her claims, combined with those of other Cabinet ministers, increased public spending by more than 12 per cent over the previous year (see Table 9, p. 189).[33] On 12 November 1974, when Healey presented his Budget, it was revealed that the estimate for the Public Sector Borrowing Requirement (PSBR) for 1974–75 was £6.3 billion, compared with the March 1974 estimate that it would be £2.7 billion.[34] Wage inflation, higher commodity prices, the increase in the money supply and sharply higher public spending all combined to produce by April 1975 a consumer price index that was increasing at an annual rate of nearly 22 per cent (up from over 10 per cent in December 1973), by far the highest rate of inflation amongst the industrial countries.[35]

Alarm bells had begun to ring in the Treasury, and work began in August 1974 under the direction of Sir Douglas Henley on a system of cash limits, to replace earlier arrangements for expenditure control. The amounts sanctioned had hitherto been in volume terms and were automatically adjusted for increases in price, even if the increase was disproportionate, giving the system an inflationary bias. The work on cash limits was coupled with the preparation of an entirely new financial information system, designed to provide an effective mechanism for monitoring observance of the limits. Once this was ready early in 1976 it was possible to extend the system, which had already been imposed on the main building programmes in the public sector in 1974–75 and 1975–76, to cover two-thirds of all public spending.[36] The effect was dramatic. Unknown to all during the whole of 1976, but more obviously in 1977, cash limits brought about a scaling down of public spending, a sharp change in the trend in public expenditure without parallel in the postwar years.[37]

Much of the work on developing the system of cash limits had taken place in 1975, and in that as in other ways that year was a watershed. Perhaps crucial to other developments, the left wing lost the June 1975 referendum on membership of the EEC: having claimed that they alone spoke for the working class, the loss of the vote (by two to one) meant that they also lost the power to insist that their political and economic wishes should dictate the political agenda. Their loss of influence would be manifestly obvious in

December 1976, when the left would be unable to prevent the Cabinet's acceptance of the proposed agreement with the IMF. But their defeat in the referendum, and the disarray in the left which resulted, must also have contributed to the trade unions' willingness to accept a new incomes policy.

Along with public spending, the other element which seemed out of control in 1975 was wage increases. Labour refused to take any powers to control wages by statute, and the only alternative was a voluntary agreement with the unions. Precedents were not encouraging, but by this time certain union leaders had begun to take alarm. At a union rally in Bournemouth early in May 1975 Jack Jones, the General Secretary of the Transport and General Workers' Union, called for wage increases to be made on a flat-rate basis, and Lionel (Len) Murray, then General Secretary of the Trades Union Congress, expressed support for this at the June meeting of the General Council of the TUC. But in early July, according to Jack Jones, the project almost foundered: there was a fall in the exchange rate of the pound and Healey 'panicked'.[38] He made an emergency statement in the House of Commons, proposing a 10 per cent limit on wage increases and the introduction of cash limits in the public sector to cover wage negotiations. This must have encouraged negotiations, with the Treasury's preference for a percentage increase pitted against many union leaders' preference for a flat-rate increase.[39] Agreement to an incomes policy – in the unions' favour – was finally reached on 11 July 1975: a pay limit of £6 per week for those earning less than £8,000 per year. This would in due course have a perceptible constraining effect on wage costs and thus on prices, and consequently on the rate of inflation.

In August there was a special Cabinet meeting at Chequers to discuss public spending priorities, and Healey warned that if spending were not cut, there were three options: import controls, devaluation or a loan from the IMF. Ministers indicated that they preferred the last-named, and tentative discussions were opened with the IMF later that month. In late November 1975 Healey informally approached the Managing Director of the IMF, Johannes Witteveen, with a request to borrow Special Drawing Rights (SDR) 1,000 million [$1.2 billion] under the new oil facility and a stand-by credit for SDR 700 million [$812 million] under first tranche conditionality.

The IMF oil facility had first been set up in 1974 as a short-term measure and, after much discussion, was established again in April 1975. Its remit was to help members of the Fund experiencing difficulty in financing oil imports after the quadrupling of the oil price in 1973 and 1974. The funds for the facility came from IMF borrowings from six of the oil-exporting countries plus several members of the Organisation for Economic Cooperation and Development (OECD).[40] Access to the oil facility would be linked with a drawing by the country from its gold tranche. The intention was to impose moderately strict conditions on an applicant, which were to include the setting-out for the purpose of Fund assessment policies to achieve medium-term solutions to its balance of payments difficulties; the country was also to describe the measures it had taken or proposed to take to conserve oil or to develop alternative sources of energy, although these measures were not subject to the Fund's assessment. The country had also to avoid restrictions on trade and the movement of capital. Yet, as the Fund's historian admits, 'in general, almost no conditionality in the form of macroeconomic policies . . . was attached to drawings made under the oil facility. As drawings under the oil facility were requested and approved, governments presented programs to the Fund, but the Fund did not seriously attempt to see that these programs were implemented', with the exception of the insistence that there be no implementation or intensification of trade and capital restrictions.[41] It is at least possible that the fact that the Fund did not insist on the conditions set out for utilisation of the oil facility misled ministers and officials into assuming that the same leniency would apply in the autumn of 1976.

By December 1975 certain UK economic indicators had improved. The deficit on current account was lower, since the trade balance had improved; this was attributable largely to the drop in world commodity prices and the drop in imports because of lower demand. Furthermore, the surplus on invisibles continued to be large. What had deteriorated was the external payments situation, as oil-producing governments and their citizens began to sell sterling. By 17 December, the day the Chancellor made the formal request to the IMF, the rate for the pound was 30 per cent lower in trade-weighted terms than at the end of 1971.

On 17 December 1975 the UK formally requested the stand-by arrangement from the IMF, whereby the UK would have the right, over a certain period of time, to draw upon a stated credit; the Executive Board considered the requests for that and for access to the oil facility on 31 December. Sir William Ryrie, the UK Executive Director of the IMF, argued that if the cost of imported oil had not gone up, the UK would have had little difficulty in financing its balance of payments deficit. 'Authorities of the United Kingdom,' he said, 'had wanted to avoid Draconian measures to curb their pay-ments deficits, partly because of political differences in the United Kingdom as to how far the authorities ought to go with deflationary policies that increased unemployment and reduced the real income of the work force, and partly in line with the request of [the IMF] in January 1974 for countries to avoid excessive deflation. Hence, U.K. officials were only now, in the latter part of 1975, beginning to take strong domestic measures aimed at correcting payments imbalances.' The Executive Board agreed with the IMF staff's recommendation that the actions of the British government met first-tranche con-ditions for using the oil facility and for the requested stand-by arrangement. On 16 January 1976, then, the UK borrowed the full amount remaining in its gold tranche, SDR 700 million [$812 million]; on 23 January it received SDR 1,000 million [$1.16 billion] under the oil facility; and on 12 May 1976 it received the further SDR 700 million available under the stand-by, the last it could receive under first tranche conditions.[42]

In early 1976 few were worrying about the exchange rate: rather, public spending was the battleground. On the one hand, the Trea-sury had fought to bring it under some semblance of control, by means of cash limits. There was still the problem of new com-mitments assumed by spending ministers, but to curb this was the task of the politicians – the Chancellor and the Chief Secretary to the Treasury – not officials. By February 1976 they had succeeded to the extent that the Public Expenditure White Paper (Cmnd 6393) called roughly for the freezing of public expenditure. Yet this decision, commended by the Treasury and the press, was bitterly attacked by many Labour MPs. The government paid the price for failing to carry its followers and lost the vote on the White Paper in the House of Commons on 10 March; a three-line whip, however, ensured that it won the vote on the Conservative-proposed confidence motion the following night.[43]

By March 1976, in spite of these blips, the Labour government could feel that it had turned a corner. The left-wing minority con-tinued to argue strongly for an alternative strategy, but their strength was not what it had been before the referendum the previous June. For the moderates and right-wingers in the Cabinet, the task now was slowly to reflate in order to utilise productive capacity and re-duce unemployment. They felt that they had made hard decisions and choices, and were now on the path to economic recovery. What they were on the brink of was a major exchange crisis, as a result of which the markets virtually refused to lend money to the government. This combination of crises would ultimately force the government to make a public recantation of some cherished economic and political beliefs. The decision to do so was made all the harder by the belief of many in the Cabinet that the whole exercise was unnecessary – they had already done enough.

CHAPTER 2

The Gathering Storm:
March–September 1976

March to October 1976 saw both an exchange crisis and a growing domestic political crisis. On 4 March the pound began its seemingly inexorable slide in value, a slide which was unintentionally triggered, but not caused, by the Bank of England. The following seven months saw various attempts by the British government to check or arrest this slide or to cope with its consequences, as they provided massive support from the reserves from March onwards, arranged a stand-by credit in early June, introduced a mini-Budget in July, and issued a warning to the Labour Party conference in September. In the end the government had no choice but to turn to the IMF for a loan, and this period ends with the announcement of the application on 30 September 1976.

One theme recurs throughout: the lack of agreement amongst all interested parties in Britain as to whether there was a crisis, and if so, what sort of crisis it was. No institution agreed within itself, neither the Bank of England, nor the Treasury nor the Cabinet. Most officials, and those politicians who paid attention, could agree that there was an exchange rate crisis, but beyond that, consensus broke down. Was it a crisis of the sterling balances, as Callaghan and Lever professed to believe? Was it a crisis over public expenditure, and if so, in which direction: was it too high, as Dell and Mitchell argued, or was it too low, as Crosland and Benn argued? Was it a crisis arising out of mistaken policies or was it primarily caused by ignorance and perverse ideology, whether of overseas politicians and officials (such as the Germans and the Americans) or of the markets, based in the City of London and Wall Street?

The consequence was a lack of agreement on what, if anything, should be done. Should the sterling balances be maintained, or should they be funded and sterling cease to be a reserve currency? Should public expenditure be cut, maintained or increased? Should there be limitations on imports? Should interest rates be raised drastically? Perhaps nothing should be done?

Connected with this is another theme, that of the somewhat optimistic notions of the Cabinet, and perhaps other parts of the government, about what the government could actually do to, or for, or in spite of, the national or world economy. Many seemed to believe in 1976 that the British economy could somehow be sufficiently insulated from the rest of the world to allow it to be reflated even as others were deflating.[1] Equally, some had optimistic expectations as to what they could convince other people (especially other countries) to do or to refrain from doing.

Or again, very little attention was paid in most parts of the government to the markets and their requirements for loaning money: the Cabinet appeared to make little connection, for example, between their own decisions on increasing public expenditure and thus the budget deficit, and the need to persuade financial markets to buy gilts and thereby fund the government's plans. It is problematical, in fact, whether many in the Cabinet knew, or bothered to consider, where the money had to come from to pay for their expenditure decisions.

The path which led directly to the coming of the IMF mission to London began in early March. On 4 March the pound began to slide against the dollar, but the question of whether it was meant to do so, and if so, who was responsible, has been the focus of some argument. Explanations have come in stages. One of the earliest, in fact, was a short American account which apparently went almost wholly unnoticed in Britain outside of the Treasury. This was a staff report prepared for the US Senate Committee on Foreign Relations and published in March 1977. Remarkably accurate in many respects, the report's comment that 'the pound's depreciation was not the result of any deliberate action on the part of the British government – although it welcomed the initial drop in the exchange rate'[2] had virtually no influence on the subsequent discussion about who was responsible.

The earliest widely noticed contribution was 'The Day the £ Nearly Died', researched and written by Stephen Fay and Hugo Young, and published in three parts in *The Sunday Times* in May

1978. This was based on newspaper clippings and interviews, and all subsequent published accounts have incorporated, or at least taken account of, their evidence and arguments.

Their argument is that Sir Douglas Wass, Permanent Secretary to the Treasury, and the two economic advisers to the Treasury, Sir Bryan Hopkin and Michael Posner, all supported a policy of limited devaluation, and that Wass in particular made the running. Wass believed it impossible to convince the Cabinet either to cut public spending more or to agree to deflate the economy; British exports had been made uncompetitive by wage inflation; the Bank and the Treasury agreed that the pound, then at just over $2, was too high; therefore, if the pound floated down just a bit, British exports would be cheaper, and this would encourage an export-led recovery. Arguing against this course were Sir Derek Mitchell, Second Permanent Secretary at the Treasury in charge of overseas finance, and Harold Lever, Chancellor of the Duchy of Lancaster, the Prime Minister's economic and financial adviser in the Cabinet. Lever in particular feared that a devaluation would unleash a run on the sterling balances. According to the authors, the Chancellor, Denis Healey, was gradually drawn intellectually to Wass's policy.

Although Gordon Richardson, the Governor of the Bank of England, agreed that the pound was perhaps too high, the argument continues, he disliked manipulating the currency downwards by market intervention, believing that if there had to be a devaluation it should be done quickly and be accompanied by public spending cuts. Britain did not have substantial enough reserves to withstand the run on the currency that would ensue if a secret manoeuvre became public knowledge.

A Governor, however, must in the end swallow his objections and carry out the instructions of the Chancellor and the Treasury. Therefore, at the beginning of March, according to Fay and Young, the stage was set for the new policy of secret, managed, limited devaluation. Interest rates were to be lowered, in order to render sterling less attractive. The authors argued that in fact, the Bank was fully involved: 'the Bank had a stratagem known as "backing into" devaluation – appearing to fight a fall while covertly seeking it. "We intended to shout 'Rape!' but not loud enough for anyone to hear," said an insider.'[3] But things went awry. On the morning of 4 March there was a flurry in the market, and the sterling rate began to rise; the Bank began quietly to sell pounds to adjust the price down; at the same time other sales were made by others independently; dealers outside the Bank did not realise that this conjunction was accidental and assumed, it is claimed, that the Bank was selling its own currency into a falling market.

The Bank then made a crucial decision. It had already planned to cut the Minimum Lending Rate (MLR) a quarter of a per cent on 5 March, in order to nudge the pound down: should this go ahead? According to Fay and Young, Richardson feared that if they did so, it would come so soon after the fall that the market would realise the authorities' strategy and a gentle fall would turn into a rout: after all, if a government clearly does not believe in its own currency, should anyone else? In the end, after talks with the Treasury and his own advisers, Richardson decided that since the cut in MLR was already so widely rumoured, cancelling it would cause more problems than letting it go ahead. The rate was cut, the market panicked anyway, and the pound fell below \$2 for the first time; within a week it was below \$1.90, effectively a 5 per cent devaluation. Had the fall stopped there, many in the Treasury and some in the Bank would have been pleased, but it did not.[4]

This, then, is how Fay and Young set the scene. William Keegan and R. Pennant-Rea published their book *Who Runs the Economy?* in 1979, and in their chapter on sterling and the balance of payments they largely follow Fay and Young. There is one significant change of emphasis, however, in that they underline the difference between the planned and the unplanned: on 4 March the Bank was not selling sterling on a falling market – it was merely trying to resist a further rise; the planned part of the strategy was the cut in MLR on 5 March. Keegan and Pennant-Rea also add one piece of information: that market sources attributed the selling of sterling on 4 March to Nigeria.[5]

In 1982 Sir Leo Pliatzky, who had been Second Permanent Secretary at the Treasury during 1976, published *Getting and Spending*. His primary responsibility had been for public spending, and thus he had little to say about the events of March, basing his account on Fay and Young, Keegan and Pennant-Rea, and the short account given in the staff report for the US Senate Committee on Foreign Relations. Nevertheless, he did add one piece of information of a technical nature:

The immediate cause which inadvertently triggered off the decline was said to have been a move by the Bank of England to 'cream off' dollars at a particular juncture when the pound was thought to be relatively strong, that is, to take advantage of this situation by offering sterling from the Exchange

Equalisation Account in order to buy a quantity of dollars to augment the foreign exchange reserves held in the EEA.[6]

Pliatzky implicitly, although not explicitly, agreed with Fay and Young when he noted that 'a prevailing economic view in the Treasury favoured progressive depreciation in order to offset the escalation of our domestic industrial costs'.[7]

There the matter essentially rested[8] until the end of the decade, when accounts by some of the principals began to emerge. In 1989 Denis Healey published his memoirs, *The Time of My Life*, but he confined any discussion of his own part in the events of March – or indeed in the events of the whole year – to a minimum. He gave no hint of his own part in any discussions, writing that 'the Treasury was beginning to think that . . . [OPEC funds] were keeping our exchange rate too high for our commercial good, and that a gentle and controlled depreciation was in order. What we got was a rout.' Healey in fact blamed the crisis on the Bank, which, he wrote, 'made two major mistakes. On March 4th, 1976 it sold sterling when the pound was already under pressure, so the markets thought it was trying to push the pound down. Next day it lowered interest rates instead of raising them, thus appearing to confirm the market's suspicions.'[9] This is a particularly unfair charge, given that any lowering of interest rates would have been agreed between the Treasury and the Bank and would certainly have required the Chancellor's approval.[10]

Of rather more interest is the brief testimony of Sir Douglas Wass, given at a conference in Oxford in December 1989 on economic policy from 1974 to 1979. He confirmed that the Bank did not set out to intervene on 4 March to nudge down the pound, but that the fall stemmed from the timing of the transactions with Nigeria. On the other hand, he noted, nothing was said to correct the market's impression. (It is worth pointing out that while no public statement was made, there was clearly some behind-the-scenes briefing of the press, as described below). Nevertheless, a 15 per cent devaluation was seen as part of the Treasury's strategy, if not the Bank's, and there was no subsequent dissent in the Treasury. Indeed, Wass's recollection was that benign neglect was seen as best, since nobody had a better solution. He noted that the Chancellor was not entirely persuaded about a policy of depreciation, and was nervous.

This perception of Healey's nervousness is supported by Edmund Dell, Paymaster-General and, according to Healey himself, 'effectively Deputy Chancellor' 1974–76.[11] Dell has written that 'through-out his Chancellorship, Healey was disinclined to policies involving the depreciation of sterling because of the inflationary consequences', although 'this did not prevent his exploiting any depreciation that occurred against his will by arguing that he was thereby doing British industry a service by increasing its competitiveness. But he disliked tinkering with the exchange rate . . .'.[12] Dell's book, *A Hard Pounding: Politics and Economic Crisis, 1974–76*, published in 1991, while utilising previous accounts, is primarily based on his own ex-periences. While undeniably shaped by Dell's own robust views, it provides a great deal of new information on the period.

One point emphasised by Dell was the intellectual split in the Treasury. This had not been ignored in the *Sunday Times* account, which had focused on those allegedly for and against a managed devaluation in March 1976, and specifically on Wass versus Mitchell. Dell, however, went much further, making it clear that there was little agreement within the Treasury on many aspects of economic policy. The result was that the Treasury was unable satisfactorily to advise the Chancellor.

Healey's disillusion began with his first Budget in March 1974: 'he felt he had been badly advised; on nothing had he received the strong advice a new Chancellor might expect from experienced officials.' Dell believed that the unreal expectations of the new Labour govern-ment 'did not excuse the lame service Healey received and which neither [Dell] nor his colleagues had expected from a Department as highly regarded as the Treasury'.[13] It seems clear in retrospect that the Treasury could not give strong advice because it could not decide within itself what to advise. Dell recounted a meeting of Treasury ministers in October 1975, where Healey revealed that he was very worried about the Treasury's changing and conflicting advice on a whole range of issues; here Dell noted that there was a 'fundamental division' in the Treasury, between what he called deflationist and Keynesian proposals.[14] The disagreement might frequently be over greater or lesser public expenditure, but in early 1976 it could also turn on the question of which policy would lead to reduced costs and increased competitiveness, to greater or lesser unemployment – deflation or a depreciation of the pound.

Talk of depreciation of the currency was much in the air, one of the single most obvious differences between the 1976 crisis and that of 1967. From 1964 to devaluation in November 1967, the Prime Minister had attempted to impose a virtual embargo on the word

'devaluation'; this was meant to prevent the Treasury from discussing the lowering of the rate as an option even within the sanctum of
Great George Street, and it was certainly never to be mentioned to
ministers. Naturally, this prohibition did not entirely work. Treasury officials thought about devaluation all the time in 1966 and 1967
– indeed, there was a Treasury committee on the subject – and Sir
William Armstrong, then Permanent Secretary, ensured that the
devaluation War Book was kept up to date.[15] Furthermore, the Bank
of England engaged in £2,000 million of forward transactions, implying more than idle discussion. Indeed, there was a fair amount of
public discussion. But it hardly dominated the public press as it
seemed to do from March to December 1976.

From 1972, however, the pound was floating, and the determination of the level at which it should float was something over which
honest men could, and did, disagree. Was it better to maintain the
rate if that could be done, which would be less inflationary than the
alternative, or to let it float down? What priority should be given to a
rate which would ensure the retention of the sterling balances, particularly when Kuwait and Saudi Arabia made it clear in June 1975 that
they would remove sterling deposits from London if the pound was
not stabilised at about $2.20?[16] Or should the rate be lower, thereby
increasing industrial competitiveness through lower export prices?

Dell described an attempt by the Treasury to propose a substantial
depreciation in sterling on 28 October 1975: 'the Keynesian leadership in the official Treasury was turning towards depreciation as its
preferred option. With the PSBR threatening to reach £12 billion and
inflation still high, there was a limit to what could be done by re-
flation. Therefore a stimulus via the exchange rate seemed an option
worth examination.' The response of the Chancellor, however,

was scathing . . . He said that if he adopted a policy of depreciation he
would at once have the Governor coming to him to complain that everything was out of control. A policy of deliberate depreciation must take
account of the effect on the holders of the sterling balances, notably Nigeria.
It could turn into a rout . . . Such was Denis's scorn for the Treasury proposal that the meeting broke up without a thorough discussion of the
options.[17]

In due course the Treasury reopened the subject. Early in February
1976 Sir Derek Mitchell, the Second Permanent Secretary, Overseas
Finance, wrote a memorandum for the Chancellor setting out the
implications of encouraging the exchange rate to fall. The memorandum was prepared for a meeting on 13 February between the

Treasury and the Bank, called to discuss whether a depreciation should be engineered.[18] Presumably ministers did not attend. It is probable that the Bank argued strongly against precipitating anything (see below).

It seems clear, then, that there was support in the Treasury in October for a depreciation of the pound as the option to deal with a number of economic problems, and to this extent all of the accounts are correct. It also seems clear that there was continuing discussion about whether depreciation should be 'encouraged'. But this is very far from demonstrating that it was government policy in March, or that a managed depreciation was then carried out. On the other hand, what is not precluded was an acceptance of such a result provoked by others. As Sir Bryan Hopkin, the Chief Economic Adviser to the Treasury from 1974 to 1977, has written,

there was in and around 1976 nothing at all out of the way in the idea of *accepting* a depreciation brought about by the forces of the market – at least up to the point that provided compensation for the excess rate of [Britain's] inflation of costs and prices compared with those of other countries generally. Indeed, it would not be too unfair to say that this *had been* the policy for some years before 1976 . . . [I]t was fairly generally accepted in most circles that thought about it, before March 1976, that a slow, unsteady, downward drift was inevitable, given the differential rate of inflation, and not to be regarded as undesirable.[19]

This is confirmed, although from a slightly different angle, by Sir Christopher McMahon, then Deputy Governor of the Bank. He has recalled that 'there certainly was a battle between those in the Treasury, especially Wass, who were depreciationists and worried about the delay in the rate's coming down, and those in the Bank [especially McMahon himself] who said "don't hurry it, it's dangerous to rush it".' The rate would come down eventually. In the previous year there had been two sharp drops in the rate followed by plateaux, and the Bank realised that this would happen again when the market decided; they should not precipitate anything. Indeed, the Treasury did not purposefully precipitate anything. But what it was doing, according to McMahon, was pushing the Bank into a position where it was being forced to cap the rate so tightly that there was a risk that the market might misinterpret what the Bank was doing.[20]

There are other arguments against the notion that the Treasury and the Bank attempted to initiate a depreciation. First of all, even though a managed depreciation would not be as public or fundamental a reversal of policy as the two post-1945 devaluations had been, the

Prime Minister would surely have had to have been consulted – and particularly Harold Wilson, whose whole career had been bound up, one way and another, with the fate of the pound. According to Bernard Donoughue, the head of his Policy Unit, he was not:

that sterling experience created the most terrible flutter in Downing Street because Wilson was all planned to resign at Easter 1976, which hadn't yet been announced, though the inner core in No. 10 knew. His view was, when sterling started to fall, that he might not be able to resign because he could not go in a sterling crisis as people would think he had been forced to resign. He was extremely neurotic about the currency anyway, so we were very upset and had quite a lot of agitated talks and post mortems on it. There was no doubt that he was unaware and had not been made aware of what was going on in the Treasury and the Bank of England.[21]

Furthermore, the most basic precaution required for a devaluation had not been taken by the Treasury: arranging for the provision of a line of credit from the central banks of the Group of Ten in case something went wrong. This had been done in 1967, and the Treasury knew the drill. Beyond this, it is inconceivable that the Americans would not have been notified if a substantial devaluation had been planned (although it would perhaps not have been considered necessary if a minor lowering of the rate via a reduction in MLR was the end in view).

Dell's account supports and extends this line of argument, pointing out that a planned depreciation would have had 'certain essential characteristics': first of all, a devaluation more substantial than the 5 per cent mentioned by Keegan and Pennant-Rea and by Donoughue as being desired by the government; secondly, more cuts in public expenditure in order to release resources for exports, which was politically impracticable at that point; thirdly, an extension of the incomes policy in order to lower inflation; fourthly, a large international loan; and fifthly, the arrangement of international central bank cooperation in order to defend any new value for sterling. He added,

All these desiderata of a planned devaluation had been discussed in the Treasury and with the Bank of England during the months preceding March 1976. None of these elements were present in March 1976 and two of them would have required stronger political leadership than the Government was then in a position to give. There was no plan and there could be no plan.[22]

Dell, of course, is perfectly correct if the issue was a substantial devaluation on the lines of that of 1967 under Bretton Woods procedures. However, as Hopkin has pointed out, 'his points would have

less validity . . . against a proposal to take advantage of market situa-
tions to nudge the rate down a few per cent at one time and to do it
again some time later'.[23]

So what is there left? The predominant element in the Treasury,
and particularly the Permanent Secretary, welcomed a depreciation
which they saw as helping the UK to regain export competitiveness,
that is, if the domestic value of the currency fell then almost certainly
so would its external value.[24] The Bank of England accepted that a
depreciation was inevitable, but was being forced by the Treasury to
adopt a tactic – a tight capping of the rate – that was too constraining
and liable to misinterpretation by the market. Neither the Treasury
nor the Bank, however, knowingly initiated the fall; nor would they
have been supported in such a move by either the Prime Minister or
the Chancellor, both of whom disliked the idea. To be sure, the
MLR was cut from 9.25 per cent to 9 per cent on 5 March, but the intention was to stimulate investment, not to lower the exchange rate.
Only in retrospect does this particular cut take on so much importance: the Bank had after all been gradually reducing the MLR from
November 1975, when it had stood at 12 per cent. In short, the events
of 4 March were clearly inadvertent: but both Wass and Hopkin in
the Treasury have made it clear that 'Whitehall' did not entirely
deprecate them.[25]

The fall in the rate of the pound presumably stimulated the market
into taking a clear-eyed look at the British economy. The value of
the pound had been gently drifting down, with a depreciation of 10.5
per cent against the dollar and of 14 per cent against the Deutschmark
between the first quarter of 1974 and the fourth quarter of 1975. Considering the news – strikes, inflation at nearly 30 per cent, industrial
decline – it is a bit surprising that the fall was not sharper, but its
value was supported by oil-related capital flows.[26] Indeed, between
October 1975 and early March 1976 the rate was flat. There was a
current account deficit of £1,500 million, but this should not in itself
have been unmanageable – Britain was, after all, about to become an
oil producer – had there been confidence in the country's handling of
its affairs. But the continuing fall in the exchange rate was a measure
of the distrust in financial markets of government policy. Once that
distrust infected first the exchange market and then holders of
sterling, the problem changed: it was no longer how to finance a declining current account deficit, but rather how to raise foreign exchange to replace growing withdrawals of capital. It was for this that
the government was obliged to turn to the IMF.

On Wednesday 3 March, sterling rose by 5 points against the
dollar and the Bank of England was thought to have bought dollars
for the reserves at a rate 15 points above the closing rate for the day.[27]
The following day, according to *The Economist*,

The foreign exchange markets received a large commercial buying order for
pounds from abroad. Rather than let the rate rise . . . the Bank of England
decided to supply the necessary funds to the market. In an unusually ham-
fisted way, the Bank allowed itself to be detected as a seller of sterling in the
market. Its intentions, not surprisingly, were misinterpreted by dealers.
They feared that the Bank was either selling pounds under instructions from
an overseas central bank, such as Nigeria, or that it was carrying out deliberate government policy to make sterling cheaper . . . . The second version
gained much credit abroad. It was carried by the American press on Friday
morning [5 March] and seemed to be fully vindicated when the MLR . . .
fell by ¼ per cent to 9 per cent at the Friday lunch-time fixing.[28]

The *Times*' correspondent, Mervyn Westlake, commenting on the
first selling wave on 4 March, reported that the market was confused
and unable to account for the fall, which at one stage reached 100
points [one cent]. The selling was thought to 'emanate from London'
and was not attributed to an outflow of oil money. There was, however, said to be one big seller of sterling. One possible explanation of
events was the expectation of a further reduction in the MLR while
American rates seemed to be strengthening.[29] Yet some dealers
thought that the authorities might 'not be entirely averse to seeing a
weaker pound' in order to restore the country's competitive
position.

When the MLR was cut by a quarter of a per cent the following
day, Norman Lamont, an Opposition spokesman on consumer
affairs and prices, echoed the same suspicion. 'Everything the
authorities are doing', he declared, 'seems designed to weaken the
pound in the most dramatic way', citing as an example 'a mystifying
cut in the MLR'.[30] The cut had been accompanied by a fall of 320
points in the rate, which was given front-page headlines in *The Times*
as the pound fell below $2. Although it reported speculation that the
Bank was using interest rates deliberately to engineer a fall in sterling, *The Times* thought it unlikely that the authorities 'would act so
clumsily as to initiate a dangerous run on the pound which might get
out of control'; *The Economist*, on the other hand, applauded the 'fortunate mistake' of the Governor in 'engineering the latest devaluation' in order 'to stimulate investment-led recovery' and 'in order
not to stifle the export-led recovery.[31]

The Bank of England's version of events was given in the Bank's *Quarterly Bulletin* for June 1976:

The authorities were reluctant to see any significant appreciation of sterling above [\$2.02] which might prove unsustainable. Thus on 4th March, when a substantial but short-lived demand for sterling appeared in the late morning and early afternoon, it was met by them. By mid-afternoon of that day, however, the dollar was strengthening sharply; and against that abrupt turnaround, the authorities' sales of sterling earlier in the day were misinterpreted by the market. The pound fell below \$2. . . .[32]

There were rumours that the sales of sterling on 4 March had been by or on behalf of Nigeria. On 3 March the UK High Commissioner had had to be withdrawn on the grounds of 'personal unacceptability', and there were rumours that the Bank of England, under instruction from Nigeria to make the necessary sales, had started off the slide in the pound on the 4th by selling £80 million on Nigeria's behalf. On 10 March the Governor of the Nigerian Central Bank announced that the country's foreign exchange reserves had been 'redistributed into various convertible currencies', including Deutschmarks, yen, Swiss francs and American and Canadian dollars, so as to provide a wider range of currencies to match the diversity of Nigeria's trade. This announcement, however, clearly related to transactions over a period of time, not merely over the preceding week. The authorities were also reported on 9 March to be trying to quash the rumours that the fall had been triggered by Nigeria; the Governor, at the monthly meeting of central bankers in Basle, had also sought to discount the rumours.

Meanwhile there was turmoil in the markets. Oil producers receiving substantial revenue payments in sterling on 11 March sold the sterling almost immediately. By that time it was estimated that the Bank had spent about \$500 million in support of the pound. *The Banker* put government support of the market at \$750 million in eleven days and *The Times* estimated the total at \$1 billion in the two weeks following 3 March, with support beginning on Monday 8 March. Other currencies were also in difficulties. Both the lira and the French franc were in trouble, and the French were blaming the Bank of England and the fall in sterling for some of their problems. There was speculation on the Continent, dating back to February, about a possible realignment of currencies within the snake, and the French, Belgian and Danish central banks had all been obliged to intervene. The West German government had already spent Dm 2 billion in February in support of the French franc and was in danger

Figure 1

Sterling – dollar exchange rate, 2–15 March 1976

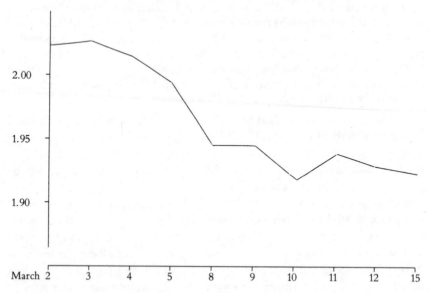

of exceeding its monetary target if it provided further support. By the middle of March France had given up the struggle and withdrawn from the snake.

In view of all the circumstances, it hardly matters who began the slide. By the beginning of March the pound was ripe for a speculative attack just as currency speculation was growing on the Continent. The persistent rise in wages and prices, combined with the step-by-step reduction in interest rates, left sterling vulnerable. There was just too much gunpowder around.

The biggest drop occurred not in the first two days, 4 and 5 March, but on Monday 8 March (see Figure 1), when there was a fall of over 5 cents in the first hour of trading – the sharpest fall since the days when the pound began to float in June 1972. In three days' trading the reduction added up to 8.25 cents and by the end of the week amounted to just under 10 cents, or 5 per cent. The fall on the 8th prompted substantial intervention by the Bank, estimated by Westlake at £50–£75 million. The volume of business, however, was said not to be as large as in previous runs on the pound. Meanwhile no public statement had been made by the authorities, but *The Times* reported that they were 'informally making it clear that they had not deliberately "engineered" the fall in the pound to create an export-led inflation'.[33]

At this point, the left wing of the Parliamentary Labour Party dealt a temporary but public blow to the government's spending plans. The government was a minority one, which made it vulnerable to pressure from its sometime supporters as well as from its opponents. On 10 March there was a debate in the House of Commons on the Public Expenditure White Paper, which had been published in February, and in which the government had set out its plans for cuts of £1,600 million in plans for 1977–78 and £3 billion in earlier plans for 1978–79. The Tribune Group, made up of left-wing MPs, called it a 'White Paper of Shame', and that night thirty-seven members of the group abstained, allowing the government to be defeated by twenty-eight votes. The following day there was a fresh wave of selling, in the course of which the pound fell to $1.91. Next day, however, the pound rose for the first time in six days, thanks no doubt to strong support from the Bank, estimated by Westlake at £100 million or more, and to the success of this government in winning a vote of confidence. The Tribune Group had indeed fallen into line during the previous day's debate on the confidence motion, and thereafter the rate remained fairly strong for a fortnight, but the market saw a government unable to guarantee the support of its own backbench members when cuts in public expenditure were an issue.[34]

This was followed within a week by the news of the Prime Minister's resignation. Wilson had apparently notified Bernard Donoughue and Joe Haines, his Press Secretary, nearly a year earlier[35] that he intended to resign in March 1976, when he would be sixty, and Harold Lever had told James Callaghan of Wilson's plan in late December 1975. By his own account, however, Callaghan did not believe that Wilson would go through with the resignation, and recalled that he had been stunned when Wilson himself told him of his intention (in the car on the way to the vote on the Public Expenditure White Paper on 10 March). Callaghan at least had some notice, a benefit not given to other possible contenders for the leadership. Just before the Cabinet meeting on the following Tuesday, 16 March, Wilson called Callaghan, Ted Short, the Deputy Leader, and Healey to his study and announced the news; the rest of the Cabinet learned of it at the beginning of Cabinet.[36] Thereafter followed a leadership contest which occupied three weeks, and which required three ballots, before Callaghan emerged the winner on 5 April.

Figure 2

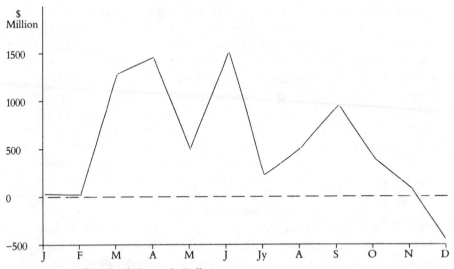

Official financing in 1976

Source: Bank of England *Quarterly Bulletin*

His first visitor was the Chancellor:

he gave me [Callaghan] a report on the prospects for a further pay agreement with the unions [the August 1975 agreement had been for one year
only], . . . warned me that inflation would . . . be increasing over the next
twelve months, and forecast that he would need to restrain the proposed
growth in expenditure for 1977/8. I was shocked when he told me how
much had been spent by the Bank of England to support the sterling exchange rate since 1 January 1976. [See Figure 2.][37]

The Chancellor added that Britain might need to make an approach
to the IMF during the summer to replace the reserves that had been
spent, but Callaghan 'did not fully take on board how significant that
comment was to become'.[38]

The pound had continued to fall. Healey was later to claim that
one-third of the outflow of the reserves was caused by 'leads and
lags'.[39] This refers to the timing of buying and selling sterling. If a
trader needs a foreign currency, he would tend to buy it as soon as
possible, before the drop in the foreign exchange value of the pound
made the foreign currency more expensive; conversely, if he was
going to require sterling, he might put off selling his foreign currency and buying pounds for as long as possible, in the hope that

pounds would fall in value and become cheaper. This undoubtedly happened, but it still left two-thirds of the outflow to be accounted for by a 'wholesale withdrawal from the sterling balances'.[40] Nor was the prognosis good. On 5 April Gavyn Davies of the Policy Unit, 'who had good contacts in the City, reported to [Callaghan] . . . that sterling holders believed a further devaluation of between 5 and 10 per cent in the value of sterling was inevitable . . . . Sterling then stood at $1.84, so a 10 per cent fall would have taken it down to about $1.66 to the pound.'[41]

The only way to stop the slide was to change the perceptions of the market, perhaps by the carrot of a change in government policies and the behaviour of the trade unions, or perhaps by the stick of making it too expensive to speculate in sterling. The latter would work only if some change in market perception could be allied with sufficient reserves to attack. Neither was then likely. The government had perforce to try the carrot, constrained as always by its perception of the reactions of the unions. Healey's budget on 6 April disappointed the market, in that no further cuts in public expenditure were introduced; but he had apparently pinned his faith on a second round of incomes policy to bring down inflation, and this priority meant that he did not want to upset the unions with further cuts.[42]

The priority over the next several weeks was the negotiation of a new incomes policy with the unions. Callaghan himself spoke to Jack Jones, General Secretary of the Transport and General Workers' Union, and probably the most powerful of the union leaders, and to the General Council of the TUC, but it was Healey and Michael Foot, then the Leader of the House of Commons, who carried on the negotiations hour after hour. While these were in process, the Policy Unit warned Callaghan before the end of April that a sterling crisis was highly likely, and that if the next pay round settled at above 5 per cent the government would almost certainly have to go to the IMF and accept its conditions. It is unclear whether this was conveyed in its exact form to Jones and the TUC, but presumably hints were given. At any rate, on 5 May 1976 an agreement between the government and the TUC was announced which set a pay limit running until August 1977 of £2.50 per week or 5 per cent, whichever was higher, with a limit of £4 per week.[43]

Yet the pound continued to fall (Figure 3), and on 12 May the government quietly purchased the final SDR 700 million from the IMF (that is, the UK borrowed $812 million) which had been made available under the stand-by arrangement in December 1975. Indeed,

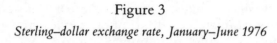

Figure 3

Sterling–dollar exchange rate, January–June 1976

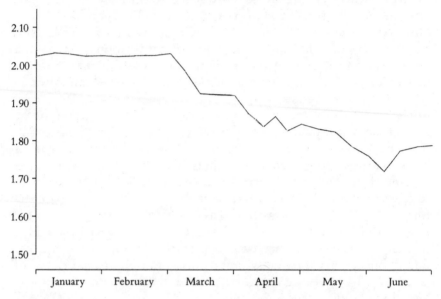

since December the Managing Director of the IMF, Johannes Witteveen, and his staff had kept in 'frequent informal contact' with Healey, the Governor, and other 'high-level financial officials', including Derek Mitchell and Douglas Wass, and of course with William Ryrie, the UK Executive Director of the IMF.[44] Keegan and Pennant-Rea reported that an IMF team visited London in May for a 'routine annual consultation' with the government, and that the view of the Fund was that public expenditure was still too high, as were the projected growth rates for the PSBR, money supply and price indices. Unless there was improvement in these areas, the Fund saw little hope of a revival of private sector confidence.[45] By the beginning of June the pound was hovering around $1.71.

It now occurred separately to a number of people that the time was ripe for a stand-by credit, the existence of which would give confidence to the market in sterling. The arrangement of such a credit was the mechanism by which the American government was brought into the matter, and it ensured that the IMF would in due course be brought in as well. Again, although most accounts agree on the essence of the matter, the story as known can be usefully amplified.

It was made clear in the previous chapter that for some time the

Americans had been concerned about the state of the British economy and in particular about the weakness of sterling. For various reasons, this concern was intensifying. First of all, the administration in Washington was Republican, facing a Labour government. Republicans, however, came in various flavours, so this basic fact need not have precluded sympathy. But in 1976 the three most important figures in this context – the Secretary of the Treasury, his Under-Secretary for Monetary Affairs, and the Chairman of the Governors of the Federal Reserve System – were all extremely conservative. William Simon, the Secretary, was a wealthy New York bond dealer with absolute faith in the market; the Under-Secretary, Edwin Yeo, was a banker from Pittsburgh who believed that national economies have balance sheets just like companies or families, and that likewise they should not spend more than they earn; and the Governor, Arthur Burns, described himself as a 'neanderthal conservative and naturally suspicious of a Labour Government. I thought it was a profligate government.'[46]

In interviews with Fay and Young, Yeo attempted to put his concerns about Britain in context.

In the winter of 1975–76, Yeo saw danger signals, in the wake of quadrupled oil prices, across great tracts of the western world. The economies in peril were marked like earthquake zones on the map – Italy, Portugal, Mexico, with France shaded in more lightly. By far the most ominous of them was Britain. 'To our great dismay,' Yeo [recalled], 'we realised we were going to have a major UK experience ahead.' Britain was not just another economy. . . . 'We feared that if a country like Britain blew up, defaulted on its loans, introduced foreign exchange controls and froze convertibility, we could have a real world depression.

Yeo discussed his fears in late 1975 only with Simon, since if the market had sensed them the result might have been a crisis. But they conditioned his approach in June 1976: ' "Our role", [said] Yeo, "was to persuade the British that the game was over. They had run out of string." '[47]

It was not only the political appointees in the US Treasury who felt this way. The view of Burns has been noted, but others in the American central banking system felt that too much of their time over the years had been devoted to concern about the pound. One such was Scott Pardee, then the Vice-President of the Federal Reserve Bank of New York and the man with responsibility for foreign exchange operations: reflecting both his own feelings and those of his contacts on Wall Street, his reaction to the possibility of yet another stand-by credit for Britain was that 'by this time a lot of people were fed up with sterling crises'.[48] Consequently he would support an attempt to make Britain agree to certain measures as the price for the stand-by.

In general terms, then, the American money men supported a tough line towards Britain, both for Britain's own good and for the good of the international monetary system. Opposed to them, however, were the State Department and, to a certain extent, the President (and his staff). Over the whole of the 1976 crisis the Secretary of State, Henry Kissinger, appears to have tried to mitigate the pressure on Britain, and certainly Callaghan perceived Ford as more ally than enemy. Britain appears to have had a sympathiser in Brent Scowcroft, Ford's National Security Adviser: upon publication of the Public Expenditure White Paper in February 1976, for example, Scowcroft wrote to the Chairman of Ford's Council of Economic Advisers, Alan Greenspan, and to the Director of the Office of Management and Budget, James Lynn, that *As we discussed, it is important to avoid criticism of the British Government's past or present economic policies in any public remarks you may make.* Any such criticism would most certainly be misunderstood and would have an adverse impact on US-British relations.'[49]

It should not be thought that this opposition of Treasury and State was a phenomenon peculiar to the US. Both Alan Greenspan and Karl-Otto Pöhl, then State Secretary in the Finance Ministry in Bonn, have described the camaraderie of finance officials. According to Greenspan, 'It is fascinating to watch them at conferences. The Treasury and Finance Ministers always appear to be on the same side; and the Foreign Ministers line up on the other.'[50] Pöhl has pointed out that at that time,

the Secretaries had a very good relationship – Yeo, Pöhl, Mitchell and Jacques de Larosière, and our Japanese colleague . . . . We met frequently, and I always said we governed the world, because we prepared all of the decisions. I was chairman of the monetary committee of the EEC, so I met Derek [Mitchell] almost three times a month or so.[51]

It is possible that Mitchell's frequent meetings with representatives of governments that believed Britain was travelling down the wrong road contributed to the growing suspicion with which he would be viewed during 1976.

Pöhl's meetings included the monthly meetings of the Group of Four finance deputies. It had been De Larosière's view that, given the importance of exchange rate relationships and the instability of markets, they should keep in close touch. The first meeting of the four was held in February 1976, and the second took place on 19 March 1976, when Yeo, Pöhl, Mitchell and De Larosière (referred to by Yeo in code as Thurber's Dogs) met in London to prepare for the economic summit scheduled for 27 June in Puerto Rico. Before they settled down to their discussion, however, Mitchell had to endure a 'close and suspicious examination' by Yeo and De Larosière of the UK's policies and motives: they suspected that there *had* been an engineered depreciation. Mitchell tried to convince them otherwise by pointing out that between 5 and 19 March the Bank had sold over $1.5 billion to support the rate, an unlikely course of action if it had wished to force the rate down. While presumably accepting this, Yeo nevertheless took the opportunity to outline to the group the fears about Britain then evolving in Washington. Mitchell, according to *The Sunday Times*, 'heard them largely without comment, and returned to Whitehall to tell his political masters', but his own recollection was of a lengthy discussion in which he explained the government's economic and political dilemmas to an unsympathetic audience.[52]

Pressure continued against the pound. The rate of exchange fell by 2.5 cents in the first fortnight of May and then by 10 cents in the next three weeks. On 3 June it touched $1.70, a lower rate than at any time for nearly four months.

Harold Lever later recalled that he

sent to Denis [Healey] a Minute with a copy to the PM, saying that we ought to have a stand-by credit so that we would be able to intervene to save the pound, and that we should get a substantial stand-by credit from the leading countries to this end . . . So, in the end, as things got more [fraught], Denis called a full meeting, the Governor was present, the officials of the Treasury, and I [Lever] put my case. Derek Mitchell, a close personal friend, was there, Gordon Richardson gave a briefing . . . he hypnotised Denis with his bloody eyebrows, I put the case for getting a stand-by credit. Derek Mitchell led the opposition, supported by everyone else there except Denis. Mitchell said [that Lever's] notion that we could get a $3 billion stand-by is . . . bizarre. . . . I turned to Denis and said let me try and I'll get it for you within forty-eight hours. So they all joined in a chorus, including the Governor, that if he [Lever] tries and fails it will leak and start a run on the pound. I said, that seems to be Catch-22 . . . . Denis turned me down.[53]

One interpretation of the event described is that Mitchell, and perhaps others, was so impressed with the strength of American feeling that, failing changes in British policy which he knew would be difficult if not impossible to obtain, he believed that the Americans would refuse to participate in a stand-by.

By the beginning of June, however, the belief was widespread that the pound was now undervalued; if this was the case, a short, sharp shock – such as a sudden rise in its value following upon concerted intervention supported by a substantial credit line – might change the market's perception. More than one version of who initiated the events of the first weekend in June are current. Lever's memory was that 'the whole project of getting the stand-by was opposed by the Governor and the top Treasury officials.'[54] Healey himself has remained silent on this episode, contenting himself in his memoirs with the bare announcement of the credit.[55]

According to Fay and Young, on the morning of Friday 4 June, Richardson spoke to Healey, and the two agreed that Richardson should telephone Burns and sound him out as to the possibility of dollar support for the pound. Burns, temperate in his enthusiasm, suggested that Richardson ask the Europeans as well. That afternoon, apparently fortuitously, Dr Jelle Zijlstra, President of the Netherlands Central Bank and of the BIS, rang Richardson: at $1.71 the pound was surely undervalued, and Britain should stop the rot by buying its own currency. He suggested that he help Richardson to raise a stand-by loan of $5 billion to be announced on the next dealing day, Monday 7 June, and after some hours, the package was agreed: $3.3 billion from European central banks plus the Bank for International Settlements and $2 billion from the US Treasury and the Federal Reserve.[56]

There is a third possibility, this one based partly on interviews, but also on documents from the Burns Papers. McMahon of the Bank remembered that Zijlstra rang Richardson 'out of the blue', and Richardson then rang Burns. According to scribbled notes in Burns's handwriting, Richardson rang him at 12.30 Washington time (5.30 p.m. London time) on Thursday 3 June; 'since then,' Burns wrote on Sunday 6 June, conversation has become increasingly specific and insistent'. Burns was writing to the members of the Federal Reserve Open Market Committee [FOMC], to inform them of what had been agreed and why, and it is clear from his notes that the Americans set out to use the occasion to attempt to force the British to change their policies.[57]

Who first had the idea of the stand-by credit or who was most instrumental in organising it is not all that important. One participant has noted that, in the circumstances, the idea would have occurred to a number of people; furthermore, these credits had been arranged so often before that the process was not difficult.[58] By the evening of Friday 4 June, according to Fay and Young, 'when it was clear that the stand-by credit would be forthcoming, the mood in London was euphoric. The Treasury, which had been sceptical of the idea of a loan, was glad to have it now.'[59]

The mood would change abruptly the following day, when Edwin Yeo of the Treasury and Sam Cross, the US Executive Director of the IMF, arrived in London. The Americans had decided to be tough. It was convenient that the US Treasury and the Fed had roughly the same ends in view, because relations between them are complicated. According to Stephen Axilrod, who in 1976 was in charge of domestic monetary policy at the Federal Reserve Bank of New York, there is a deep distinction in the US (unlike in the UK) between international and domestic monetary policy: the Fed is 'totally and utterly independent when making a domestic monetary policy decision'; not only is there no clearance with the Treasury – to attempt it would cause a constitutional crisis. The international arena is more complicated: here the extent of the Fed's independence is unknown and has not been fully tested, but in practice it is limited. 'The Treasury controls international finance, so [they] could have prevented the stand-by; it required their agreement.' In most other countries, as in the UK, these were matters for the central banks.

According to Axilrod, the Fed has a better legal basis for making independent foreign loans than for intervening in the exchange markets: 'foreign exchange market operations are not so clearly authorised in law and it takes a peculiar interpretation even to permit the Fed to do it. The Fed wouldn't do anything the Treasury didn't want; if the Treasury wants the Fed to do something, the Fed has a little bit of leverage' because it has to get the vote at the Federal Open Market Committee.[60]

The Treasury is constrained in another direction as well, in that in international relations, links between the Treasury and the State Department assume a greater importance – and even more so the re-lationship between the Treasury and the White House. In these cir-cumstances the Treasury has to ensure that the Fed does not under-mine foreign policy because of 'technical considerations'. Axilrod noted, however, that during the Ford administration the Federal Reserve and the New York Federal Reserve Bank were given more

flexibility on technical matters (such as terms of agreements or exchange market interventions) than was the case, for example, during
the Reagan years.[61] Indeed, the relationship between Burns and
President Ford could even be termed a bit peculiar, possibly owing
to the fact that Ford lacked the fundamental self-assurance which
comes from having been elected president (he had succeeded to the
presidency when President Nixon was forced to resign in August
1974).[62] Burns himself has described the relationship: 'Mr Ford . . .
was truly angelic. I met with President Ford frequently, alone in the
privacy of his office. He never inquired about what the Federal Reserve was doing. He never even remotely intimated what the Federal
Reserve should be doing.'[63]

Burns, then, had a good deal of independence, arising from the
traditions of the governorship, his strong personality, his relationship with the President and, in this context, from the fact that the
Treasury wanted his cooperation in moving against the British.
Simon and Yeo decided to use the British need for the stand-by to
force them to change their policies. The American government as
such could not tell the British what to do, but Simon, Yeo and Burns
trusted that the IMF could enforce the financial and political discipline which they believed the British so sorely needed. As Yeo later
said, the Americans 'put up the money "for the bait" – i.e. to hook
the UK economy into IMF control when it had to be repaid'.[64] The
Treasury would need Burns's agreement to its plan, but in this case it
was pushing at an open door. Burns's own inclination was strengthened, if that was necessary, by urgent advice from his subordinates
to impose measures on the British as the price of the stand-by.[65]

Nevertheless, Burns did ensure that the Treasury paid a price for
his cooperation: it had to provide half of the money. Under the
General Arrangement to Borrow (GAB), as agreed by the ten major
industrial countries in 1962, the Bank of England theoretically could
draw on a swap credit (a short-term credit from another central
bank) of $3 billion from the Federal Reserve, and of this they asked
for $2 billion; under the final arrangement the Fed provided $1 billion
and the US Treasury provided $1 billion from the only source it had,
its Equalization Fund. In his notes for a letter to the FOMC Burns
made it clear that this split was his idea, noting that 'I have asked
Treasury to become a partner', and giving as one of his three reasons
[two are illegible] the wish 'to minimize criticisms' of the Federal
Reserve.[66]

The curious nature of this arrangement piqued the curiosity of

Alex Brummer and Hamish McRae, who published the following in the *Guardian* newspaper in London on 9 June:

On Sunday the Governor of the Bank asked Dr Arthur Burns . . . if Britain could activate $2 billions of the $3 billions swap line. Dr Burns felt $1 billion was as far as the Fed was prepared to go, and approached the US Treasury for a contribution. The Treasury chipped in with its $1 billion only after it was clear that if it did not Mr Richardson would not get the $2 billions from the U.S. he was seeking . . . . Why did the Fed refuse? There are at least three possible reasons. First, Britain has been slightly unpopular with the Fed since the late 1960s when Britain allowed one credit, nominally for three months, to run for more than a year. Second, the Fed itself came under fire in Congress in 1971 for the ease with which it had made credit available to foreign governments. And third, individuals in the Fed are anxious that swaps – which are essentially short-term credit – are being used when long-term policies would be more appropriate. The real importance of the Fed refusal, though, is that it demonstrates two things: that although foreign central banks are unanimous that sterling has been undervalued by the market, not all are happy about the UK Government's approach to its problems; and that if the UK want to go back to the Fed for another $2 billions – the amount which is available in theory over and above the latest package – it might get an unhelpful reply.

A copy of this article made it to Burns's desk on the same day, and whether or not the details were correct – and the Chancellor for one denied it[67] – the spirit certainly was.

When Yeo reached London on Saturday 5 June, he went straight to Number 11 Downing Street for talks with Healey and Wass. Speaking for Simon and Burns, he insisted that the stand-by was for three months, with only one renewal possible; in no circumstances would it be extended. (It is worth emphasising that a three-month stand-by with one three-month renewal was absolutely standard, and not a new approach invented by the Americans.) According to Fay and Young, Yeo was escorted through the connecting door to Number 10, there 'to confront a militantly combative Prime Minister'. As Yeo later described the meeting, 'Callaghan tried everything to prevent the six-month time limit . . . . First they didn't want any limit at all. When I wouldn't have that, they wanted a longer limit. And when I wouldn't have that they wanted a long take-down, which means that the six-month period would not begin until they started drawing the money.' When Yeo would not budge, the British began to shift their position to one of emphasising the irrelevance of the six-month condition, and in the end agreed to it. Over the weekend Healey wrote a letter to Simon acknowledging the six-month condition, and promising that if by then Britain could not re-pay what it had used of the stand-by, the government would apply to the IMF for a longer-term loan. Yeo carried the letter, which con-stituted a legal commitment of the British government, back to Washington with him.[68]

It can be argued that there was a certain amount of over-dramatisa-tion here, whether by Yeo or by *The Sunday Times*. McMahon has emphasised that stand-bys of this nature are central bank arrange-ments, and those kinds of arrangement are always short term. The condition of turning to the IMF was implicit in the acceptance of the stand-by: the UK's reserves were very low (less than £3 billion, having fallen by 30 per cent between February and April), and if the stand-by was used there would be no means of repaying it other than with a loan from the IMF. Therefore, once the stand-by was utilised, the UK was hooked.[69] It is possible, of course, that even after all of his experience as Chancellor from 1964 to 1967, Callaghan did not realise that central bank stand-bys were always short term; it is more likely that he was testing the boundaries.

From Burns's scribbled notes, the promise to go to the IMF, extracted from the British, was the primary condition of the loan; furthermore, he wanted it to be publicly accepted. Accordingly, when Healey announced the credit to the House of Commons at 3.30 on Monday 7 June, he admitted that 'if any drawing on [the credit] could not otherwise be paid on the due date,' the British Govern-ment would be 'prepared to seek further drawing from the Inter-national Monetary Fund.'[70] He was considerably more disingenuous when he insisted that there were no strings attached to the stand-by, since this statement was open to different interpretations.

First of all, and most obviously, the conditions imposed on the re-newal of the stand-by, although standard operating procedure, were thought by some to constitute a string. On the other hand, to Pardee and others who had been pushing for strong public 'measures' of a monetary or fiscal kind to be attached to the stand-by, there were, disappointingly, no strings.[71] But thirdly, according to Burns's notes, there were 'informal' negotiations, which took place on 5 and 6 June, and 'informal' agreements. First of all, he had a telephone call from Richardson, during which Richardson agreed that the informal agreements were (1) that the government must bring down public expenditure (Burns noting at this point that the take-out [the six-month limit] would force this); and (2) that they must take steps to mop up excess liquidity. Burns clearly felt particularly strongly about the second point, because Healey added the following to his letter of thanks of Burns on 7 June: 'Incidentally, I gather Gordon has now talked to you about your message to me of 6 June. As he has explained, he passed on your views about excess liquidity to me very clearly and I am glad to say that there was no confusion about that.'[72]

While the final negotiations were going on over the Sunday, Pardee talked several times with his contacts in the Bank of England. Subordinates in both banks had been left on the margin during these negotiations, which were being handled at a 'very senior' government-to-government level, and their discussions centred on how the markets should be handled when the agreement was announced. Pardee was in the New York Bank waiting for the text of the agreement, because Burns was eager to have it as soon as possible. It arrived on Sunday evening, and was to be announced on Monday at 10.30 a.m., New York time.[73]

The stand-by credit of $5.3 billion was duly announced on 7 June. It consisted of $1 billion each from the Federal Reserve and the US Treasury, $800 million from the Deutsche Bundesbank, $600 million from the Bank of Japan, $300 million each from the Bank of Canada and the Banque de France, and $1.3 billion from Switzerland and the Bank for International Settlements. According to the IMF, the UK promised that it would impose no import restrictions, in addition to the promise to turn to the IMF if necessary to enable repayment of the stand-by to be completed by 9 December 1976. When the announcement came, Pardee in the New York Federal Reserve Bank, and his counterpart at the Bank of England, Derek Byatt, were ready: there was an open line between the two trading rooms for half an hour, and they worked together, with New York taking the cue from Byatt. The intervention worked, and sterling rallied sharply, gaining 1.5 cents against the dollar to $1.74 (see Figure 3).[74]

The point of the stand-by was to buy time, either (as the Cabinet hoped) to allow the measures already taken to work, or (as the Americans hoped) to allow the British to cut public expenditure and mop up excess liquidity. At the meeting beginning on 27 June of the Group of Seven industrial countries in Puerto Rico, Callaghan tried to convey his sense of political reality to President Ford, while Simon kept up the pressure. According to Fay and Young, Ford and Callaghan were due to meet at San Juan, for which Simon briefed Ford to warn Callaghan that a fundamental shift in British economic policy would be necessary. Callaghan, for his part, planned to emphasise that economics could not be divorced from politics, that

Labour knew that changes were necessary and some had in fact already been made, but that things would take time. The two leaders chatted together for ninety minutes, during which Ford explained that he simply wanted to inform himself.

It was only when they were joined by Healey and Simon that the US Treasury's warning was conveyed to the British. Simon told them that they had a respite of a couple of months, since Europe closed down for August, but that they should not waste the time, thereby implicitly reminding the British of their 'informal' agreements. '"We said the markets were waiting and hoping" . . . "If tough steps haven't been taken to restore confidence in the pound", Simon told the Prime Minister, "it's going to hit the fan after Labor Day."'

In spite of his unvarnished talk, Simon felt in retrospect that the UK did not receive a firm warning: Kissinger was more sympathetic than Simon to Callaghan's political problems (the two were friends from Callaghan's period as Foreign Secretary), and Simon believed that Kissinger muffled his warnings. Certainly they made little impact on Callaghan and Healey: according to Fay and Young, 'they found Yeo and Simon almost totally unbelievable. The two bankers, they concluded, were so Right-wing that they were in danger of falling off the edge.'[75]

Within a fortnight Healey would be deep into a round of public expenditure cuts. During June, according to Healey,

the Conservative press was screaming for cuts in public expenditure; its frenzy was not discouraged by the Treasury's own misleading statement that public spending was taking sixty per cent of Britain's GDP and by the official Treasury forecast, which over-estimated that year's PSBR [for 1976–77] by over £2 billion . . . . The PSBR forecast for 1977/8 also turned out to be much too high, but it was all I had to go on, and it was worrying the markets. I was determined not to go to the IMF for a conditional loan if I could possibly avoid it.[76]

This last was possibly a reference to the repeated arguments of Richardson that the government should now go to the IMF. Dell in fact links the July public expenditure cuts directly with the plight of the pound: 'once more sterling was on a knife edge. In the circumstances the Prime Minister reluctantly accepted advice from the Treasury and the Bank of England that a further round of public expenditure cuts was needed.'[77]

Dell had some sympathy with Healey's frustration with market reaction, noting that there were more grounds for confidence than the markets had shown (see Chapter 7): in his book he points out that there was renewed optimism in British industry, since its liquidity position had become more favourable; there were rapid reductions both in the rate of inflation and in the current account deficit; there was also clear evidence of overseas recovery, which meant export markets for British goods. But 'the market is moved by what it knows', and its perception was that the UK was still running a current account deficit, outflows from the sterling balances would have absorbed the May loan from the IMF, inflation was higher than that of Britain's industrial competitors, the government was too complacent about trade union pressure, public expenditure and the PSBR were too high, and economic management 'was the subject of intense disagreements within the Government accompanied by threats of general import controls and attempts to borrow by menaces'.[78]

On 2 July the Cabinet Committee on Economic Strategy met at Number 10 to consider the situation. The members of the so-called EY Committee included the Prime Minister and the Chancellor; Anthony Crosland, the Secretary of State for Foreign Affairs and a former economics don; Roy Jenkins, the Home Secretary and a former Chancellor; Michael Foot, second to Callaghan in the leadership election, Leader of the House of Commons and darling of the left; Anthony Wedgwood Benn, Secretary of State for Energy; Edmund Dell, now Secretary of State for Trade; and Harold Lever. Healey had not produced a paper for the meeting, but at the request of Callaghan he 'talk[ed] through the matter'. Possibly he informed the Committee of the Treasury forecasts, of the pressure on the exchange rate, and of the call by a section of the Treasury (for example Mitchell) for public expenditure cuts of £3 billion for 1977–78. He may have revealed that he proposed to present a programme of cuts totalling a bit more than £1 billion, since Dell objected to the number, saying that the cuts were not enough and the Chancellor would need more, 'presumably £2 billion cuts'.[79]

One member of the committee, Tony Benn, *had* produced a paper, in which he argued against cuts: firstly, they would lead to unemployment, which would limit growth; secondly, the economy was in recession, and therefore there was plenty of room for expansion – there was no need to cut to make room for it; and thirdly, 'the real solution should be to go to the IMF and to sell them the validity of our policy, get them to agree.' Dell said 'he didn't understand me [Benn] and was amazed when he read my paper, why I should be in love with the IMF and suggest we go and see them now. I replied that I was not in love with £2 billion worth of cuts either.'[80] Crosland argued for the basic strength of the economy, pointing out that the pound was undervalued, and that they had the social contract with the unions. Foot warned about unemployment and its impact; Lever supported the Chancellor.

These positions, staked out on 2 July, would be held for the succeeding months of the crisis, and in some cases beyond. Benn, with the help of one of his political advisers, the economist Francis Cripps, developed what he and others called the 'alternative strategy' (see below), a strategy which would have demanded a rather different view of and approach to Britain's external relations. It failed in the end to convince a sufficient number of Cabinet ministers to be adopted as government policy, and indeed, it slipped rather lightly over a number of difficult problems. But there is no doubt that at this point in the gathering crisis, Benn saw with clarity what would be one of the Cabinet's central problems over the succeeding months: 'I told the meeting that my paper emphasised that the survival of the Government depended on the maintenance of a relationship of confidence both with the TUC and the IMF.'[81]

On Tuesday 6 July, the full Cabinet spent more than three hours discussing the paper submitted by Healey and the Chief Secretary to the Treasury, Joel Barnett: it called for (1) a cut of £1.25 billion in public expenditure, which would reduce the PSBR for 1977–78 and (2) the abolition of the Contingency Reserve (set aside for unforeseen spending requirements), by requiring all the extra spending bids (totalling £1.6 billion) to be constrained within the approved White Paper total by making cuts of equal amount.[82] The two together would come near to the £3 billions' worth of cuts demanded by the Treasury minority and the Governor.[83] According to Benn's diary, 'Denis presented his paper, describing the problem of confidence, playing down the resource argument a little, still making a strong case. He said that it would be fatal to go to the IMF unless we had decided what we wanted to do in advance, which would have to be what they wanted us to do.'[84] It seems clear, then, that the conditions of the stand-by had dictated further public expenditure cuts. The market was nervous and likely to put pressure on the pound; a sustained attack on the pound would require support, which would mean drawing on the stand-by; and the only way a drawing could be repaid by December would be by means of a loan from the IMF.

According to Barnett, on 6 July 'there was then a very serious, but good-tempered, debate'[85] – good-tempered, presumably, because only the principle of making cuts was to be decided: the fight over whose departmental programmes would suffer the cuts would come later. Benn presented his own paper, which he had had Cripps draft after the discussion at the EY Committee on 2 July. This was the first time that the full Cabinet heard Benn set out his 'alternative strategy', but the gist of the argument would be repeatedly advanced over the following months:

I said my alternative was as follows: there should be a normal time for public expenditure surveys, preliminary discussion now and the rest in November; that we should prepare contingency plans to restrict imports to allow us to re-equip our industrial capacity but not import masses of consumer goods; that we should increase the tax on imported good[s], such as oil, alcohol and tobacco; that we must provide a means by which the investment generated by higher profits could be got selectively back into manufacturing industry, which had never happened before and there was no guarantee that it would happen in the future. I concluded that we were in a much stronger position than we realised. The IMF do not want speculation against the pound. They do not want to see the Social Contract break down because they know that if we were replaced by a government that couldn't handle the trade union movement then Britain would become a serious threat to the international monetary system.[86]

Benn had supporters for some of his points, if not for his whole argument: both Shirley Williams, Secretary of State for Prices and Consumer Protection, and Albert Booth, Foot's successor as Secretary of State for Employment, feared the effects of the cuts on the social contract, while David Ennals, Barbara Castle's successor as Secretary of State for Social Services, 'strongly supported' Benn. Jenkins, on the other hand, while complimentary about the paper, 'thought it would be fatal if we drifted through the Autumn with the possibility of a sterling crisis and panic action'. Fred Mulley, Secretary of State for Education, 'said we should do nothing, we always mutilate ourselves unnecessarily, the cuts wouldn't affect us till the Spring, why do anything now? We had to think politically, he said, because if we lose the Election because of all this, the Tories will pick up all the gains.' Eric Varley, Secretary of State for Industry, thought that the unions could be brought to support the Chancellor's strategy if they were told that it was necessary for Labour's industrial strategy; Reg Prentice, the Minister for Overseas Development, also supported Healey. Michael Foot argued against the cuts, while Lever strongly supported them. In the end, after everyone had commented, Callaghan summed up by saying there was a majority for the cuts: now there should be bilateral talks to sort it all out.[87]

The task of deciding on public expenditure cuts falls in the first instance on the Chief Secretary: he carries out the negotiations with the spending ministers, who may not appeal to the Chancellor against him, but only to the Cabinet. As Barnett later wrote, 'if the actual £1 billion decision seems to have been taken comparatively easily, in just one tough Cabinet, there is a world of difference between obtaining the initial agreement on a total, and the final agreement as to how it should be shared between different departmental budgets. The difference in this case spelt much anguish.'[88] He had particular difficulties with Peter Shore, the Secretary of State for the Environment, who controlled very large budgets in the local authority field which Barnett felt were eminently cuttable; Shore appealed to the Cabinet, with some success. Williams also fought hard, in her case against cutting food subsidies.

On 13 July the Prime Minister took the Cabinet through the proposed cuts item by item; but 'this Cabinet did not reach the really tough decisions, and the Prime Minister obviously wanted to "play it long", so as to avoid serious trouble.' The second Cabinet came on Monday 19 July; Cabinets normally do not meet on a Monday, and 'a Cabinet on such a day is always a sure sign of crisis'.[89] There were sessions in both the morning and the evening, at the end of which only a provisional £887 million had been agreed. Further Cabinets followed on 20 and 21 July. 'We still did not finish and we went round and round the same problems.' Eventually,

with a little extra here and there, we were at £954 million, which the Prime Minister was prepared to accept as being near enough. Denis Healey, however, continued to press to get nearer the £1 billion. [He had previously been warned by Mitchell that cuts of £1 billion itself came to too low a figure to satisfy opinion on 22 July,[90] so an even lower figure might have been disastrous.] So we adjourned to a final Cabinet in the evening. Fortunately, this did not last long, as Denis agreed to make up the difference by saying the cuts would 'cut' the estimated Debt Interest by £60 million, getting him over his magical £1 billion. This was something of a subterfuge, but that is how it was done.[91]

The addition at the last moment of a 2 per cent surcharge on employers' National Insurance contributions, which was intended to raise another £1 billion, enabled Healey to report to the House of Commons the following day that £2 billion had been cut from the PSBR for 1977–78, reducing it to £9 billion.

According to Fay and Young, Callaghan, and most other mini-sters, thought it would be enough to stabilise the pound and 'give the economy a firmer base. They also believed that the Labour Party would simply refuse to stomach a single penny more off public spending.' The Americans, however, 'were unimpressed. Although Simon and Yeo made helpful noises in Washington, neither believed the Budget went far enough; Britain's economic problems were not going to be solved by higher taxes.'[92]

Nevertheless, the main goal of the Americans was slowly but surely being accomplished: much earlier than was publicly realised, Britain was turning to the IMF. As noted earlier, Benn in July had argued for going to the IMF and convincing them of the correctness of the government's strategy; by 2 August he was referring to 'the IMF, where we'll have to borrow anyway . . .'. At a meeting of the EY Committee that day, Foot asked what conditions would be im-posed if Britain went to the IMF? According to Benn, 'Denis said we could borrow on existing policy which confirms that his whole idea was to get the conditions agreed by us before he went to the IMF.'[93] As noted above, Healey had made no secret of this to Cabinet.

In fact, by August

U.K. officials and the Fund management and staff were engaged in secret exploratory discussions about a stand-by arrangement. Since U.K. officials expected that they could not deliver the necessary forecasts of economic de-velopments until late October, it seemed to the Fund staff even in August that any stand-by arrangement could not be in place until late December at the earliest. In August and early September, informal discussions took place on possible amounts of an arrangement . . . . An amount of SDR 4,060 million, less the SDR 700 million [$812 million] of the first credit tranche already drawn [in May – see Chapter 1], or SDR 3,360 million [$3.9 billion], could thus be involved.

As the Fund's historian adds, however, 'it was by no means certain . . . that the Executive Board [of the Fund] would approve such a large amount. Much depended on the policy package that could be put together.'[94]

These talks were exploratory because the British government had not yet finally decided that it would have to turn to the IMF – per-haps something would turn up? – or at least had not finally decided when it would have to do so. One Treasury official has noted, how-ever, that over these months there was an increasing sense of in-evitability that Britain would have to apply.[95] The decision was forced by renewed attacks on the pound, and these renewed attacks seem to have been triggered by concerns of a monetary rather than a fiscal nature.

The Chancellor had two separate markets which he had to pacify, the foreign exchange and the gilt-edged markets, who might or might not react similarly to the same stimulus. ('Gilt-edged' is short-hand for public sector debt sold to the non-bank domestic sector, for example to pension funds, insurance companies and private citizens.[96]) Most of the discussion over the months had focused on the foreign exchange market, since the rate of exchange of the pound had, since 5 March, been treated as the public thermometer measuring the health of the economy. A vitally important component was the central monetary authorities of oil-exporting countries, whose sales of sterling (£1.1 billion between March and September 1976) had contributed to the sharp decline in the balances.[97] Much of the attention of the Governor, if not of the Chancellor, was concentrated on maintaining the value of the pound in order to keep the confidence of these and others holders of sterling.

The foreign exchange market had been more or less behaving itself during the summer months, in that, while losses of foreign exchange continued, the rate of exchange had not fallen sharply. The same could not be said of the gilt-edged market. There had effectively been a buyers' strike since early July: sales of tap stock on 17 August were the first for six weeks, with no further sales until the latter part of September (see Table 15, p. 207).[98] According to one account, perhaps the most widely read book in the City during 1976 was Joseph Gold's treatise on IMF conditionality, *The Stand-By Arrangements of the International Monetary Fund*; the market therefore knew what the IMF would demand of the government should they turn to it for a loan. The assumption was widespread that the government would very soon have to do so, and would then have to pay a higher rate of interest for its money. The market sat back and waited.[99] Indeed, anecdotal evidence suggests that the reluctance was as strong in New York as in London: bankers there consulted their friends and contacts in London, and on London's advice refused to buy.[100]

There were strong connections between the willingness of the gilts market to buy, the growth of the money supply, and the rate of inflation. Interest rates were a very important, but not the sole, concern of the market. MLR rose from 9 per cent to 10.5 per cent in April and from 10.5 per cent to 11.5 per cent in May, but still gilt sales declined and their yields rose, the latter an undeniable sign of lack of confidence in government debt. Fear of inflation was one cause,

while another was apprehension about the growth of the money supply (M3). In July the government set a target of 12 per cent growth in
M3, but by the third quarter (July–September) M3 had risen to 17 per
cent per annum,[101] causing general alarm. The buyers' strike in the
gilt market contributed to this, since the growing cash balances held
in lieu of buying gilts constituted part of the money supply.

By September gilts brokers in the City were advising their clients
not to buy: the government would almost certainly have to raise interest rates in September, and buyers should wait.[102] Higher yields,
amongst other measures, were forced on the government during the
month, partly because of stagnation in the gilts market and partly
because of turbulence in the foreign exchange markets. On 1 September the New York Federal Reserve Bank confirmed that, up to 30
June, Britain had drawn about $1.1 billion of the stand-by; according
to Dell, this information strengthened the belief in the market that
Britain would soon have to turn to the IMF.

Meanwhile the drain on the reserves had recommenced. The
policy of the Bank had been to hold the rate at about $1.77 and it had
done so from June to August by utilising the stand-by credit. During
August things had been relatively quiet. Towards the end of the
month, however, market sentiment began to turn against sterling
after an easing of disturbances affecting continental currencies and
fears that a long period of drought might lead to a three-day week in
some sectors of industry. The foreign exchange market was also
alarmed by the money supply figures and by signs of a renewed increase in inflation.

At the beginning of September there was a wave of wildcat strikes
in the motor industry. These combined with fears of a seamen's
strike to stimulate heavy selling of sterling on 7 September, which
continued the following day when the National Executive Committee of the Labour Party announced proposals to nationalise major
banks and insurance companies. On the same day balance of payments estimates for the second quarter were published and showed a
sharp decline in non-resident sterling balances.[103] On 8 September
the National Union of Seamen called a strike. The following day the
Bank stopped supporting the pound – it was estimated that it had
used over $400 million since the beginning of September to maintain
the rate at $1.77[104] – and it fell within minutes, touching $1.735 before
recovering a bit.

According to Callaghan, although the Governor would have preferred to continue supporting the rate, 'the reality was that as soon as

the Bank repaid the $5 billion loan, it simply would not have the re-
sources to sustain sterling at $1.77. This seemed to both the Chancel-
lor and me to be conclusive',[105] and they decided to call a halt. On 9
September they told the Governor to discontinue support –
although, as can be seen from Figure 2, there is evidence that support
was soon resumed.[106] The following day MLR was raised to 13 per
cent and a call for special deposits was made on 16 September,
although neither produced much lasting effect. By 24 September the
pound had fallen by nearly 7 cents in three weeks, in spite of the
settlement of the seamen's strike on 22 September. A short burst of
sales in the gilts market in response to the rise in interest rates soon
petered out. Only when MLR was raised to 15 per cent on 7 October
did the gilts market really come back to life.[107]

Both the Governor and the Chancellor were fearful about what
would happen to the pound once the market realised that the Bank
was no longer supporting it. What seems clear in retrospect was that
no matter what the government did, short of repudiating both its
history and its supporters, the market would continue to demonstrate its total lack of confidence, unless and until an approach was
made to the IMF. The Chancellor and Prime Minister did not look at
the problem in quite that light, however: their concern was to find
the money to repay the stand-by in December and, beyond that, to
finance a balance of payments deficit which the Treasury was apparently estimating at £3 billion for 1977 – a forecast much at
variance with that of the National Institute for Economic and Social
Research, a well-respected independent forecasting body.[108]

The question then becomes, when did the government finally
decide formally to apply to the IMF? Gavyn Davies of the Policy
Unit appears to place it in early September:

The thing was triggered in the end . . . by the drop in the pound which
went back under $1.80.[109] There was also the knowledge that we had only
two 3-month rollover periods on the standby credit. We didn't actually use
much of the standby credit up but we'd come to the end of the first 3-month
period, and . . . Callaghan had been told he wasn't going to get another extension beyond a further 3 months. That was when the decision was
taken.[110]

On the other hand, Fay and Young reported Wass of the Treasury as
believing that, although the UK probably could not avoid going to
the IMF, the rise in the MLR to 13 per cent made the situation much
better and the terms ought not to be too drastic. The implication here
is that the decision had still not been taken by mid-September.

In fact, the only hard evidence is Benn's diary entry for 23 September, in which he described an afternoon meeting of the EY Committee: 'the third item was this whole question of the Chancellor's paper in which he said he'd have to go to the IMF and he might introduce import deposits.' Slightly softer, because no date is given, is Dell's recollection that a week before the Labour Party conference (due to begin on 27 September), Healey warned the EY Committee that a sterling crisis was impending and that the government must quickly apply to the IMF for another loan. This was agreed, but no announcement was made as Healey did not wish it to be known before he attended the annual IMF conference, scheduled for the same week as that of the Labour Party. According to Callaghan, the Cabinet then gave authority for an application to be made to the IMF later in October, although (according to Fay and Young) Healey expected to begin negotiations the following week at the IMF conference in Manila.[111]

Widespread selling of sterling recommenced on Tuesday 28 September just as the Labour Party conference opened. The Chancellor was due to leave for Hong Kong for the Commonwealth Finance Ministers' meeting that morning (he planned to then go on to the IMF meeting in Manila), but when he reached Heathrow airport, the news of the morning's trading in sterling was so appalling – it fell 4.5 cents that day to $1.63 – that he returned to London and rang the Prime Minister at the conference in Blackpool. He told Callaghan that the experts at the Bank were forecasting that sterling would continue to fall a cent a day at least until it reached $1.50, and it might not stop there. In other words, sterling was in free fall (see Figure 4). He said the Bank was considering selling a large number of dollars to support the pound, and he was uncertain whether he should leave for the Far East at that moment. Callaghan was willing that Healey should remain in the UK if he thought that it would help (in fact, it caused panic in the markets for forty-eight hours), but he was not in favour of spending a substantial sum from the reserves to support the rate. Callaghan asked Healey whether a public announcement of the intention to apply to the IMF would steady the rate; if not, he would prefer 'to sweat it out'.[112]

Later that day, Callaghan made his own contribution to steadying the markets with a speech which flashed around the world:

For too long, perhaps ever since the war, we postponed facing up to fundamental choices and fundamental changes in our society and in our economy.

Figure 4

Sterling–dollar exchange rate, July–December 1976

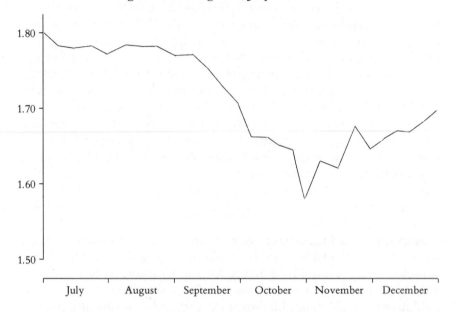

That is what I mean when I say we have been living on borrowed time . . .
We used to think that you could spend your way out of a recession and increase employment by cutting taxes and boosting Government spending. I
tell you in all candour that that option no longer exists, and that insofar as it
ever did exist, it only worked on each occasion since the war by injecting a
bigger dose of inflation into the economy, followed by a higher level of unemployment as the next step.[113]

The reaction to the speech was mixed. Judging from Benn's diary,
it did Callaghan no good at all with the Labour left, but from
Callaghan's point of view at that moment, this was probably more
than balanced by the reaction of the Americans. He rang President
Ford the following day, and the President greeted him with 'Jim,
you made a helluva speech yesterday.'[114] Robert Hormats, the senior
staff economist to the National Security Council, was later quoted as
saying that 'That speech, which was echoed by Healey subsequently,
demonstrated to us that the UK had changed course. Without that
speech it would have been difficult to obtain support in the US. With
it, we could point to a genuine turn-around in thinking in Whitehall
which merited our support.'[115] Callaghan would soon attempt to
mobilise that support.

Meanwhile, at a meeting in the Treasury, Healey and his advisers decided that he should announce his intention to apply to the IMF for a loan, and Callaghan agreed. Johannes Witteveen, Managing Director of the IMF, was informed in advance as he was travelling to Manila; according to the Fund's historian, the absence of Healey and Richardson from Manila 'meant that Mr Witteveen was unable to talk directly to them at that time about the terms of a stand-by arrangement. The lack of frank, face-to-face talks at this stage may have added to the difficulty of later negotiations.[116] The British officials who did attend Manila probably regretted Healey's absence as well, if only because they caught the backlash. The British team was led by Wass, and included Ryrie and Mitchell, as well as McMahon from the Bank of England – no minister was present. Ryrie has recalled that 'I can still remember squirming through a meeting in which Arthur Burns . . . just gave us a hell of a time . . . . The gist of what we were saying was, we need some more money, we need some more time, we need an extension of the stand-by credit, and Burns was saying "no way".' McMahon remembered the meeting as 'appalling'.[117]

On 29 September Healey announced that Britain was applying to the IMF for a stand-by credit. His approach – which he emphasised the following day at Blackpool – was that he was going to the Fund on the basis of 'existing policies'. The chances of an application on this basis being successful were virtually nil. Britain would have to apply on the basis of third tranche conditionality: this would require a full review of her economic policies by Fund specialists and an agreement with the IMF on these policies as a precondition to Fund financing.

But Healey could hardly have been expected to stand up in front of the conference in full cry on 30 September and tell them that, on behalf of Britain, he was prepared to throw over cherished policies in exchange for a handful of dollars. As it was, Benn's reaction to his performance was disgust:

Denis had arrived . . . with a terrific flurry of cameras. There were hisses and boos when he came forward to speak and said, 'I have come from the battlefront.' He then went on to shout and bully and rule out all alternative policies, saying this was the only way forward . . . . The Conference was pretty hostile but when he finished, it having been such a bold and vigorous speech, parts of the Conference cheered him . . . . I couldn't even clap him, his speech was so vulgar and abusive.[118]

And so, at the end of seven months, the Cabinet tacitly admitted defeat and agreed to apply to the IMF for a stand-by credit which could conceivably carry a heavy price. Those outside of Whitehall and Westminster may have inferred that there was no alternative, but the government was hardly bowed under a weight of guilt. On the contrary, a majority in the government believed that the house had been put in order, the policies were correct and only time was needed to demonstrate this – and as in the case of the Group of Ten stand-by in June, the IMF stand-by was intended to buy this time. The IMF, and those with a predominant influence in formulating its policies, intended otherwise.

CHAPTER 3

The Crisis Breaks:
October to December 1976

By October 1976 the British government believed that the crisis was one of confidence, not of fundamentals. The Chancellor had announced that he was going to the IMF on the basis of 'existing policies', and the general, although not unanimous, feeling in the Cabinet was that further cuts in expenditure were unnecessary. What they wanted the IMF to do was to look at the estimates and forecasts, publicly announce that the UK's existing policies were correct and extend the loan. Confidence would then reanimate the market, the exchange rate would stabilise, interest rates could decline, gilts would continue to sell, exports would increase, industry would pick up, unemployment would decline and in due course the Labour government would win the next general election. Only after several weeks of negotiations did the Cabinet accept that things were not going to be that straightforward.

The Prime Minister had an additional goal. Believing as he did that the primary cause of sterling's exchange rate instability was the existence of the sterling balances, he wanted the other industrial countries to agree that they be funded and to help finance the funding; he also hoped to discourage the future use of sterling as a reserve currency. In June he had entertained the hope that such an agreement might preclude the need to turn to the IMF; by November his hope was that such an agreement might be announced simultaneously with that with the IMF; but in the end he had to accept that only after an IMF agreement was secured would discussions on the sterling balances take place.

During October preparations for the coming negotiations were made by all sides. The Treasury in London beavered away at the

National Income Forecast, the basis both for Cabinet spending decisions and the negotiations with the IMF mission; at the same time
Treasury officials went to Washington to try to ascertain just what
the IMF would require. The Chancellor took steps to reduce the
growth of the money supply, which also temporarily stabilised the
pound. The Prime Minister attempted to mobilise international political aid, by trying to convince President Ford and Chancellor
Schmidt that they should do what they could to lighten IMF pressure
on Britain; the US Treasury attempted to counter this.

On 1 November the IMF mission arrived in London. Not a great
deal happened during the following two weeks, but then came a fortnight of intensive discussions between the mission and the Treasury.
At the same time discussions took place in the Cabinet, both offi-
cially within Number 10 and unofficially amongst Cabinet members
of various political hues. By early December the Cabinet had decided
it must accept certain IMF conditions, which included cuts in public
expenditure planned for 1977–79, and the subsequent ten days saw
further painful Cabinet meetings as these were thrashed out. On 15
December the Chancellor announced the results.

The month following the Chancellor's dramatic announcement at
the Labour Party conference on 29 September saw preparations made
and positions staked out by all sides. The Treasury continued the
preliminary talks with the IMF which had begun in August. The
object then had been to try to ascertain just what the IMF would require if an application were made for help; the question was now no
longer hypothetical, and early in September Treasury officials flew
to Washington to continue the talks.[1]

Meanwhile, the Treasury in London worked at drawing up the
National Income Forecast (NIF). This would have had to have been
done in any case, since it would form the basis of the government's
Public Expenditure White Paper: only when the Treasury had estimated the size of revenue could they begin to estimate how much the
government would need to borrow the following year (the PSBR).
There was continuing tension between Treasury officials and ministers over the numbers; as the Chief Secretary to the Treasury has
written, 'one four-hour meeting with officials indicated some disagreement, but all favoured large, if varying, levels of cuts in the
borrowing requirement (PSBR). They thought this should be done
through what I considered politically unrealistic cuts in public expenditure.'[2] Callaghan has noted that the Cabinet were 'restive': just

over two months earlier they had gone through the agony of agreeing to public expenditure cuts, and they assumed that 'what they had
then agreed would put the Government back on course'.[3] Treasury
ministers knew that the fight within Cabinet was going to be difficult enough, without their having to propose a clearly unacceptable
level of cuts.

While the Treasury concentrated on drawing up the NIF, the
Chancellor worked to bring the money supply under control. In the
third quarter of 1976 M3 had increased by 4.2 per cent (as compared
to 1.9 per cent and 2.7 per cent in the first and second quarters respectively); one reason for this was the drop in the sales of debt to the
non-bank domestic sector over the three quarters, from £1,419
million to £1,048 million to £665 million (see Table 15, p. 207).[4] The
Bank of England was very worried, and the Governor advised
Healey to raise the Minimum Lending Rate 2 per cent at one shot to
15 per cent: this would be so attractive a rate that enough gilts could
then be sold to get the money supply under control. (The Governor
also persuaded him that within a year the MLR could be brought
down to 10–12 per cent, the rate of inflation.)[5]

Healey briefed Dell on 1 October, and called him in again on the
6th: according to Healey, Dell was 'the only member of the Cabinet
on whom I could count'.[6] His support was particularly important at
this juncture: as Callaghan told Benn the following day, 'when Denis
came to me last night and said the Bank of England wanted to raise
the MLR 2 per cent today, I said I didn't agree with him and I argued
and argued with him and in the end I said "Well, you can put it to the
Cabinet and I won't support you. You will have to put it on your
own authority."'[7] Healey threatened to resign if the Cabinet failed to
support him. Callaghan let him spin in the wind for a bit, but about 7
p.m. that evening, while Dell was with Healey, Kenneth Stowe,
Callaghan's Principal Private Secretary, put his head around the door
and told Healey that if he was really determined on the rise, he
should go ahead: Callaghan had only been testing his resolve.[8]

The following day, at the meeting of the Cabinet's Economic Strategy (EY) Committee, Healey announced that the Bank of England
wished to raise MLR to 15 per cent. The Treasury was also urging
this, arguing that without such a rise, 'the pound would go down the
drain'. There was no open Cabinet revolt, partly because the Cabinet
does not determine interest rates, partly because the Chancellor had
the reluctant acquiescence of the Prime Minister and partly because
he had the support of some other ministers as well. The reaction in

the market was a rush to buy gilts.[9]

The Prime Minister had agreed to the rise, but he bitterly resented it. He feared that it would jeopardise further economic growth, with rising unemployment as a consequence. Various writers have claimed that from this moment he took control of economic policy.[10] It is unclear just what this might mean: on most major decisions the Chancellor needs the agreement of the Prime Minister in any case, and even if, strictly speaking, he did not, any prudent Chancellor would obtain it. Certainly Callaghan did not stalk through the doors to Number 11 and take over the shop, but he did search for ways to outflank the Treasury. The conviction apparently grew in him that there was a conspiracy between the US and UK Treasuries to use the IMF as a weapon to force undesirable changes in British government policy. (This argues that he did not know the UK Treasury very well, since Sir Douglas Wass, the Permanent Secretary, shared many of Callaghan's beliefs in neo-Keynesian approaches to policy-making.) In any case, Callaghan's response to this 'conspiracy' was to try to mobilise the American and German political leaderships to neutralise the finance ministries.

He had already telephoned President Ford on 30 September, when Ford complimented him on his speech to the Labour Party conference. Callaghan explained that he needed two things: an early indication that a stand-by loan would be forthcoming from the IMF, and a safety net for the sterling balances. Ford 'readily undertook to do everything in his power to be helpful on both matters'. He knew of Healey's intentions to reduce the PSBR and to try to improve the balance of payments, but 'he raised one more serious point': were the British contemplating import restrictions? Callaghan's response was 'not at the moment, but this is the alternative strategy that is being dangled in front of people.' Ford pointed out that the Americans would have reservations, and Callaghan noted that 'if the alternative strategy were adopted it would call into question Britain's role as an Alliance partner which I am anxious to preserve.' This elicited a slightly anxious response, which Callaghan was probably angling for;[11] at any rate, he had planted a fear, which he would try to exploit later in the crisis.

On the same day, Ford received pressure from another front on behalf of the British. This was a letter from George Meany, President of the AFL-CIO, the American equivalent of the TUC: 'The collapse of the exchange value of the pound underscores and reflects the continuing economic and financial crisis faced by America's oldest and most steadfast friend in the world, Great Britain and her people.' Meany then explained the crisis in a manner which would have been wholly acceptable to most of the Cabinet:

That crisis emerges, in large part, from causes beyond the direct control of any policy or program that the United Kingdom, acting alone, can reasonably be expected to follow. Her people have responded to this new common danger in their best tradition and have accepted burdens, conditions and constraints in a manner which warrants general praise rather than carping criticism.

Meany then made the following points: Britain's fate was irrevocably linked with that of the US; the US had to place its strength and resources on the side of Britain; and Ford should declare that the US placed her 'full faith and credit'[12] behind the British people. He urged that the US should proceed, in consultation with the British government, to 'devise and initiate concrete measures in the form of whatever guarantees, loans, or other programs of aid may be required to overcome this emergency and to restore confidence in the future of the British economy'. If possible, the US should work with the other democracies; if not, 'we must nevertheless act, strongly and soon.'[13]

Meany sent a copy of the letter to Callaghan, who was 'immensely moved by this spontaneous expression of goodwill'.[14] As far as one can tell, emotion, and a public statement of support for Britain by the President, was about all that it engendered. Ford's reply to Meany on 2 October gave nothing away:

I have been in close touch with Prime Minister Callaghan on this problem, as have other officials of the Administration with their British counterparts. I have welcomed [his] firm resolve and his decision to begin discussions with the International Monetary Fund. [He] understands that the United States will support an agreement between Great Britain and the Fund. . . . We will continue to work closely with Great Britain in the framework and spirit of the 1975 and 1976 economic summits, and we will coordinate our approach to continued economic growth with the other industrialized democracies.[15]

There was nothing in this letter that could not have been written by Simon or Yeo, a comment both on their strength and on the weakness of the influence of organised labour in the US, particularly on a Republican administration.

Callaghan had continuing faith in Ford's desire and ability to help, writing in his memoirs that 'I never had cause to doubt Gerald Ford's word or his good faith.' His explanation for their ability to work 'so confidently' together was that 'both accepted that the interests of our two countries and of the Alliance transcended political differences'. Unfortunately, as Callaghan writes, when Ford lost the election to Jimmy Carter on 2 November 1976, 'his influence quite naturally waned, at the time when we most needed his help.'[16]

There must have been a further reason. Ford was a Republican president, with very conservative financial and economic advisers, in particular Simon, Yeo and Burns; all of them believed strongly that Britain had to be forced to change her economic policies, and all believed that IMF pressure was required to force it. Thus they were unlikely to transmit requests from the President or his advisers to the IMF to lessen this pressure. Even those advisers whose remit was the political and diplomatic had, as noted in Chapter 2, very great worries about Britain and the British government's policies. In short, all those surrounding Ford believed that Britain could not go on as she had been: they only differed over the extent of the pain required.

Callaghan must have realised this, but he put his faith in Ford's political nous and will. Yet, even if Ford and, say, Kissinger, believed that Britain should be helped in some way, there was little Ford could have done of a tangible nature on his own. The independent power of a president does not approach that of a prime minister – and particularly the power of an unelected president who is then rejected by the electorate. Callaghan was doomed to disappointment later in November, when he sent Harold Lever on a mission to Washington for help.

He seems to have been more successful with the Chancellor of the Federal Republic of Germany, Helmut Schmidt, whom he also rang on 30 September. By one account, Schmidt had 'always had a special relationship with the British Labour Party since his days as a Hamburg politician', and Callaghan appreciated the Schmidt brand of social democracy. Schmidt believed the British economy had deep problems, but he also believed that Callaghan was the 'last best hope' of changing course.[17] Schmidt was in the midst of an election, but if he won, he said, he would come over to London to talk things over, an offer which Callaghan gratefully accepted. He won, and the German Chancellor spent the weekend of 9 and 10 October at Chequers.

Fay and Young reported that Callaghan persuaded Schmidt that the deflation likely to be required by the IMF could destabilise the British political system. Furthermore, public spending was now under tight control: the problem was the money markets, and their antics were bound up with the sterling balances.[18] According to Callaghan, Schmidt had offered friendly advice from the outset. He believed that the trade unions' restraint on pay was a step in the right direction, but he also believed that further steps, unspecified in Callaghan's account, were necessary in budgeting and currency policy. Callaghan of course wanted German help, presumably through the German Executive Director of the IMF, in lessening the anticipated pressure on Britain, but that was a problem which became more acute in November and December. At this point, Callaghan was more concerned about the sterling balances. Accordingly, he asked Schmidt 'what help Germany could give to assist the long-term stability of Britain's overseas sterling holdings'.[19]

In his reply, Schmidt 'unfolded the picture of the German currency reserves. They were largely held in dollars and financed the American deficit, a subject on which he was lengthily and disapprovingly vocal. If Germany were to recall part of her dollar reserves this, together with similar assistance from the United States and one or two other countries, would make it possible to devise a plan that would offset the instability of the sterling overseas balances, and bring much-needed relief. He promised to follow up this idea with the Americans, and did so, but once more,' Callaghan wrote, 'we were foiled on the political front by the hiatus that arose following President Ford's defeat on 2 November.'[20]

On 5 November Callaghan and Schmidt again spoke on the telephone. From this, according to Callaghan,

emerged an unexpected offer that was to be of tremendous reassurance during the difficult weeks that followed . . . Schmidt said he felt Germany must be ready to act when required, in order to make the British Government feel a little more secure. Therefore, on a personal basis, he undertook that if ever an acute danger of necessity should arise, Britain could draw upon Germany within twenty-four hours, and the German Government would make whatever improvised arrangements were necessary.[21]

Callaghan does not say what the scheme was. Schmidt had asked him to regard the assurance as a personal one, and therefore the only member of the Cabinet who was told was the Chancellor of the Exchequer. Callaghan arranged for the Secretary to the Cabinet, Sir John Hunt, to pay a private visit to Bonn to determine just what both sides should do if the assistance was ever required. Schmidt was the Chancellor of a coalition government of his Social Democrats and the Free Democrats, and he told Callaghan that he would have to clear the understanding with his partners. He had, he said, already begun to explain something of the situation to them, 'so that there would be fuller understanding if such a step were ever required'.[22]

It is likely that Schmidt was offering financial guarantees for the sterling balances, but it is questionable whether he would have been able to deliver. Karl-Otto Pöhl was at that time State Secretary in the Finance Ministry and Schmidt's closest adviser on international monetary matters; although he does not know what the two discussed, he has commented that 'Schmidt always made promises of that kind at this time, committing the reserves of the Bundesbank to people like Callaghan . . . but he was not empowered to do that.' Schmidt had done this before, in 1973, when he 'wanted to persuade Britain to join the snake, and he persuaded the German Cabinet to accept a huge – about $5 billion – standby credit for Britain in order to guarantee the sterling balances, which I think was impossible'.[23]

The reason Pöhl said that it was impossible was that the German government does not control the German reserves. The Bundesbank Law of 1957, by paragraphs 3 and 12, makes it the 'protector of the currency' and 'not subordinate to the Federal Government'. Consequently, the reserves cannot be allocated by the government, but only by the Central Bank Council of the Bundesbank.[24] Schmidt may have proposed, but the Council – guided by the powerful voice against of Dr Otmar Emminger, the Deputy Governor of the Bundesbank – would have disposed. Callaghan, presumably, did not concern himself with such niceties, but depended on the precedent of 1973, when the Germans had made their offer of guaranteeing the balances. It might have been thought that Harold Lever, the financial expert of the Cabinet, would have been aware of the constitutional situation, yet he was apparently encouraging Callaghan in his hopes. He told Benn on 18 October that 'the Germans have reserves of $45 billion and they could fund the entire OPEC sterling balances in London without any difficulty at all.'[25]

By 27 October David Owen, Minister of State at the Foreign and Commonwealth Office, was reporting to Benn that the Treasury and Foreign Office were 'furious' with Callaghan

for trying to negotiate on a bilateral basis with Helmut Schmidt a Common Market loan to fund our sterling balances over a long term to avoid the rigours of the cuts. He said Jim was saying nothing to the FO or the Treasury and was engaged in private negotiations of this kind and David himself was pressing the same course in the FO but the FO and the Treasury were in general out of touch with Jim's line and Jim really distrusted the Treasury.[26]

Certainly Callaghan distrusted the Treasury: as he wrote in his memoirs, in the labyrinth of the Central Banks and the Treasury, there was never any real enthusiasm for such a solution. They used the excuse that they wished the completion of the IMF negotiations to take place first. These officials were so shortsighted that they were unable to understand that the announcement of such a scheme would have made these negotiations more acceptable and enabled us to conclude them with less political difficulty.[27]

According to Pöhl, Schmidt was very deeply involved in the crisis, 'because Callaghan called Schmidt nearly every evening and asked him to support Britain in its negotiations with the IMF. And Schmidt, who always liked this kind of crisis management,' later sent Pöhl on trips to London and Washington to help Callaghan.[28] Certainly the rumours that surfaced during October worried the US Treasury: after Schmidt's visit to Chequers reports appeared in London, Washington and Bonn that he thought it would be wrong 'to let Britain go to the wall'. Washington's concern was heightened by Callaghan's remarks when he appeared on the BBC television programme *Panorama* on 25 October: without notifying the UK Treasury in advance, he advocated the elimination of the sterling balances. '"I would love to get rid of the reserve currency," he said. "I am not sure that everybody in the Treasury would, or maybe in the Bank. But from Britain's point of view I see no particular advantage in being a reserve currency at all." He added that the IMF loan was subsidiary to this priority. Get rid of the balances, he said, "and then we would be able to get back and look more readily at our long-term strategy."' By the end of the month, reports were reaching Washington that Schmidt had been won over to the idea of a sterling balances deal as an alternative to an IMF agreement, and Yeo flew to Germany to see Schmidt. He apparently found, to his relief, that whereas Schmidt might be sympathetic to Callaghan's pleas, Schmidt's advisers were insisting that Germany must not undermine the IMF: so Germany would not act unilaterally to help Callaghan.[29]

Yet it can be argued that in the end Schmidt helped to deliver what Callaghan wanted: the IMF requirements were much less onerous than they might have been, possibly in part because the German Executive Director of the IMF, Herr Pieske, had instructions to argue for restraint;[30] the balances were funded (although not when Callaghan wished); and a further Eurocurrency loan was arranged with substantial backing by the German banks.

As the time for the arrival of the IMF team drew nearer, a series of events served to remind the public of the issues. First was the exchange rate. It had remained reasonably steady since the increase in

MLR on 7 October, but it plunged again on Monday 25 October. The cause was a story by Economics Editor Malcolm Crawford in *The Sunday Times* reporting the terms of a $3.9 billion stand-by, allegedly agreed by the IMF and the US Treasury, to include a devaluation of the pound from the then $1.64 to $1.50. The rate fell 7 cents on the Monday, and William Dale, the Acting Managing Director of the IMF, and William Simon, the US Treasury Secretary, both issued emphatic denials.[31] The fall, however, continued until 28 October when the rate touched bottom at $1.535 (see Figure 4, p. 56). From then until the end of the year it improved steadily.

By one account, Crawford later believed that two depreciation options were being considered, an opinion based on having seen a leaked IMF briefing paper about the British economy. The same account reports that a senior IMF official later commented that at an earlier time the Fund believed that the pound should be devalued, and therefore that the story was probably a delayed one.[32] But Alan Whittome, who was to lead the IMF mission to London, has stated emphatically that 'no one was talking about $1.50.'[33]

Callaghan himself kept the tension up with his appearance that same Monday evening on *Panorama*. At the same time as depreciating the sterling balances, 'he pointedly raised the NATO bogy, always a sensitive subject in Bonn and Washington. If Britain did not receive the kind of international help she wanted, he insisted, it might not be possible for British troops to remain in Germany.' According to Fay and Young, 'the broadcast caused consternation in the Treasury', on the grounds that, until then, 'no one there understood the depth of Callaghan's commitment to a course so different from the one they were pursuing.'[34] This may have been the case with regard to his comments on the sterling balances; but according to Benn, Healey told him on 28 October that Callaghan 'had cleared his comment on Panorama about NATO with the Treasury[35] but it was intended as a warning and not as a threat'. Benn added that his son Stephen Benn had rung that evening from Washington and said 'that he had reason to believe that in the Defence Department, that statement had been taken amiss'.[36]

On 1 November the six-man IMF mission arrived in London. It was headed by Whittome, formerly Deputy Chief Cashier at the Bank of England, and then the head of the Fund's European Department. His chief assistant was David Finch, a plain-speaking Australian, and the team also included a New Zealander, a German, a Greek and an American; William Ryrie, the UK Executive Director of the

Fund, accompanied them. The mission were checked into Brown's Hotel under assumed names, and refused the Treasury's suggestion that they hold a short press conference.

The usual mode of operation of an IMF mission is this: the mission goes through a country's books, decides what is going wrong and informs the country's ministers and officials; it then invites the country to propose the cure. The implication is that the IMF does not impose a course of action upon a country: rather, it helps the country to implement the course of action it itself proposes. All of this usually takes about a fortnight. In the case of Britain, much of this went awry. It is likely that the IMF anticipated some difficulty, since Callaghan had gone out of his way to say that changes in domestic policy were not required, but perhaps not how much.

It is worth noting that the IMF also had its own concerns in the negotiations. First of all, it had gone into something of an eclipse after currencies began to float in 1972: the Fund had been established in the first place to act as the mechanism to facilitate exchange rate adjustments, and this task ceased with the ending of fixed exchange rates. Furthermore, with the sharp rise in oil prices in 1973 and the consequent flood of funds into the Eurocurrency markets, countries with balance of payments difficulties had the alternative of borrowing in the money markets before turning to the IMF with its conditions. A successful outcome to their negotiations with Britain would re-establish the Fund's utility to the industrial powers, the main shareholders in the Fund, and hence its future.[37] Secondly, Britain was not the only country that had called upon them for help: there were also Italy, Portugal and Mexico. Indeed, Whittome had only just returned from a mission to Italy. (According to Joel Barnett, 'having come straight from Italy, Whittome not unreasonably did not believe anything he saw in any country's books.'[38]) There was concern that they should not be accused of leniency towards Britain, for fear of making it harder to hold the line in other, perhaps more difficult, cases. In more general terms, the Fund was acutely conscious that Britain must be seen to have to fulfil the same conditions as any other country. As explained in Chapter 1, after the IMF came to an agreement with Britain in 1967, a number of Third World countries complained bitterly that the Fund had imposed less harsh terms on her than on others. Consequently, the IMF was very aware that it must not show favouritism and was particularly sensitive to the political pressure which Callaghan, with some success, encouraged German and American politicians to put on them. Arthur

Burns, however, 'stressing that it was important that the "rule of law" be observed for all members, helped the Managing Director [of the IMF] resist such pressure'.[39]

Finally, the historian of the Fund implies that IMF officials saw this mission as a test in a more general sense:

Officials of the United States and of the Federal Republic of Germany were relying on the Fund management and staff to assess the specific measures needed and to get U.K. officials to agree with them, thus putting the Fund in a key role in financial negotiations with the U.K. Government. U.S. Treasury officials, especially [Simon] and [Yeo], had come to regard the Fund as the only multicountry instrument that could make a serious attempt to lend on conditional terms and that might persuade a country to adopt the policies it recommended.[40]

In short, a successful set of negotiations with Britain could help to ensure a successful future for the IMF as international bank manager, but this meant that the talks could not fail – a point of pressure for the UK government.

The first meeting between the Chancellor and the head of the IMF mission took place on 4 November, during which Healey told Whittome that the short-term economic forecasts were not ready. According to Fay and Young, 'it was the first of many obstructions which hampered the team. In the early days of their visit, they had to spend hours waiting in their hotel rooms wondering[,] with some reason, if doors were being closed deliberately and the British were consciously delaying.'[41] Whether or not this was the case – and the Chancellor for one thought things had to be concluded in November – the Treasury at least was making clear the lack of priority accorded to the mission. Mitchell has confirmed that they did tend to let the mission 'hang around' and to let people know that this was happening. The point was to try to reassure the Cabinet and the Parliamentary Labour Party that the Treasury was not in thrall to the IMF.[43] The full IMF team did not meet the full Treasury team until 10 November, and even when discussions got under way, 'the early parts of the discussions . . . were handled by fairly junior officials, by Geoffrey Littler, then an Under-Secretary.'[44] This in itself was not unusual, however, in that negotiations of this sort were built up from the bottom; so fielding an Under-Secretary in the early days was not intended as a snub to the Fund.[45]

Skirmishes had already begun in the newspapers. The Treasury's estimate of the PSBR for 1977–78 was leaked to *The Financial Times*, which published it on 6 November: the suggestion was a PSBR of

£11.2 billion. Two days later, an article by 'our economic staff' in *The Times* argued that with the economy already in such difficulties, the IMF surely could not want to cut the budget deficit (and by implication the PSBR).[46] But the public debate only reflected the uncertainty in the Treasury, an uncertainty with a very straightfoward cause: the uncertainty of the estimates themselves.

On 3 November the Chancellor had given the EY Committee 'a series of unpalatable forecasts which suggested higher unemployment, high inflation, together with a substantial cut in living standards. Though output was now more buoyant, unemployment was still rising and seemed likely to remain above 1 million for a long time ahead.'[47] He gave some indication of the range of options, saying that

there were very uncertain forecasts, the drought and depreciation had made it worse, inflation was cutting demand and there were flatter forecasts. There were three variant forecasts in which the central one was a 10 per cent wage scheme, another was wages or earnings of 20 per cent, and there was another more optimistic one but the central forecast was the one referred to in his paper . . . We must get the IMF borrowing for 1977 and fund the sterling balances if we can. He said it was a formidable task and we must reach a conclusion in November. We must show the IMF the forecasts and head them off from wanting to disrupt the industrial strategy or the social contract. . . . [M]eanwhile the PSBR had risen to £11 billion from £9 billion where it was in July because of unemployment and the MLR but there would be some balance of payments improvement. He said we had to cut the PSBR without deflation and he had a number of possibilities . . . . He said we should not make an offer to the IMF now but hope to avoid a demand by them for fiscal measures.[48]

The implication is clear: the front presented by the Treasury may have seemed obstructive and it may have been arrogant, but it masked a desperate indecision on the part of the Chancellor and his officials. First of all, they had yet to decide which forecast to accept, and until that decision was taken they could not know the basis for their presentation to the IMF. But Dell places emphasis on an even more fundamental split in the Treasury: a significant section, presumably including the Permanent Secretary, believed that on economic grounds, further cuts were unnecessary, although they would have to be accepted as the price for a loan,[49] while another significant section, possibly including Alan Lord, Second Permanent Secretary, Domestic Economy, and certainly including Derek Mitchell, believed that such cuts were vital to Britain's economic and even political health.[50]

The split within the Treasury was a matter of comment within Whitehall and Westminster, but much of the comment took the form of conspiracy talk. The IMF came to be seen as an enemy by many: in Benn's diary, for example, it gradually mutated from an organisation which might be called upon for help and which could be dealt with to the organisation which proposed to attack the working class. What then happened was that those who had earlier dealt with the IMF or with its supporters, particularly if they themselves seemed sympathetic to what the IMF was requiring, gained the reputation of being fellow travellers, if not actively traitorous.[51]

The man whose face seemed best to fit, and who attracted most of the comment, was Derek Mitchell. He was the Treasury official whose remit covered the pound, and who frequently met his opposite numbers abroad (Thurber's Dogs).

Peter Jenkins in the *Guardian* suggested that British officials were selling Britain short in the United States. John Pardoe, the economic spokesman for the Liberal Party, picked this up and soon the conspiracy developed an identifiable villain, Sir Derek Mitchell . . . . Richard Crossman's description of him as a civil servant who was 'pretty anti-us' conformed to the view emanating from No. 10.[52]

According to Nicholas Kaldor, a Cambridge economist who acted as an adviser to the government, 'it was Alan Lord and Derek Mitchell at the Treasury who were putting the knife in.'[53] On the other hand, the US Treasury Under-Secretary, Edwin Yeo, has denied the charges: 'Callaghan got madder than hell at us. I know he thought there was a conspiracy between the British and American Treasuries, but there was not. Derek Mitchell fought all the way. He never once said "This is what they think, but I think this".'[54]

There is some evidence to suggest that Mitchell's style contributed to his isolation. He himself has said that 'he had rubbed in what the Americans and others were saying about us (that they wanted the UK to be put through it) and that this had excited some doubts'. David Walker, Mitchell's subordinate at the Treasury, was even asked by Wass to check on Mitchell's reports.[55] Pöhl remembers him as being very sad and depressed: Healey blamed him for being too IMF-minded, partly because he objected to the treatment being meted out to Whittome.[56] If this was the case, it could well have meant that the arguments of the Treasury official who was most strongly in favour of dealing with the IMF were discounted by the Chancellor.

However the deck was cut, the Treasury was internally riven. A Treasury divided within itself, unable to receive guidance from a divided Cabinet, could give no lead to the IMF mission. Therefore the announcement by Healey to Whittome on 4 November that 'the forecasts were not ready' was no more than the simple truth. The Treasury also knew that whatever package the Chancellor finally proposed would have to satisfy an increasingly suspicious Cabinet, and Parliamentary Labour Party, as well as an already sceptical IMF mission.[57]

On 10 November the full Treasury team, headed by the Chancellor and the Permanent Secretary, met the IMF mission for the first time. They discussed the PSBR estimates for 1977–78 and 1978–79, and the target for domestic credit expansion (DCE), a measure of credit generated in the domestic economy alone. The IMF mission had decided to urge a borrowing requirement for 1977–78 of £6.5–7 billion, as well as an expansion in domestic credit of about £1–2 billion less than the Treasury estimated would develop under existing policies. Presumably these were laid out at the meeting.[58] The Fund's historian also notes that

the size of an initial drawing under a stand-by arrangement was also debated [although it is not clear whether the debate took place at this meeting]. U.K. officials understandably wanted to be able to have as large a 'front-loading' as possible, while the Fund management and staff considered that SDR 1 billion (£1,160 million) was more appropriate as a first drawing under the stand-by arrangement.[59]

According to Barnett, Whittome refused to believe many of the forecasts; for example, 'he was certain we had increased the unemployment forecast to avoid having to deflate'.[60] Whittome, of course, knew how these things worked, and there is some evidence that he was right. Bernstein quotes an anonymous Treasury minister as follows:

There is no hard evidence of [manipulating the PSBR], but it would have been hard for a Labour government to get further cuts in public expenditure – since even bigger cuts had been made in the previous twelve months than were eventually made for the IMF. So everyone knew that further cuts would be difficult and there was the temptation to make the figures worse than they actually were. Deliberate fiddling to exclude items wouldn't be done, but there are a million and one ways to massage the figures. For example: you need an estimate of total public expenditure outturn, you need figures for the shortfall. These can be juggled. The same is true of the contingency reserve. I and my officials both did it. So we weren't trying to make the figures look good.[61]

According to Fay and Young, 'the exchange rate bulked large in their argument. A fall in the rate had been high among the Fund's preferred remedies for Britain ever since the loan application . . . [and] it had already been vigorously pressed by the team, especially by the Australian, David Finch.' Indeed, according to one source, Finch preferred an exchange rate cap of $1.55. Looking back thirteen years later, Whittome denied that the IMF thought that the pound should be lower.

We don't pretend to know where it should be in this place [the IMF], but we did have a strong bias – which is now more open to debate – that for most countries sustainable growth comes primarily through a strong export position. One element is price, and the price of currency plays a part. We were not saying that $1.50 was right at all, and things were moving like a yo-yo over the year at any rate, but some of them were thinking that back to $2.12 was desirable, while we were saying no, somewhere about $1.70–1.80 was right, more competitive. I don't know if we were putting any figures on it, but no one was talking about $1.50.

Nevertheless, according to The Sunday Times, Healey told the IMF team that lowering the rate 'had already been tried, and since it had failed, he was not about to try it again'.[62]

That evening the two sides dined together at the Hyde Park Hotel, by which time it was quite clear that their negotiating positions were far apart. Furthermore, the Treasury refused to follow traditional procedures for IMF missions of this sort, which was for the country involved to suggest solutions to the problems, to which the IMF mission would respond. According to Fay and Young, Wass told Whittome and his colleagues that 'since the IMF had made so drastic a diagnosis . . . they should come up with their own cure, because the British government was contemplating nothing on the scale which it proposed, especially on the exchange rate.'[63]

According to The Sunday Times, 'for Alan Whittome, this was the first of several depressing rejections. As the leader of the IMF's European department, he was simultaneously involved in negotiations over a loan to Italy. Confused and tired, he flew back to Washington, away from suspect telephone-lines, to talk face-to-face with Johannes Witteveen, his managing director.' Tired he undoubtedly was, and he would grow more tired still, but the dash was not quite so dramatic as Fay and Young made out. As Whittome later explained, if you leave on Friday for Paris to catch Concorde, and then meetings here [Washington] all Saturday and then catching Concorde back . . . you are dead on your feet . . . . We certainly feared the security of communications . . . .[64] But also I don't like to have a boss at my shoulder, I like a very free hand, but the price of that is you keep the boss informed. And I knew perfectly well the political pressure he was under – he was constantly being contacted by Ed [Yeo] or whoever, saying where are we – so the least I could do to keep my own freedom of manoeuvre was to get over here and tell him exactly what was happening and get his views.[65]

On 11 November, the day following the first full meeting with the IMF, the Cabinet met to try to agree on the Public Expenditure White Paper. The White Paper is an annual fixture, setting out the proposed expenditure of the public sector for the following year. In this case, the Chief Secretary was engaged in battles with several colleagues to make cuts in their proposals: a number of them had assumed that the cuts in July had settled the matter and more should not be imposed. There was an added question involved in this round: should the Cabinet approve cuts before the IMF requirements were known? That is, should they offer them in the hope of staving off further IMF requirements, or should they wait, in the hope that the cuts might be less than anxiously anticipated? Enough members of the Cabinet thought any further cuts were unnecessary to make the second option a reasonable one.

The PSBR, in spite of the July cuts, had crept up again and it looked as if the 1977–78 figure would be about £10 billion and possibly £10.5 billion. (For the purpose of negotiations with the IMF, internal Treasury discussions contemplated agreement on a PSBR of £9 billion on the basis of a further cut of £1 billion in expenditure in 1977–78.) By the end of Cabinet, the White Paper had been agreed. However, it was riddled with asterisks, which denoted 'further cuts if needed', and, as Barnett notes, 'we were all on edge with the knowledge that the really big battles were to come'.[66]

During the 11 November Cabinet, Callaghan stated that 'we needed . . . to look at political as well as market considerations'.[67] This was almost certainly because he had not yet given up hope that political pressure might be mobilised to lessen the IMF requirements. In spite of the fact that Ford had been defeated in the American presidential election on 2 November, he hoped that he, and his Secretary of State, Henry Kissinger, might yet hold back Simon and Yeo – who, after all, were equally lame ducks. He needed someone to talk to Ford; he could not leave the UK at this juncture, and besides, a journey by the head of government would invest the mission with too much political weight: failure would be catastrophic. What he decided to do was to send someone whom he knew he could trust, and who better than Harold Lever, the member of the Cabinet who was both financially literate and a keen proponent of funding the sterling balances?

Callaghan described Lever as 'an old friend of many years' standing, always cheerful and bubbling with new and fertile ideas, generous with his friendship, ingenious in finding new solutions to old problems. A splendid raconteur, he possesses much worldly common sense.'[68] A wealthy man, he had, as many said, made and lost two fortunes and married a third. When people said that Lever had married his beautiful Lebanese wife only because she had $2 million, he replied that no, he loved his wife: he would have married her if she had only had $1 million.[69] He had had a stroke in the autumn of 1972, but both Harold Wilson and Callaghan valued his advice, and both had him in the Cabinet as Chancellor of the Duchy of Lancaster with an office in Number 10.

The office is non-departmental, which allows the holder to take on any tasks the Prime Minister wishes; in Lever's case his tasks all tended to have a financial angle (for example, in 1976 he took over responsibility for the gilts market). Healey wrote that 'I found his understanding of the financial markets invaluable . . . [but] he had certain prejudices . . . . The most important was that Harold would never have the Government spend its own money if it could borrow someone else's.' According to Healey, Lever eventually became his man as much as Callaghan's – 'by the end he had become something of a double agent, helping me as much as the Prime Minister'[70] – and presumably the source of this access and influence was 'the seminar'. According to Lever, 'the three of us [Callaghan, Healey and Lever], of whom I was the least important, formed a group called the seminar, there were no minutes, but all the Cabinet rubber stamped what we had decided . . . . It gave me a hearing at the highest level.'[71] It sounds as though Lever was included in the usual discussions which take place between a Prime Minister and a Chancellor on economic policy; he might also have conflated personal discussions with his later attendance at 'the Seminar', a secret, mixed ministerial/official committee set up in 1977 to discuss major decisions on interest rates and sterling.[72] Whichever was the case, it meant that he was completely aware of developments, and would know how the Prime Minister would react to any negotiations that might take place in Washington.

Shortly after the American elections on 2 November, Callaghan sent Ford at letter in which

he stressed the intense political difficulties which harsh IMF loan conditions would create and proposed again that the only way the pill could be made less bitter was by creating a safety net for sterling which would enable Britain to follow a more expansionist economic policy. Moreover, an agreement to that end should be announced at the same time as the IMF loan agreement.

He asked Ford to receive Lever as his political emissary. The White House apparently received the letter on Tuesday 9 November, the day before the first formal meeting between the IMF mission and the full Treasury team. The White House telexed an invitation, and Lever and his wife flew to Washington on 14 November.[73]

Washington was riven with its own divisions regarding Britain. The Treasury under Simon and the Federal Reserve under Burns were united in their determination to prevent Lever from accomplishing what they imagined his mission to be: to secure Ford's approval of Callaghan's wish for a sterling balances agreement which would be a substitute for an IMF agreement. According to Yeo, 'For a while it looked as though we were going to get our tail kicked . . . . At this stage we regarded the sterling balances as a Trojan horse, because an agreement about them would have made the Fund irrelevant.'[74] They had no truck with apocalyptic references by Callaghan and Lever to the dangers to parliamentary democracy or to NATO if Britain were pushed too far.

Others were more susceptible. William Rogers revealed that in the State Department,

we all had the feeling it really could come apart in quite a serious way. As I saw it, it was a choice between Britain remaining in the liberal financial system of the West as opposed to a radical change of course, because we were concerned about Tony Benn precipitating a policy decision by Britain to turn its back on the IMF. I think if that had happened the whole system would have come apart. God knows what Italy might have done; then France might have taken a radical change in the same direction. It would not only have had consequences for the economic recovery, it would have had great political consequences. So we tended to see it in cosmic terms.

These fears extended to the National Security Council, where Brent Scowcroft, the President's National Security Adviser, was quoted as saying that 'I spent more time on this matter during those weeks than anything else. It was considered by us to be the greatest single threat to the Western world.'[75]

According to *The Sunday Times* (presumably based on interviews with Lever), 'Lever wanted to warn the Americans that there were grave dangers if the IMF pressed conditions too harshly on Britain, but this was subsidiary to his main objective, which was to get an agreement in principle on funding the sterling balances as soon as the IMF negotiations had concluded. He also wanted to get an agreement for a simultaneous announcement on the IMF terms and the sterling balances.'[76] Accompanied by William Ryrie, the UK Executive Director at the IMF and Economic Minister at the British Embassy in Washington, Lever's first meeting was with Simon, 'who was like a brick wall, but I [Lever] knew he was fixedly opposed'.[77] They then went to lunch with Arthur Burns, 'and I said, "Be careful, Arthur, if you push too hard you'll get your cuts but they'll include major defence cuts. Besides, I said, "we're going to come to terms with the IMF, but they must be sensible terms." And he said, "Well, I'll think about it." '[78]

The following day, Monday 15 November, Lever was scheduled to see Henry Kissinger at 11 a.m. According to Lever,

Henry phoned me at the Embassy where I was staying and said come half-an-hour earlier and we'll have a coffee and a chat. I went to his private room, and he says 'Harold, you've come on a hopeless mission. You've been sent to fail.' 'Why do you say that, Henry?' He said, 'Because the President told me yesterday that he has it from the highest intelligence authority that you're the only member of the Cabinet who's in favour of this.' I said, 'But the Prime Minister sent me here. And I've got a letter to give to the President.' And he said, 'Harold, you've read your *Hamlet*.' So I said, 'When you say that I'm the only member of the Cabinet in favour of this, it's true. No other member of the Cabinet knows about it, only Denis Healey who's opposed to it, and he's only opposed because he's a bloody stooge of his Treasury officials. Jim is very enthusiastic, he's at least as enthusiastic as I am.' So he said, 'If that's really true, get Jim to telephone the President . . . on the hot line, tell him how keen he is, if you're right.' So I said, 'Well, I am right.'[79]

According to Ryrie, the meeting with Kissinger was difficult: 'Lever was trying to explain to him about how everything was absolutely fine in the UK, and Kissinger listened through a long spiel, and then said, "How come you got a crisis then?" '[80] Certainly he became impatient when Lever began to outline the complex economic problems:

'Harold,' he said, 'I don't understand the technical talk; give me the brief you're reading and I'll have my experts look at it.' 'But Secretary of State,'

Lever replied, 'I can't; it's an aide-memoire, and I've been told not to part with it. We're afraid it might leak.' 'Give me the paper, Harold. There's only a 50 per cent chance it will leak,' said Kissinger, taking it gently from Lever's hand.[81]

Lever continued by elaborating Callaghan's end-of-democracy scenario, adding the hint of cuts in the British Army of the Rhine in Germany. 'He threw in the possibility of import controls as the grave and perhaps inevitable consequence of a "siege" atmosphere in Britain,' and with these arguments he apparently made more of an impact.[82] Helmut Sonnenfeldt, Kissinger's assistant at the State Department, remembered that '"Lever was very dramatic in presenting the effects of what was happening in London, and said he could not in good conscience support British acquiescence to the IMF." Kissinger's sympathy was translated next day, in news reports, into an American acceptance of the principle of funding of the sterling balances, and this alarmed the US Treasury.'[83]

When Lever returned to the Embassy he telephoned Callaghan.

I told him, 'Somehow they've got the notion, the President has been informed . . . he'll listen to me courteously and then say this is a complex decision, I'll let you know. Somehow you've got to speak to him, telephone him tomorrow before I see him.' He said, 'Don't worry, I'll do that.' So then [the following day] I rolled up to the White House and was shown into the Cabinet Room, and then to the Secretary of State's room off the Cabinet Room, and out of that room emerges Kissinger. 'The President's hopping mad,' says Kissinger, 'he called me in twenty minutes ago. Jim's been on the telephone, telling him how much importance he attaches to this' and so on, and the President asked Henry, 'Why am I always so ridiculously misinformed by intelligence about these matters? I was told he was lukewarm, and he's red-hot about these matters.'[84]

Lever's account then deviates a bit from the documents. According to him, he saw the President on his own in the Oval Office, but Scowcroft's brief for the President makes it clear that this was not the case, unless Lever had an additional separate meeting which went undocumented. Both Kissinger and Simon attended the meeting, as well as an aide to Ford (presumably Scowcroft), but the briefing for Ford had clearly been approved by the Treasury:

Your meeting provides an opportunity to indicate our belief that every effort should be made to reach early agreement between Britain and the IMF because we believe that such an agreement is capable of providing the basis for a solution to Britain's economic problems and that we will do everything possible to facilitate a UK agreement with IMF once it is reached. It will also enable you to underline our position that we cannot outside of the context of such an agreement lend support to any proposals designed to finance sterling balances as we do not believe that such a step would address the basic problems faced by the UK or constitute an appropriate way of providing any needed additional financing.[85]

According to Fay and Young, 'a precariously balanced policy had been designed' for Ford to follow when he met Lever. There would be no interference with the IMF. According to a White House source, '"We couldn't take too soft a line because that would weaken Healey's position . . . . But Callaghan would be offered some hope on the sterling balances."'[86]

When Lever and Ford met on the morning of Tuesday 16 November, Lever gave the President a three-page letter from Callaghan.[87] Then, according to Lever,

I told him [Ford] that this was quite separate from the IMF, we would be settling with the IMF if they could agree reasonable terms. He was a sensible man . . . though he was a lame duck, he said, 'Well, I'm very sympathetic to your arguments, you know there's opposition here as well as support, but you have my sympathy.' And I said, 'Well, I've come a long way, Mr President, I hoped to go away with something more substantial.' And he said, 'Well, you know, I don't control on these matters, you know, the IMF is not in my control and the central bank is not in my control.' So I said to him, 'I want your firm undertaking that once we reach agreement with the IMF you would do everything in your power to bring this about at the earliest date.' So he said OK, and I couldn't get out quick enough, I'd got a firm undertaking from him.[88]

According to Fay and Young, during the meeting Lever calmed some of the US Treasury's fears, by making it clear that Britain was not

seeking the sterling balances deal as an escape from the IMF; he did not even want to discuss the details . . . This clearly relieved Ford, whose response, according to one White House aide who was present, was sympathetic on the principle . . . . But the timing was a more sensitive issue. 'Lever proposed a kind of parallelism. His presentation placed emphasis on the sterling balances, and on a simultaneous announcement. We had to get the message that even if we didn't announce the sterling balances agreement at the same time as the IMF agreement we still had to give Callaghan reason to believe that there would be a sterling balances deal eventually.

According to the same witness, Ford '"did in principle indicate a reaction which could have led Lever to believe that the sterling balances was a good possibility". . . . It was the principle which mattered most to Lever', rather than the timing, which had been left rather vague. Consequently, the Treasury and the White House both were concerned that 'Lever might have interpreted Ford's positive tone as conceding "simultaneity" as well as the principle'.[89]

This does not seem to have strictly been the case. In retrospect Lever stated only that he had called a press conference 'in which I said that I was very confident of American support', [90] but it certainly gave rise to twenty-four hours of classic Washington politicking. As described in *The Sunday Times*,

Lever had gone back to the British Embassy cock-a-hoop. The Ambassador, Sir Peter Ramsbottom, telexed news of an agreement in principle to Callaghan with some optimism about simultaneity. Word of Ford's half-promise soon spread round the official network, creating consternation at the Treasury. The White House advisers wanted to soften the impression Ford had given. 'There was a feeling,' says one, 'that the President had been more forthcoming than he actually was and we wanted to pull Lever back. Our worry was that the British should get the signals exactly right.

Robert Hormats, Economic Adviser to the National Security Council, telephoned the British Embassy twice: his message was that 'there really was a good probability that it would all work out, but the administration was making no final commitment until the IMF terms had been settled.'[91]

Helmut Sonnenfeldt, dining at the British Embassy that night, made the same point, and Lever blew up: did he now have to tell the Prime Minister that the President was going back on his word? After dinner Sonnenfeldt contacted Kissinger, who swung into action. The following morning Hormats, Sonnenfeldt and Kissinger all telephoned Lever at the Embassy. Hormats and Sonnenfeldt said essentially the same thing: that Lever seemed to have misunderstood the messages transmitted to him. 'The administration would keep its commitment on the sterling balances – but there was still a question of the mechanics and the timing of the funding.' Kissinger gave a final reassurance: Lever should go back to London content. 'He should just try and understand that Washington like London had inter-departmental difficulties. These included disagreements about what Ford had actually told Lever, but Kissinger would sort things out.[92]

According to Fay and Young, he did so.

Hostilities in Washington continued after Lever's departure. The [US] Treasury was incensed by the agreement in principle and aghast at any possibility of ambiguity on timing. The White House was locked in discussions with the Treasury, with Kissinger intervening. But at the end of the week, a coded message was sent direct from the White House to Number 10. It infuriated Arthur Burns by appearing to accept the principle of a sterling balances agreement . . . .

But though the US Treasury and the Fed were displeased, they had also secured general American agreement to their fundamental position: 'that the IMF terms should be agreed first, unsoftened by an agreement on the balances; and Callaghan would not have the sweetener of a simultaneous announcement'. [93]

In the end, then, what was the significance of the Lever mission? Had it been worth the time and energy spent on it? According to Ryrie, Lever 'did a spiel here [in the US] which just didn't seem to be taking the basic problems seriously, and this just confirmed the US view that we had to go through with this. This was the last throw to get some American influence to moderate the IMF line, and I think it convinced Callaghan that it wasn't going to succeed and he had to bite the bullet.' Dell seems to agree that the mission made it clear to Callaghan that American political leaders were not going to help the UK evade IMF conditions. [94] Indeed, this was the case as well with future American political leaders. During Lever's visit to Washington, a lunch was arranged at the Embassy attended only by the Ambassador, Lever and Fred Bergsten, an economist in charge of international economic issues for the Carter transition team. For over two hours Lever tried to convince Bergsten that Carter should somehow lighten the pressure coming from the Ford Treasury. Bergsten's answer was no. [95] If Callaghan had truly expected – rather than hoped – that the Americans could be persuaded to allow a sterling balances agreement to be a substitute for an IMF agreement, the mission was a resounding failure.

But assuming Callaghan's obsession that the basic cause of Britain's difficulties was the existence of the sterling balances, particularly now that wage increases and public spending were under control (through the incomes policy and cash limits respectively), then the mission was a success. The US government had in some sense agreed that they would help the UK government to secure a sterling balances agreement, although whether it included help in funding the balances or a safety net is not clear. The existence of this high-level political agreement would be crucial in late December, when negotiations over the sterling balances took place. Yeo continued to fight against an agreement, and it is probable that the existence of the commitment from the White House to Downing Street

helped Kissinger and the State Department fight off the US Treasury. As Lever put it, 'a couple of weeks before or three weeks before
[the end of the term of office] he [Kissinger] called in Yeo and told
him that he'd given his word, and that the American Government
has to be behind this, and that must be understood, and that's how it
went through.'[96]

In terms of the crisis, then, Callaghan and the government had
secured medium-term but not short-term help. Meanwhile, formal
negotiations between the UK Treasury and the IMF mission opened
in London on 19 November, while Cabinet negotiations, both
within and without formal Cabinet meetings, began in earnest on 18
November. Callaghan had decided that he would not show his hand
until the very end, nor would he push the Cabinet to take a decision
before it was ready: he feared that if so pushed, the government
would split, and then the Parliamentary Labour Party would split.
Therefore he encouraged all sections of the Cabinet to air their
views. This had the incidental result of leaving the Chancellor on his
own, arguing with the IMF mission on behalf of the government and
arguing with his Cabinet colleagues on behalf of a settlement with
the IMF. It was a harrowing and thankless task since, without the
support of the Prime Minister, he was doomed to fail, and this support was withheld until the very end.

During the fortnight before serious talks began, Callaghan made
certain that the mission was aware of what he considered the political
realities. First of all, the Prime Minister indicated to the mission his
idea of an appropriate settlement, insisting that he was not willing to
go beneath the PSBR of £9 billion for 1977–78, which the Cabinet
had accepted in July; 'the IMF took this badly'.[97] Secondly, he
strengthened his defences by calling in Lionel (Len) Murray, the
General Secretary of the TUC (who was also a Privy Councillor),
and talking to him frankly about the state of negotiations and the
prospects. He wanted to ensure TUC support for the government as
well as to ensure that the mission would learn that the TUC supported the government. In due course, Murray himself suggested
that 'since the unions were seen in Washington as Britain's bogey-
men, it might be as well if the IMF heard from them directly'. On 25
November he met with Whittome and his team and told them that
the social contract, pay policy and industrial strategy were the best
that it was possible to achieve, and that if the IMF imposed conditions that were too onerous, the incomes policy would collapse.[98]
Finally, on 10 November John Methven and Donald MacDougall,

the Director-General and Chief Economic Adviser respectively of the Confederation of British Industry, met with Whittome and Finch. According to MacDougall,

one of the things which came up was the pay policy in year 3 between the summer of 1977–8. We said, based on our in-house work and also the views of CBI members, we thought a savage deflationary policy would be quite counter-productive from the point of view of the TUC and moreover it would be bad for business confidence. We later sent him some notes about the parlous state of company finances.[99]

There is no evidence that these meetings particularly influenced the IMF.[100]

The IMF mission had not, as noted above, been given any kind of lead by the UK Treasury; when Leo Pliatzky, the Treasury Second Permanent Secretary in charge of public expenditure, had a pre-liminary meeting with Whittome and Finch on 11 November, he told them that he had no authority to discuss reductions in public expenditure with them. [101] Possibly the IMF mission concluded that it was to be involved in especially adversarial negotiations; at any rate, its opening bid was pitched high. The first formal meeting between the Treasury public expenditure team and the IMF mission took place on 19 November. As Pliatzky put it,

conceding that we had performed a small miracle in bringing public expenditure under control, the IMF proposed that further reductions should be made of £3 billion in 1977–78 and £4 billion in 1978–79 at 1976 survey prices . . . . The figures put forward . . . represented cuts of 6 per cent rising to 8 per cent on public expenditure programmes totalling something like £50 billion. It was never on the cards that Treasury Ministers would put such proposals to Cabinet, let alone succeed in getting approval for them. . . . This did not mean that . . . nothing could be done . . . [T]erms had somehow to be worked out which on the one hand would produce agreement with the IMF and on the other hand would not destroy the Government.[102]

Within the Treasury, the situation was apparently much as it had been during the search for expenditure cuts in July, 'the same scene, and the same actors, but with an increasingly weary and frustrated Whittome now in the wings, and the same internal debates, but more intense and going on longer, late into the night and over the week-ends'. There were severe limitations on what could be cut, beyond the fact that any easy cuts had already been made in July. First of all, the largest single spending programme was social security, and this was virtually untouchable; not only that, but unless new legislation could be passed – and the political judgement was that it could not – the main benefits would go on rising in line with prices (and pensions with earnings). They also had to leave untouched another large area, the current expenditure of local authorities, 'for the practical reason that there was no way of ensuring that cuts in this expenditure would take place'.[103]

While talks within the Treasury and between the Treasury and the IMF continued, Cabinet discussions began in earnest. At the meeting of the Cabinet EY Committee on 17 November, the Chancellor told them that 'I want a mandate to talk to the IMF . . . . The PSBR is the key [to the IMF loan]. The IMF think we may be pessimistic about an £11 billion PSBR, that it might be slightly less. . . . [W]e have to have a contingent agreement on the PSBR from the Cabinet by next Tuesday [23 November] and it will take two weeks to implement and we should aim to agree to something not less than a £9 billion minimum target.'[104] The following day at Cabinet Callaghan stressed that the PSBR had to be agreed the following Tuesday,[105] but he also reassured Cabinet members that there would be no agreement with the IMF without their approval.[106]

That evening a small private meeting was called by the Prime Minister at Number 10. Those attending included Healey, Dell and Anthony Crosland, a former economics don and author of *The Future of Socialism* who was now Foreign Secretary, and a number of Treasury officials. According to Dell, the purpose of the meeting 'was to run over the ground, and to discover whether there was any meeting of minds between those identified as the main contenders'. Healey said that it was vital that the negotiations with the IMF be successful, and that required further cuts in public expenditure. Crosland argued that there was no economic case for such cuts, and that everything was now in place for the recovery of the economy. Dell pointed out that even if that were true – and Crosland could not know it – the disbelief of the market could undermine and even bring down the government before Labour could reap the benefits. The market's lack of confidence had forced the government to go to the IMF, and the government had to negotiate successfully with the IMF or be swept from office.[107]

Over the next several days word began to leak out that the IMF was trying to impose heavy deflation on the government and 'the cabals had been forming'.[108] On the evening of Monday 22 November, Shirley Williams organised a meeting of the social democratic group in Crosland's room at the House of Commons (Crosland him-

self was attending a dinner for the President of Venezuela at Buck-
ingham Palace). Later that evening Roy Hattersley telephoned him
to report. According to Susan Crosland, 'Harold Lever, Shirley
Williams, David Ennals had been there, and Bill Rodgers had come
in halfway through. All opposed cuts. But their opposition was
based on different arguments. Ennals and Shirley wanted to protect
their departments' budgets. Lever, like Hattersley – and Tony –
thought the whole exercise unnecessarily deflationary.' She further
reported that the same evening, another opposition group met in
Peter Shore's room at the House; Shore, Michael Foot, Benn, John
Silkin, Stan Orme and Albert Booth all agreed to oppose the cuts.[109]
Fay and Young also reported that the 'left-wing group' had the first
of two meetings that evening, but Benn does not mention it in his
diary, an uncharacteristic omission.[110]

On the following day the Cabinet met for a difficult, critical but
inconclusive discussion. The Chancellor had put in a paper calling
for £1 billion in cuts from the PSBR for 1977–78 and £500 million to
be raised by the sale of British Petroleum shares. When the Cabinet
came to discuss the IMF terms (after a discussion about Rhodesia),
the Prime Minister proposed that Healey should be authorised to
negotiate with the IMF on the basis of a £9 billion PSBR in 1977–78,
adding later in the discussion: 'let's be clear that £9 billion is more
than the IMF wanted in the first place.'[111]

There was a great deal of opposition. Lever and Elwyn Jones asked
for clarification on points,[112] and then Crosland passed a message to
the Prime Minister, asking to speak next. He repeated the arguments
he had made at the private meeting on 18 November.

There was no economic case for the cuts, he said. With 1¼ million un-
employed, nobody could say that there was not enough spare capacity to increase exports. Far from reducing the PSBR, the spending cuts would mean
higher unemployment, which would in turn mean higher social security
payments and lower tax revenue, thus actually increasing the PSBR. In any
case, the Treasury forecasts were unreliable; other experts' forecasts were
much lower than the Treasury's.[113] The cuts would massacre the industrial
strategy . . . . The only serious argument for cuts was one in terms of international confidence. But what would happen to confidence if . . . the
Government could not deliver the cuts in the House of Commons? The
Government had made its negotiations too public to do nothing now. He
was prepared to see cuts – mainly cosmetic – of one billion pounds, half a
billion coming from the sale of shares of Burma Oil, the other half to be
found in the least deflationary way possible.

(In 1974 the government had rescued Burmah Oil from severe financial difficulties, and as part of the package of support the Bank of
England, on behalf of the government, bought Burmah's holding of
shares in British Petroleum.) Crosland then suggested that the IMF
and its backers be threatened:

The Government should then say to the IMF, the Americans and the Germans: if you demand any more of us we shall put up the shutters, wind
down our defence commitments, introduce a siege economy. As the IMF
was even more passionately opposed to protectionism than it was attached
to monetarism,[114] this threat would be sufficient to persuade the Fund to
lend the money without unacceptable conditions.[115]

According to Benn, he ended with 'our weakness is our strength . . .
it is a test of nerve, and the IMF must give us the loan.'[116]

Foot said that Crosland's alternative 'was an important one and we
should accept his approach'. Therefore the Chancellor should not be
authorised to discuss a PSBR of £9 billion with the IMF. Ennals,
Lever, Shore, Orme, Hattersley, Benn, Williams and Silkin all
agreed, although not all fully agreed with the Crosland approach.
Only Reg Prentice and Dell supported the Chancellor.[117] The result
was inconclusive and 'it was clear that the Cabinet would have to return to the question, perhaps with the benefit of advice from President Ford and Chancellor Schmidt.'[118]

The failure of the Cabinet to decide to support the Chancellor's
proposal generated activity in several areas. Callaghan telephoned
Schmidt and Ford, warning them of the strength of feeling in the
Cabinet by relating his suspicion that Crosland, a Cabinet heavy-
weight, would regard the break-up of the government as the lesser
evil.

Giving myself a little margin, I told them that the Cabinet would agree to
nothing less than £9.5 billions for 1977/8. There was strong objection to
substantial deflation with higher unemployment, which would utterly destroy our hard-won agreement with the TUC on pay. Moreover, I would
not be able to carry it in the House of Commons. I asked them to talk to
their representatives in the IMF. Helmut Schmidt recognised our political
difficulties and was fearful of the world moving down a protectionist path.
He undertook to telephone President Ford, but in Washington Secretary
Simon's influence was paramount, and the President could not deliver.[119]

He also asked Schmidt to send over an envoy to 'cool down
things'.[120]

Healey saw Whittome, and then Whittome saw the Prime Minister and the Chancellor together. He heard from them their fears of

deflation, and the dilemma they faced between retaining the confidence of the TUC on the one hand and the confidence of the markets on the other. Whittome asked the British to look at three scenarios for 1977–78, with PSBRs of £8.5 billion, £9 billion and £9.5 billion. Callaghan was to report this to the Cabinet on 25 November, calling for a decision at the next Cabinet meeting on the following Wednesday, 1 December.[121]

Meanwhile the Chancellor's Cabinet opponents scented blood, and alternative plans began to take formal shape. According to Fay and Young,

when the social democrats met again on November 24 and did their arithmetic, they discovered that, between left and centre, there was actually a Cabinet majority against a deflationary package, although Bill Rodgers was growing lukewarm. He was being told by his parliamentary secretary, John Horam, that in the parliamentary party there was more support for Healey than was reflected in the Cabinet . . . . [Rodgers] was particularly incredulous of Harold Lever's proposal that Callaghan should threaten Schmidt with the withdrawal of the British Army of the Rhine unless the IMF's terms were realistic. It seemed crazy to Rodgers.[122]

David Hill, Hattersley's political adviser, approached Frances Morrell, who was Benn's, to propose a united front against the Treasury's deflationary package, but Morrell replied that 'the Bennites were not willing to play that game with the Crosland group.'[123]

Crosland in fact was, with the help of Roy Hattersley, hard at work that day on a paper incorporating a concept which might well draw him, and others in the centre, nearer to those on the left: import restrictions. Central to Benn's 'alternative strategy', which had first been articulated in July and was about to make another bow, import controls had not hitherto attracted either Crosland or Hattersley. 'But now they decided that import restraints might be preferable to IMF-induced deflation. They wrote a paper putting forward an import deposit scheme, which they thought that Healey could use at least to frighten the IMF.'[124]

That same day, Benn himself 'decided to dictate a Cabinet paper, with Frances [Cripps – Benn's economic adviser] by my side, to be classified as Top Secret, in which I spelled out the choices facing the Cabinet, the dangers of the IMF route and the alternative strategy, ending with a long passage on the problems of implementation.' He took this paper, entitled 'The Real Choices Facing the Cabinet', with him when he met with Foot, Shore, Booth and Orme at 5.30 p.m. 'We agreed that we would have to stand firm, and they were all very optimistic about Tony Crosland's position, saying we should rally around him . . . . Michael was worried and thought Jim was going to come down against Denis, and Denis might resign. Of course if he does resign, the pound will go through the floor, even if we get the IMF loan.' Benn later found out that someone had sent the paper to Number 10, and the Prime Minister had decided that it was not to be circulated to other ministers. Callaghan relented, however, announcing in Cabinet the following day that it would be circulated the following week;[125] it would in fact be discussed on 1 December.

Import controls as a way of avoiding too much deflation became of prime concern to various members of the Cabinet over the following several days. Indeed, the idea of such controls had attracted a number of people over the previous months, in spite of the fact that when arranging for the June stand-by, the UK had promised not to levy import restrictions. In early September, for example, when the Bank had agreed to cease supporting the pound, the Governor had suggested that instead they should continue its support, at the same time introducing a system of import deposits. On 13 October the Chancellor had proposed an import deposit scheme, which would have required 100 per cent deposits for three months. (The proposal was deferred.)[126] Indeed, on the morning of 25 November, Benn learned indirectly from Nicholas Kaldor that 'the Treasury [had] a complete plan for import controls and exchange controls – a full wartime plan locked away in a cupboard. It was known as "the unmentionable".[127] The argument against such controls, of course, was dominated by the belief that trading partners, and particularly fellow members of the EEC, simply would not allow them. This argument was presumably less compelling for those who had opposed Britain's joining the EEC, such as Benn and Peter Shore, but in a number of cases the belief persisted that trading partners could be persuaded to accept such a scheme.

Crosland and Hattersley presented their plan for import deposits to the Cabinet on 25 November, but no decision was taken. Benn's plan would be presented to Cabinet on 1 December, and on the same day Peter Shore, also busily writing, would present a paper 'drawing attention to the circumstances in which the GATT permitted import controls'. During the crucial Cabinet on 2 December, the Prime Minister would allow the possibility of import deposits. Whittome has confirmed that the IMF would probably have been prepared to accept an import surcharge, although 'I remember telling the Americans, the Germans and the French that it might come up, and it being received with raised eyebrows'. In the end it was not part of the agreement.[128]

Meanwhile, what of Whittome and his team? According to Fay and Young, the team 'was steeped in gloom. By November 25 they had met Wass five times in nine days; Whittome had drunk much whiskey with the Chancellor'; and Callaghan 'would have me around at midnight to soft talk [me] into taking a softer line'.[129] He saw trade unionists, but 'I saw no one on the Conservative side, ever.'[130] But the Chancellor could not budge, and Whittome would not.

On 26 November Schmidt's emissary, Karl-Otto Pöhl, arrived in London.

The first thing I did was to go see Denis Healey. I thought they would be excited seeing me, helping them, but on the contrary, Healey was very cool, if not rude: 'What do you want here? This is our business.' I wasn't aware that there were very different views between Callaghan and Healey . . . I was just trying to do my duty. So I was very angry and I went home to my hotel and I tried to get in touch with my friend Alan Whittome . . . for whom I had the greatest sympathy, because he was trying to apply the right conditionality to Britain. I was very much in favour but my in- structions were the opposite, so I called him and I said what are we going to do? And he said my position is very delicate and I would rather not be seen with you, they are always behind me and they treat me very badly . . . . After a long talk on the telephone he said 'I'm sure they bug my phone here,' so we met in the darkest corner of the bar of the hotel where I stayed . . . . Whittome said that he was really angry that the German government had sent someone like [Pöhl] to try and influence him, and then he told me the whole story. How they treated him was awful . . . it was like a con- spiracy, and I was really upset.[131]

Whittome, however, was undoubtedly relieved by his talk with Pöhl: according to Fay and Young, he had assumed that the Germans wanted him to 'cave in', but Pöhl told Whittome that the German government was not going to ask the IMF to weaken its position.[132]

The following day another visitor arrived: Simon, on an official visit to Moscow, decided to stop over in London on the way to try 'to break the log jam . . . . The Press were all over the place and I told them: "I'm just here to see the sights" . . . . The pound was pretty well down at the time and I hadn't bought any new suits for a while, so I called Ed Yeo along to my tailor's, Wells of Mayfair, and we talked there for so long that I ended up with four suits that I didn't need.'[133] He also met UK Treasury people there, 'and there was generally a small parade of folks in and out of this tailor'.[134] Simon and Yeo then 'went off and talked to Whittome for a few hours', encouraging him not to give way, and then met 'all the senior government officials' at a dinner given by US Ambassador, Anne Armstrong. The British were hoping that Simon would talk about a compromise, but he stated that there was no alternative.[135]

Pöhl was still in London and he and Simon got in touch with each other. Simon said that perhaps they'd better not talk on the telephone, so he sent Yeo to see Pöhl at the German Embassy. Yeo and Pöhl agreed that they should put pressure on the British to fulfil the conditions set out by the IMF and not make an exception. The pull of different loyalties represented by his mission – Schmidt's instructions to help the British versus his own deep belief that the IMF was doing the correct thing – left Pöhl frustrated and angry.[136]

He returned to Germany and

was asked by Schmidt to go to the US to talk to the Americans, to try and weaken the conditions. So I [Pöhl] went to Washington, and I was really, really frustrated there, depressed really, because I was in such an awkward position. I went first to Ed Yeo, and I noticed that he was very cool with me, and we were close friends . . . . So I asked what was going to happen, and he said 'Let's go see Arthur Burns', with whom I also had a very close, personal relationship. And Arthur received me almost hostilely . . . And then Burns said 'Have you seen the letter Helmut Schmidt wrote to President Ford?' I said no, and Burns said, 'Never in my life have I seen such a letter! I always thought that the Germans were prudent people.' The letter simply said to President Ford that they should give up their tough position via London, and Schmidt hadn't shown me the letter. . . . [I]t put me in a terrible position – I was so *upset*, I will never forget that. I said 'Arthur, I'm a civil servant, I have to obey orders, and I have instructions to tell you that we are supporting Callaghan and the British for political reasons and because of the partnership in Europe, and all this kind of thing', and I did it very formally. Arthur and Yeo understood that, but they didn't like it, and I understood that they didn't like it.[137]

Events were rapidly coming to a climax. Both the Germans and the Americans – and the IMF – understood that to bring the British to a decision, the key man in Britain whom they had to convince was the Prime Minister, and the only way he was going to be convinced was to be told this himself by the top men. This they proceeded to do.

When Pöhl returned to Germany, he told Schmidt that he could not put pressure on the IMF to lighten conditions on Britain, because he would destroy the IMF. Schmidt may have accepted the justice of this stricture; equally he may have believed that nothing good would be served for anyone to draw out the negotiating process any longer. At any rate, he took the opportunity of Callaghan and Crosland's attendance at the European Council at The Hague on 29 and 30 November to speak frankly.

On the morning of the 30th Schmidt, Callaghan and Crosland breakfasted together. According to Callaghan, the German Chancellor

again expressed his fear that the world was moving down a protectionist route, and that a decision by an important trading nation like Britain to take protectionist measures would set the ball rolling with adverse consequences for every country. Helmut Schmidt knew my views thoroughly from our conversations and my telegrams, but I took the opportunity, while Tony Crosland was there, to enquire if he would be willing to intervene with the IMF to secure better terms. He made a temporising reply, but it was obvious to Tony that he believed we should reduce our borrowing requirement and was politely saying 'No'. I was not surprised.[138]

Callaghan now knew that the Germans would go no further.

On the flight home he pressed Crosland to make a decision, informing him that, as he had told him before, he would back the Chancellor at the crucial Cabinet meeting.[139] Crosland was 'sad about his conversation with Jim on the flight back . . .'. Other support was beginning to crumble. According to his wife, after supper that evening Crosland

went off to the House of Commons for divisions. Hattersley had arranged for Tony's group to meet again in his room. It was a disappointing meeting. Bill Rodgers had gone over to the Prentice-Dell hard line. Shirley and David Ennals were undecided what was best to do since they now seemed likely to save some of their departmental budgets. Shirley was talking of putting together a 'compromise' paper to satisfy Healey and the Crosland group and perhaps even Benn. Tony and Harold Lever and Roy Hattersley alone were unchanged in their opposition to the IMF's terms.[140]

The array of forces would be clearer at the next Cabinet, due at 10 a.m. the following morning, 1 December.

In the event Cabinet did not begin until 10.30 a.m. In his diary, Benn speculated that the cause was a row between Callaghan and Healey. The cause was indeed a row, but not between the Prime Minister and the Chancellor: it took place between the Prime Minister and the Managing Director of the IMF himself, Johannes Witteveen.

According to one account, William Simon had rung Witteveen while he, Simon, was still in London: 'the IMF, he said, should close in for a deal, while President Ford could be held. Witteveen packed his bags and came to London himself, with little notice.' According to another account, that of the Fund's historian, President Ford had continued to take a close interest in the crisis, and *he* asked Witteveen to fly to London to persuade Callaghan to support a reduction in the PSBR. She makes a point of this, because of the difficulties this visit caused to relations between Witteveen and the Fund's executive directors: Witteveen broke the Fund's rules of procedure by going off without the permission of the directors (because of the need for secrecy). According to Whittome, it was clear to both Witteveen and himself that the former was going to have to be brought in at some stage, although he does not say who suggested it at this particular moment.[141]

At any rate, it was all very dramatic. Several conflicting versions of the meeting or meetings exist, although it is regrettable that Callaghan chose not to allude to the incident at all in his memoirs, and it is not wholly clear which version should stand. According to Ryrie,

at the final stage . . . there was to be a Cabinet meeting at which the final decision was to be taken. Whittome and I were back in Washington, and Witteveen heard that this was happening. Witteveen immediately said 'I'm going to London,' and I got a message saying please arrange for the Managing Director of the Fund to see the Prime Minister tomorrow morning [1 December], before this Cabinet meeting. I got myself on the same plane, and we flew over. It was a fantastic journey, because first of all, the plane was very late out of Washington, and I thought we were going to miss the meeting, and then we had record tailwinds . . . and we arrived early, then being escorted to No. 10, the whole of the M4 was a traffic jam, and again I thought we were going to miss the meeting, and some police cars winkled us out, and led us along the hard shoulder and through red lights, and we drew into Great George Street at 8.45 in the morning.

[Callaghan] postponed a Cabinet meeting, made a little time, very unusual . . . . What [Witteveen] intended to do was to go to Callaghan and say, these are my terms, I'm not going to move any further, and then get back on the 12 o'clock Concorde and come back to Washington, just to make quite clear that he wasn't negotiating. He did that; and Callaghan said, delighted to see you Dr Witteveen; would you please wait until we've had our Cabinet meeting and then I'll have another word with you. Witteveen said no, I'm getting on the 12 o'clock Concorde, and I've said what I've got to say; and he did. And after flying overnight, and then back, he'd arranged a party at his own house that night, which he kept.[142]

According to the Fund's historian, when Witteveen arrived at Number 10, officials had a copy of the charter of the GATT on the table. (Callaghan later told the Cabinet that he had read Article 12 of GATT, which provides for exemptions, to Witteveen.[143]) Witteveen pointed out the disadvantages, both for the UK and the world economy, of using import restrictions to help the UK balance of payments deficit, and they discussed possible adjustment measures. Witteveen, Whittome, Callaghan and Healey continued talks over lunch, and 'afterwards, just before the Cabinet was to meet, Mr Callaghan finally agreed to support a reduction of the public sector borrowing requirment.'[144]

According to Whittome,

I was over here [Washington] that weekend when Callaghan had made an appeal to Ford and talked to Schmidt. Simon had been warned by the White House about what had happened, and Simon immediately got on the phone to Witteveen and said the only way I can get the President out of this is to be able to tell him that you're on your way now to see whether something can't be arranged. And so Witteveen and I flew over . . . and we went straight into the Cabinet Room, and there was a tense meeting with Healey and I fairly silent and Callaghan and Witteveen . . . during which Witteveen made the presentation. He was well up to it, he was a first-class intellect and a politician [he had been Finance Minister in Holland before going to the IMF], and he knew it, he'd been briefed. Callaghan turned around at the end and said 'You never mentioned the word unemployment,' . . . and Witteveen mumbled something as one would that in the short term it may be higher than it would otherwise have been, but ultimately, surely, it will be better, and Callaghan said, 'Well, if that's all you can say you'd better get back on the next plane to Washington.' Then Healey and I came in with some remark which allowed it to get going again. But basically at that meeting I can't remember that we settled on figures; perhaps we did, but we certainly settled where we'd have to end in broad terms . . . Witteveen went away that very night.[145]

Finally, according to Fay and Young, Witteveen

arrived quite unannounced in the Treasury . . . and said that he would like to see the Prime Minister. [He] had decided to intervene personally after hearing a face-to-face account of the mess in London from . . . Whittome. Negotiations had been effectively broken off the previous week when four of the team returned to Washington, leaving only two behind to disguise any impression of complete collapse. Whittome felt that Callaghan had to be personally involved and that only Witteveen could do that. His conclusion was enthusiastically supported by Ed Yeo.

Callaghan hoped to engage [Witteveen] in an intimate political discussion which would put the purely mechanical details of the loan conditions in a broader prospective, and maybe soften them . . . . But [Witteveen] was a bank manager now, not a politician, and he refused to discuss Callaghan's apocalyptic vision of a British political collapse which would ricochet throughout Europe. Their meeting, according to one report in Washington, was 'highly unpleasant'. Callaghan suggested that Witteveen would be personally responsible if democracy was undermined. Witteveen replied that Britain simply could not expect special treatment. He explained that there would be no loan without some collateral, and the collateral would be the conditions, though he tried to persuade the Prime Minister that these were less onerous than he believed: the package would not be as deflationary as it looked, because it would lower interest rates; it would also, he said, pointedly, stabilise the pound. Once Callaghan had conceded the principle of conditionality, Witteveen added, he would be willing to discuss terms. The Prime Minister curtly asked him to stay a couple of days: he had a lunch and a busy afternoon ahead. Witteveen refused, forcing Callaghan to rearrange his diary to fit in a second meeting.

At the afternoon meeting, Callaghan finally accepted that there had to be conditions. That done, Witteveen offered his concessions: the Fund, he said, would be content with public spending cuts of £2.5 billion, over two years – as long as the economy did not overheat – which, with the BP sale, was 25 per cent lower than £4 billion, the sum Whittome's team first thought of. [This is in accord with Pliatzky's figures of the IMF's opening bid, as noted above, which were reductions of £3 billion in 1977–78 and £4 billion in 1978–79. By one account, however, Pliatzky's were based on contemporary Minutes, and they can presumably be taken as correct.] Before this decisive accord, Healey had in fact prepared the final Treasury paper, also proposing £2.5 billion. After it, according to reports received in Washington, Witteveen and Callaghan shook hands on the bargain . . . . Witteveen went straight back to Heathrow, flew to Paris and caught the Concorde flight to Washington, where he was host at a cocktail party that evening, just as if nothing had happened.[146]

It is still unclear precisely what happened at this apparently climactic meeting. It may have been that Callaghan had continued to argue for a PSBR of £10 billion or more, while knowing that Witteveen must know that, as noted above, he had continually told both Ford and Schmidt that he could go no lower than £9.5 billion. Therefore, he might have allowed Witteveen to beat him down to £9 billion – the implication of a cut of £2.5 billion over two years – which, according to his memoirs, had been his own baseline since the beginning of the crisis; it would have allowed the IMF to believe that it had squeezed another £500 million to £1 billion off the PSBR. On the other hand, Callaghan himself told the Cabinet on 2 December that

Witteveen 'was very unyielding and he wants £2 billion of real cuts', although he did not say whether they were all to fall in 1977–78 or could be spread over two years: if the latter, he might have been trying to scare the Cabinet by withholding the concession.[147] Healey has written that Witteveen came to see him in the Treasury and asked him for £2 billion in spending cuts for 1977–78, but he told him it was out of the question. 'I took him to see the Prime Minister. Jim reinforced the message, but for the first time said he would support me on cuts of £1 billion.'[148] According to Donoughue, the head of the Prime Minister's Policy Unit, 'the Prime Minister told me that he had successfully persuaded the IMF to ask for smaller cuts but that the minimum had been reached. His political job now was to persuade his Cabinet to agree to an amount close to that minimum.'[149]

Fay and Young noted that Healey's paper prepared for that day's Cabinet also proposed reductions of £2.5 billion, but according to Donoughue, this was at least partly Downing Street's number:

Mr Callaghan [had] asked me to set the Policy Unit to work on producing possible cuts packages which would achieve the required cuts in a form that would be politically acceptable to Ministers and that would have the minimum recessionary impact. The Prime Minister knew from long experience that the political dimension was usually missing from the Treasury's presentation of even commendable policies. . . . [T]he Policy Unit produced an alternative package of cuts which met Mr Callaghan's suggested minimum net total of £2 billion – still below the minimum figure indicated by the IMF but the minimum which he believed Ministers might find acceptable. The Unit's proposed package was for £3 billion of gross cuts in 1977–9, £1 billion of which would be used for the launch of a major investment programme. In economic terms, this would cut the PSBR to £9 billion. Politically, it would minimise the employment consequences and, on the plus side, would boost investment. The Prime Minister expressed satisfaction at our suggestions and asked the Chancellor to include them in the proposals to be put to Cabinet.[150]

Great preparations had been made for the 1 December Cabinet, with at least fourteen papers submitted by various ministers. In the end, most attention was focused on proposals put forward by Benn, Crosland and Shore. Benn and his advisers had hoped that the Cabinet would reject the cuts and then turn to consider his alternative.[151] This was just what Callaghan was determined to prevent, and he called Benn first. However, Dell and Benn wanted a report on the negotiations with the IMF, and Healey took the opportunity to try and puncture an illusion or two:

I talked to Simon and a German official, and trying to bully the Fund won't help us. The US are being very difficult, there is no bilateral borrowing available to us, even if the Fund helps us, but if a safety net is required, the US would be prepared to look at it. Henry Reuss, the Chairman of the House Banking Committee, is being very helpful. If the Fund does provide a loan, he'd try to clear it through Congress.

In response to a question from Ennals, Healey replied that 'they would look on import deposits with disfavour.'[152]

Callaghan then invited Benn to speak. He did so at some length, setting out his ideas and their political context, and then summarised his prescription as follows:

I suggest we follow the alternative strategy which is of import controls fed in by a period of import deposits, and exchange controls which would certainly be necessary in the short run. This would permit us to have a differential interest rate for official holders of sterling. We'd need a capital issues committee, control of bank borrowing and to keep an eye on the direction of investment – and planning agreements under reserve powers – more money for the NEB. But the most important thing is that we should consult the TUC.

According to Benn, 'I was then subjected for about half an hour to the closest cross examination', which he describes in some detail in his diary.[153] This was not accidental. According to Fay and Young, 'without a Treasury behind him, Benn was pulverised. Even non-economic Ministers, primed with briefs from No. 10, joined in to expose the weaknesses of his argument.'[154] Peter Shore referred during the discussion to Benn's being teased and hounded, but 'Jim wouldn't accept that I was being teased and hounded – I didn't think so either – but I suppose that's how it looked.'[155]

Peter Shore was called next, and he argued that they had two alternatives: the earlier policy had failed, and they could go either for deflation or import controls. Shore argued that the UK was not paying its way, and the easiest way to deal with it was import controls. 'The GATT and EEC provisions allowed any country to take these protective measures where there was a risk to its currency or to forestall a fall in its monetary reserves.'[156] According to Fay and Young, Shore's alternative, which involved import controls but of a less ferocious kind than Benn's, was more persuasive.

His case was devoid of ideology; protection was not in itself a good thing, he explained, but Britain had no alternative. In fact, Shore said, Britain would be doing the rest of the world a favour if the Cabinet decided that Britain would not take any more imports – not cut them, just prevent them increasing, for a two-year period – and balanced its trade. His sophisticated argument had attractions, which were politically reinforced by the fact that Crosland's paper outlining an import deposit scheme was still on the table, as a possible weapon if the IMF did not relent.[157]

Healey came in near the end of the discussion on Shore's proposal, saying that the UK might get an agreement on import deposits of some kind, but Callaghan shut him up, saying that it was all very secret.[158]

According to Benn,

The third gladiator in the ring, Tony Crosland, began with marvellous arrogance. 'I think the proposals I wish to put forward will command more support than Tony's or Peter's. I want us to stick to our existing strategy . . . But we live in the real world of expectation and there are two scenarios to consider. One is the £1 billion net cut which is unacceptable, and the IMF won't really press us for it. If they do, we should resist and threaten a siege economy, or talk about our role in Cyprus or our troops in Germany, or our position in Rhodesia, membership of the EEC, etc. Schmidt and Ford would soon give way. The other alternative is tolerable: to get £1 billion off the PSBR by selling the Burmah oil shares, having import deposits which are a bit deflationary and have political advantages, and to do a presentational job to the IMF'. 'What if the IMF say no?' [Benn] asked. 'We won't accept it.'[159]

According to Fay and Young,

Crosland had seized on the idea of import deposits – making importers put up cash in advance – as an alternative to brutal public spending cuts. It was a shrewd way of turning the flank of the Treasury. It would cut the PSBR by £1 billion, and any variety of import controls ought to win the support of the left. He hoped he could piece together an unnatural alliance of the left and right, and now he had an influential ally. The policy unit at No. 10 . . . also put up a paper on import deposits which had influenced the Prime Minister.[160]

There was further discussion on Crosland's ideas, and on a compromise proposal from Williams, which was attacked by all sides.[161] Most of the members of Cabinet commented one way or another, and at the end Callaghan said that they

were ready for a general decision tomorrow [2 December] on the AS [alternative strategy] but the majority were not agreed on the size of the package. Tomorrow we would discuss the quantum and the make-up of it generally. He said he supported the Chancellor in saying the IMF should know the position tomorrow and then we'll allocate it. He was seeing the TUC Social and Economic Committee tonight. He now hoped the Party would come together on this.[162]

According to Susan Crosland, 'at Wednesday's Cabinet the ten Ministers who hadn't spoken before said they would support the Prime Minister in whatever he judged to be best.'[163] Benn went back to his office and, with the help of his political advisers, worked out his own list of who was on which side, which seems less straight-forward than the Crosland statement.

The line up is as follows: the Healey strategy is supported by John Morris, Edmund Dell, Roy Mason, Fred Peart, Bill Rodgers? [sic], Elwyn Jones and Reg Prentice; the Jim Callaghan strategy is supported by Merlyn Rees and Eric Varley with Eric probably moving towards Denis; the Crosland soft option is supported by Ennals, Mulley, Millan, Lever, Williams and Hatters-ley; the Benn group is Shore, Silkin, Orme, Booth and Foot. If you break this down more carefully, it's Healey 8, Callaghan 3, Crosland 7, Benn 6. On the worst possible analysis with all the others up against the AS, we'd be defeated 18–6. On the best analysis we'd pick up Millan and Hattersley and it would be 8–16. On the other hand if you take Healey's position, he could be at worst defeated by 16–8 with his basic 8 and the best he could hope for is 18 to 6 which is against the AS. Crosland's best hope is 13 to 11 if he gets all our group and his groups against Jim and Denis. His worst position is 9 to 15 if he finds that he can't carry the rest of the Cabinet. Jim, if he goes with Denis, loses 11 to 13, and if he goes with Crosland, he wins 16 to 8.[164]

That evening in the House, the Crosland group met to consider the position, and Crosland discovered that his support was begin-ning to melt away. One member of the group, on his way to the meeting, had noticed Shirley Williams writing furiously. '"I knew that she was lost," said one of the group advisers later. "Whenever Shirley resorts to paper you know she's trying to work out a com-promise."' Apparently she was trying to find a method of meeting the IMF's PSBR target with the least damage to public spending and jobs. But on import deposits she was implacable, on the grounds that they were protectionist and would damage Third World countries.[165]

When he met Crosland, according to Fay and Young, 'Lever was openly hostile. Not only were import deposits objectionable to a free trader, he said, they were deflationary. But Lever had already been converted by the Chancellor; he let it be known that Healey had promised him that public spending cuts in December would be matched by income tax cuts in the spring. This, to him, was best of all. He would support Healey.'[166]

While the opposition groups were meeting, the Prime Minister was also touching various bases. He had spoken to Michael Foot on 30 November, after which he concluded that Foot believed it would be better for the Labour Party to stay together than to remain in government: Foot joined Benn (and Callaghan) in being slightly obsessed with the precedent of 1931 (when the then Labour Government had resigned over cuts in public expenditure, and the Party had split). But more cheering news came on 1 December. After the lunch with Healey, Witteveen and Whittome, Callaghan saw Jack Jones and Len Murray (separately). Jones 'warned me strongly about the consequences to the Social Contract if there was a large increase in unemployment or reductions in social benefits, but he gave me every encouragement to maintain a Labour Government, even if it meant taking some decisions the TUC would not like and would oppose.'[167] Callaghan must have taken great comfort from this, since it was precisely what the Cabinet would have to do. He also had Jones's comment in his armoury if required for the decisive Cabinet meeting the following day. Further good news came from Crosland. By the end of the meeting in his room, it was clear that the only firm supporter he had left for his strategy was Hattersley; therefore he trotted down the corridor to Callaghan's room to confess defeat. However, he clothed his capitulation in structural terms: he did not believe in the proposed policy, nor admit that his own might be un-workable; rather, since Callaghan proposed to support the Chancel-lor, he said, the Cabinet had to back the Prime Minister, or the government would fall. He would make his position clear during Cabinet.

The other consideration for the Prime Minister was the Parlia-mentary Labour Party. Labour were a minority government, and furthermore, a minority government supported in the House by a number of restive, left-wing supporters. As noted above, certain options in drawing up the cuts had been deemed non-starters pre-cisely because they would never make it through the House; indeed, when rumours flew around Westminster that, for example, cuts in social security were mooted, the reaction was enough to convince any doubters.[168] Callaghan's last caller on 1 December, Michael Cocks, the Chief Whip, underscored the problem. Callaghan asked him for an assessment of the mood of the party.

He said there was pretty general despondency with a left-wing group almost certain to vote against any particular piece of legislation which involved a reduction in public expenditure. They might however sit on their hands in a vote on the package as a whole, if it was an issue of confidence in the Government; they did not want the Government to fall.[169]

At 10 a.m. on Thursday 2 December the decisive Cabinet began, but somewhat slowly, with parliamentary business followed by foreign affairs. Finally, Healey opened the discussion on the IMF. The government must borrow less in the following year, not because of the demands of the IMF, but because a need to borrow £10.2 billion, the current Treasury estimate of its PSBR in 1977–78, would be highly inflationary, and would cause a further collapse of sterling. He emphasised that the drawing on the stand-by of $1.6 billion had to be repaid by the following week [on 9 December]; if it was repaid without an IMF drawing, it would leave less than £2 billion of usable reserves. As the Cabinet had requested earlier, options of cutting the PSBR to £9.5 or £9 or £8.5 billion had been discussed with the Fund, and he now recommended that he put the following to the IMF negotiators: a £500 million sale of the British Petroleum shares acquired from Burmah Oil; a net reduction of £1 billion in the PSBR for 1977–78, mainly by cuts; another reduction of £1.5 billion in the PSBR for 1978–79. Therefore the PSBR for 1977–78 would be £8.7 billion, which would reduce the Gross Domestic Product by a half per cent, but it would rise by 3.5 per cent in 1978; it would only add a half per cent to the Retail Price Index; unemployment would rise by 30,000 by the end of 1977 and by 100,000 by the end of 1978, but these would be offset by various micro measures.[170]

Callaghan now made it clear that he supported the Chancellor, although he emphasised the political and economic uncertainties: the package might require legislation, but the Chief Whip had warned that it might not get through. He called for a 'three-legged stool' approach, comprising a cut in the PSBR for 1977–78 of £1 billion, a safety net for the sterling balances, and import deposits.

Michael Foot remained of the same mind as on 30 November. According to Benn, Foot 'spoke for the first time this week. He began very quietly by saying he was grateful to the Prime Minister, "But I must tell you that your proposals are not satisfactory. £2 billion cuts and all the consequences that will flow from that are inconceivable."' But the impact of this was presumably muted by Crosland's announcement that while he remained unconvinced by the economic arguments, his political judgment was that, given the position which the Prime Minister had taken, it would not be right to press the issue. The unity of the Party depended upon sustaining the Prime Minister; if it got out that he had been rejected, sterling would crash and the Government would fall.[171]

Discussion continued for a couple of hours, but as it drew near to 1 p.m., Callaghan went around the table one by one, asking each member of Cabinet for his or her opinion. He noted in his memoirs that at the end it was obvious that while there was a substantial majority for the Chancellor's proposal, a minority found it unacceptable. According to Benn, he then said that

I want now to sum up as best I can by saying that I put in the import deposits because I thought it would make it more acceptable. Of course, it also provides another £1.5 billion reduction on the PSBR. So I now think we should authorise Denis to offer to the IMF £1 billion in cuts, £0.5 billion in sale of shares, and test out the import deposit argument. Denis replied, 'Let's be clear, we have not yet persuaded the IMF that we can get away with as little as £1.5 billion with only £1 billion cuts.

Foot wanted to make certain that the Cabinet would have the final say once they knew what the IMF would agree and how the cuts would be allocated, and Callaghan agreed.[172]

Finally, the Cabinet had taken the decision. Healey forbore to rub in the obvious point that they had accepted on 2 December precisely what they had rejected on 23 November. Between the two dates a lot of anguished discussion and drafting of alternatives had gone on, and Callaghan clearly was right that ministers had to wear themselves out before accepting that there was no alternative. Of course, as Healey did point out, just because the Cabinet had agreed on a proposal did not mean that the IMF mission would accept it: in fact, if Witteveen were indeed insisting on £2 billion in cuts for 1977–78 alone, the likelihood was that they would not. He would find out the following day, when he was scheduled to meet Whittome and his colleagues at noon.

The accounts by the Chancellor and the Prime Minister of that meeting agree in essence but differ in detail. According to Healey, he finally got Whittome to accept cuts of no more than £1 billion [presumably for 1977–78], and thought Witteveen had agreed; but the latter rang from Washington and asked for another billion. Healey says he told Whittome to tell Witteveen to 'take a running leap', and Whittome smiled and said 'We seem to have reached an impasse.' Healey then says that he told Whittome that if the IMF persisted, they would call an election on the basis of the IMF versus the people, and Witteveen surrendered.[173]

According to Callaghan, the IMF mission had been given written instructions by Witteveen in Washington that in the opinion of the Fund, British expenditure would need to be cut by £2 billion in 1977–78 and by up to £3 billion in 1978–79. The Chancellor had then

delivered a brisk homily to the IMF indicating how far the Cabinet thought it right to reduce expenditure, emphasising that they could go no further than they believed to be necessary to get the economy into balance. If the IMF then refused a loan, the Government would ask the Queen to dissolve Parliament and we would call a general election on the issue of the IMF versus the people. With this message ringing in their ears, the IMF negotiators had made a hurried departure for Washington. I had not given the Chancellor any authority to threaten a general election but I was quite happy that he should have done so.[174]

From these two descriptions, the inference could be drawn that Witteveen had *not* in fact agreed to cuts of £1 billion only at the meeting on 1 December, as Fay and Young have written. In this case, the IMF was merely insisting on its previously stated terms. The Chancellor, on the other hand, now had the support of the Prime Minister and a Cabinet majority behind him, and could exercise his oft-honed threatening manner. It would be strange if the threat of a general election in itself had much influenced the IMF: why should they care if the British held an election on the subject? It is more indicative of the intense self-regarding focus of the UK government at the time, and especially of the Chancellor, that the threat should have been made, and should subsequently have been thought to have worked. But the two sides had now set out their final terms and, that done, Whittome presumably caught his usual Friday flight to Washington.

The IMF decided to cede ground on this leg of Callaghan's footstool (although the Chancellor and the Prime Minister would discover them to be immovable on the other two legs). By this time all knew that there had to be an agreement: too much had been invested in negotiations for them to fail. Presumably this had been Healey's appraisal, and his brutal negotiating manner at least made it clear that a line was drawn in the dirt. The following morning, Saturday 4 December, Callaghan arrived at Chequers and received an unexpected message: the IMF negotiators had reported back in Washington and had shortly afterwards telephoned London, suggesting a renewal of contacts between them and the UK Treasury, to which Callaghan of course agreed. The IMF mission flew back, and negotiations resumed 'almost at once'.[175]

According to Bernstein, what helped to break the bargaining deadlock was the substitution of a two-year programme, which would allow for some flexibility, for a one-year programme. She quotes an anonymous interviewee as follows:

The breakthrough was when Whittome suggested that if at the beginning of the second year it seemed likely that growth would be more than 4%, we'd make further cuts – so the PSBR wouldn't crowd out private investment. We didn't believe there would be such a sharp recovery . . . . The IMF reduced their demand for cuts in the second year with the proviso that if we expected 4% growth there would be additional cuts. That was the breakthrough since it introduced a bit of flexibility.[176]

Over the weekend there had been massive leaks from the Cabinet to the press, and *The Economist, The Financial Times* and *The Observer* all carried detailed stories. When the Cabinet met on Monday 6 December at 3.30 p.m., in order to begin the 'agonising process of cutting', the Chancellor told them that the leaks had made negotiations with the IMF much more difficult. He reported that when he had met with Whittome on the previous Friday, Whittome had told him that Witteveen wanted another half-billion in 1977–78 and another billion for 1978–79 [yet another version]. Healey assured them that he had told the IMF to take a running leap. But they had agreed to the Cabinet's proposals of a PSBR of £8.7 billion for 1977–78 with £500 million from the sale of British Petroleum shares, and £8.6 billion for 1978–79. He also reported that the IMF believed that the agreement would so raise confidence that the cuts would not be deflationary, and that 'if the balance of payments surplus came earlier we could end the IMF tranches though that was to be kept very secret'. Then began the Cabinet negotiations over cuts, which Callaghan said had to be decided by the following afternoon at the latest. The Chief Secretary managed to ensure that decisions covered the two years 1977–79.[177]

That evening a dispirited group of left-wingers, Foot, Shore, Stan Orme, Albert Booth and Benn, met in Foot's room in the House. Foot, Benn and Shore did not want to resign, but Orme had nearly talked himself into it. In the end all but Benn went to dinner. After a bit more work in his room he went to the tea room and talked things over with Brian Sedgemore, Norman Buchan, Frank Judd, Audrey Wise, Andrew Bennett and others. Left-wing backbenchers all, they told him he should resign. Resignation decisions are infinitely easier if one is not in office, and Benn himself could not see the point of resigning.[178]

Cabinet resumed at 10.30 a.m. on Tuesday 7 December, with the emphasis now on cuts in individual programmes. The room was soon full of cries of pain and rage. After going through the list of spending departments, and then the nationalised industries and the Foreign and Commonwealth Office, the argument came to selling BP shares. Benn argued against and Healey was in favour. 'Crosland said it was crazy but we should do it. I [Benn] raised a point of order and asked if it was really right for Cabinet Ministers to say things were crazy but they still supported them. Jim said I couldn't make the point.' They were clearly getting punch-drunk, but they still had only £954 million out of the £1 billion required.[179]

According to Barnett,

at 1 p.m. Jim appeared to lose patience. I say 'appeared' because he was always cool on these occasions, and in total command, so I assumed it was carefully planned. He said, as we could not agree, he and Denis would go away, make up a package and present it to the House and the Parliamentary Party. If it was thrown out by the Party, that would be that; if it was approved, then those Cabinet Ministers who wanted to resign should do so then, but not before. There was an appalled silence before Michael Foot, Peter Shore and a number of others said there was no need for that and that we were not far from agreement. So we were to meet yet again at 8 p.m.[180]

The Cabinet resumed in the Prime Minister's room at the House, since there was to be a Division at 10 p.m. The Chancellor had put in a new paper, now asking for £1,199.25 million in 1977–78 and £1,700 million for 1978–79. In other words, he was asking for £200 million more in cuts for each year to allow 'add-backs' to help industry and unemployment (this was found by increasing excise duties on tobacco and alcohol by 10 per cent and would therefore not affect the net figures). In the end, decisions were taken. They included an end to food subsidies, an end to the Regional Employment Premium (except for Northern Ireland), and a six months' postponement on all new starts in a range of programmes such as roads, health and water and sewage. Defence took a substantial cut, and the defence chiefs complained to the Prime Minister, but by then it was too late. Housing took a large cut. In fact, virtually everything cuttable – that is, excepting social security and local authority expenditure – was cut. The result was a reduction in public expenditure of £1 billion in 1977–78 plus the sale of £500 million of Government-owned BP shares, reductions of £1.5 billion for 1978–79, and a further fiscal adjustment of £0.5 billion for 1978–79 provisionally agreed.[181]

Callaghan's later assessment was naturally more positive, emphasising that expenditure was not wholly reduced by mechanical cuts
across the board. Furthermore,

the Cabinet agreed to increase the resources of the National Enterprise
Board and the Scottish and Welsh Development Agencies, as well as
schemes for encouraging industrial investment and training for employment. The main social security benefits were not reduced. The effect of
these measures did much to mollify the minority of Ministers who had
opposed the package as a whole.

He was correct here. Some ministers unwound in Foot's room after
the Cabinet, and their assessment according to Benn was that 'we
haven't done badly - we have fought off the emotive things like
social security and prescription charges'.[181]

The Cabinet had agreed, but what about the Parliamentary Party?
Benn assumed that the package would be 'absolutely widely un-
popular'[183] with the party, and this was a real danger. Therefore Callaghan's next step was to call in the sixteen whips, led by Michael
Cocks and Walter Harrison. When they arrived in the Cabinet room,
he told them it was neither 1931 nor 1951: the government would stay
together, and there would be no election. Would the Parliamentary
Party stay together? 'They told me that it was demoralising for the
Party to have agreed to a set of measures in July, and then to learn
that more was required in December, and a group of those they
called "kamikaze" members might vote against the Government on
specific issues.' The government would win on an issue of confidence, but possibly not on reductions in expenditure that required
legislation: the government should avoid this, for they could not
guarantee a majority. Given a choice, [the whips] would prefer
measures to reduce unemployment rather than to increase social expenditure, and they believed this represented the view of the party in
the country, who understood the government's problems and the
priority of avoiding a Conservative government. This was all dis-
tinctly encouraging.[184]

The details of the policy package and of the stand-by arrangement
were worked out on 11 and 12 December, and on 14 December the
Cabinet met to consider the result, the draft Letter of Intent from the
Chancellor to the IMF. This set out commitments on conducting
economic policy during the two-year life of the agreement; the Cabinet received it accompanied by the Treasury's economic forecasts
(which excluded that on unemployment).

Denis described the letter of intent and said that the domestic credit expansion was the key and we would have to promise not to introduce import restraints or exchange controls. Crosland said 'What about the import deposits and what about the safety net, what news is there there?' Then Denis said, 'The last two days of discussions have taken place in the Bank of International Settlements but they want a dollar guarantee and the US Fed and the US Treasury are being very unhelpful and Ford insists on an IMF settlement first. [See Chapter 5.] Then they want sterling permanently funded and Burns of the Fed is being very unhelpful and Kissinger is helpful but loathed.'

Benn rightly summed it up: they had as yet no safety net, nor had they the right to introduce import deposits. 'Jim said he was disappointed. He said Ford and Schmidt had let him down and that Burns of the Fed was most unhelpful and it was the first time in his life that he felt anti-American.' Crosland asked specifically whether import deposits were ruled out by the Letter of Intent, and Callaghan confirmed that they were.[185]

Dell's reaction was more robust. 'The Letter of Intent was a constraint as it was intended to be.' Besides import deposits, it also ruled out further exchange controls. It said that

An essential element of the government's strategy will be a continuing and substantial reduction over the next few years in the share of the resources required for the public sector. It accepted that 'It is . . . essential to reduce the PSBR in order to create monetary conditions which will encourage investment and support sustained growth and the control of inflation.'

The draft letter then set out the agreement as described above, with the addition that the 1978–79 commitment included a provisional undertaking to make a further fiscal adjustment of between £500 million and £1 billion if growth exceeded 3.5 per cent per annum.

In addition to fiscal measures, the IMF had insisted on setting monetary limits – the source, according to Donoughue, of some conflict between the Treasury and the Policy Unit, with the latter allegedly catching out the Treasury trying to sneak tighter limits on credit past the Unit. Domestic credit expansion – like M3 a measure of monetary expansion, but which represented banks' assets rather than liabilities, and was restricted to money or credit generated by the domestic economy alone – was to be progressively reduced from £9 billion in 1976–77 to £7.7 billion in 1977–78 to £6 billion in 1978–79. It was also expected that the increase in M3 would be between 9 and 13 per cent.[186]

Dell notes that 'there was great concern in the Cabinet about the effect of the Letter of Intent on the level of unemployment.' Benn wrote that 'I tried to raise the question of unemployment and this was ruled out.' Barnett reported Shore as saying angrily that 'there is no will in this Cabinet to tell the IMF to take a running jump, even if unemployment rose to 2 million.'[187] This concern did them great honour, but by this time the Cabinet had very little room for manoeuvre; yet it is worth noting, in this context, that Shore later conceded that 'in the event, unemployment hardly moved, and the economy began to move forward again really fairly shortly afterwards'.[188]

The Cabinet had little room for manoeuvre because no one was going to reopen the negotiations. First of all, all energy, if not all passion, was spent. Secondly, the IMF would probably not have agreed to resume talks. But thirdly, and this must have been in some minds, if not in those of the spending ministers, the bill had fallen due. The $1.6 billion from the stand-by had had to be repaid on 9 December, and if they did not receive the $1.5 billion from the IMF drawing fairly quickly, the reserves were going to be in trouble.

And so on 15 December the Chancellor rose to make his statement to the House of Commons.[189] He emphasised that the measures would further national recovery, and would cover two years rather than one, in order 'to avoid excessive strains' the following year.[190] They would accord with the medium-term strategy set out in the February 1976 White Paper (Cmnd 6373), which had indicated the government's intention to reduce the share of resources going to the public sector, by a rigorous application of cash limits and a refusal to accept new commitments which would breach the Contingency Reserve. He then detailed the measures, both the cuts and the 'add-backs', promised cuts in taxation if wage claims continued to show restraint, and set out the monetary targets agreed with the Fund. He then announced promising negotiations over the sterling balances, and revealed that in addition to the IMF loan, the UK could draw on a £500 million swap agreement with the US, and the Bank of England could draw on a standby facility of $350 million from the Bundesbank. He ended with an optimistic forecast of the country's economic prospects.[191]

According to Dell, 'he met less hostility from his backbenchers than expected', although Barnett reported that

his credibility was at a very low level, and the House was unsympathetic: he was received with jeers by the Tories and stony silence from our side. The parts of the statement making forecasts, or expressing some optimism, were greeted with general derision. Any other Shadow Chancellor would

have destroyed him, but once again he was saved by an indifferent performance by Geoffrey Howe.

According to Healey himself,

the Conservatives did not know whether to attack me for giving in to the
IMF or for not doing enough. The Tory press had no doubts: I had not done
anything like enough. 'Chicken Chancellor' screamed the *Daily Mail*.
'Britain's Shame', shrieked the *Sun*. The *Financial Times* was kinder: 'The
first thing to be said . . . is that it can in no way justly be called, as Sir
Geoffrey Howe called it, an IMF budget.'[192]

On the other hand, the pound was stable, and support came from
various quarters. The same day the TUC General Council responded
with what Callaghan called a 'markedly understanding public statement' to the effect that there was no real alternative to seeking financial support.[193] (Murray later confirmed to Benn that 'if the Cabinet
can stick together, so can we.') Simon issued a statement in which he
described the UK programme as 'a responsible and sustained
approach which represents a sound and realistic strategy for the
United Kingdom rather than a one year transitory effort'.[194] Such
praise from Simon probably confirmed the programme's opponents'
view that they had been right to object, but short of trying to bring
down the government, there was nothing they could do about it.

On 16 December the Parliamentary Labour Party met, and it became clear that the party would not split. Healey made a statement,
ending with 'The package I introduced was introduced on behalf of a
united Cabinet.' (Benn told his diary, but not the assembled throng,
that this was a bloody lie.) There were a number of speeches
questioning and attacking, but Callaghan's winding-up speech apparently calmed things down and invited acceptance, if not active
support. He emphasised that

in the Cabinet all the views were expressed, and the alternative strategy and
the papers to back it up were presented to the Cabinet, and the great majority of the Cabinet agreed to reject. We didn't agree about the outcome but
we came out intact . . . . I must warn the Party you can't support the
Government in general and vote against individual measures because of our
credibility . . . . Remember this, unlike the Tories we haven't cut the social
benefits, that's the first thing the Tories would have gone for. I shall need
help from the PLP, from the NEC, from the Tribune Group and from the
Manifesto Group. Let's have unity and get together.

Benn thought that 'it was an extremely skilful speech and said with
great relaxation and he has put on the record that there was a big

argument in Cabinet and that, in a sense, is all one wants people to know.'[195] By the time the economic debate took place in the House, on 21 December, Healey had recovered some of his old resilience and, in spite of interruptions by left-wingers on the issue of un-employment, his speech went 'reasonably well'.[196]

All that could be done in Britain had now been done, and, owing in great part to Callaghan's political and management skills, the government and the Party remained united. The fate of the IMF loan, and of the funding of the sterling balances, was now in the hands of the Group of Ten. The request by the UK was for a draw-ing so large that the IMF had to turn to its larger shareholders to finance it, and although the British assumed that the decision was a foregone conclusion – and it probably was – the IMF had still to get it approved. Callaghan's particular bee, the sterling balances, posed more of a problem, in particular because Burns and Yeo were deter-mined that the UK should not be able to wriggle out of its IMF com-mitments by means of an agreement on the balances. Thus, a short but ferocious battle was still to be fought, but the venue was now abroad.

CHAPTER 4

Getting Rid of the Sterling Balances

On 25 October Callaghan publicly advocated the elimination of the sterling balances, announcing on the BBC's *Panorama* programme that it would be to Britain's great advantage if sterling ceased to be a reserve currency. He believed that this was more important to the economic health of the country even than an IMF loan, and he attempted to convince the Germans and, in particular, the Americans, to agree to help to provide a safety net for the balances and to facilitate their funding. The US Treasury feared that Callaghan wished to substitute a sterling balances agreement for an IMF agreement, and refused to agree to anything before the UK and the IMF had come to terms. The White House, however, agreed that once the IMF agreement was in place, they would support Callaghan in his efforts.

The two agreements, therefore, were bound up together. The Germans were already preparing for a sterling balances agreement by late October, after Callaghan's public plea, but the Americans only began to prepare after the Lever mission and President Ford's promise of support. Burns and Yeo continued to fight against an agreement, and then against an agreement without very strict safeguards. The arguments by one account were ferocious, and no less so for taking place largely out of the public eye. An agreement was finally announced on 11 January 1977.

Both the IMF stand-by and the sterling balances arrangement were to last for two years: on the whole the former fulfilled expectations while the latter did not. There was one early hiccup: a political crisis blew up in March 1977 when the time came for the House of Commons to agree to the public expenditure cuts required by the IMF

111

agreement. The government decided that defeat was certain, and to evade it they entered into a pact with the Liberal Party. This sustained them in power long enough for the medicine to work – indeed, it was hubris of a sort which encouraged the government to embark in 1978 on one incomes policy too many, losing them the support of the trade union movement and thereby costing them the next election.

Callaghan began his campaign to put an end to the sterling balances during the visit of Chancellor Schmidt to Chequers on 9 and 10 October 1976, when he asked Schmidt what help Germany could give. As described in Chapter 3, Schmidt unfolded a grand plan to fund the balances, the development of which, as far as Callaghan was concerned, was abruptly curtailed by the defeat of President Ford's bid for re-election on 2 November. Nevertheless, the German government was sensitised to the importance of the issue for the British Prime Minister, an importance underlined by Callaghan's public call, during his appearance on *Panorama* on 25 October, for the elimination of the sterling balances and the end of sterling's role as a reserve currency.

Unknown to Callaghan, apparently, the Bank of England and the Treasury had already begun to consider the issue. Callaghan has always argued that the Treasury and the Bank worked against his wishes in this matter;[1] evidence has emerged about the Treasury's and the Bank's activities in this connection which make it clear that he was wrong. In the middle of September 1976 the Overseas Division of the Treasury produced a memorandum suggesting that negotiations begin that autumn for a safety net for the sterling balances. There should be a medium–term credit facility provided by the major developed countries, probably managed by the BIS, for the UK to draw on to the extent of reductions in the balances. Such a facility should cover both official and private balances.[2] A copy of the memorandum was sent to the Prime Minister soon after it was written. It is likely that discussions on the proposal were held with the Bank; certainly, just after the *Panorama* interview, Christopher McMahon, the Deputy Governor of the Bank, visited the Bundesbank for talks with Dr Emminger, the Deputy Governor, on the issue. In preparation for this visit the Bundesbank had produced a paper, dated 27 October (two days after the *Panorama* programme), setting out the case for assistance for Britain; and the Bank of England produced a background paper, probably incorporating the points in the Treasury memorandum, which looked towards negotiations on the balances (a copy of this went to the Bundesbank).

The early support of the Bundesbank for an arrangement to help Britain relieve herself of the balances is perhaps not so surprising. During this period the Bundesbank was strongly against the Deutschmark's taking on a reserve role, simply because it believed that any currency assuming this burden was bound to get into difficulties. In particular, it thought it a bad idea for a country to rely on this role to cover its deficits.[3] (This stricture, of course, could have applied equally to the US.) Therefore Callaghan received early help in his campaign. What he did not receive, however, was any encouragement from the Bundesbank in his hope that such an agreement could be a substitute for an IMF loan.

In its paper dated 27 October, the Bundesbank argued that while an agreement on the balances, contrary to Callaghan's belief, would not be enough in itself to change market sentiment towards Britain, nevertheless there were good reasons to look at the problem of the sterling balances in a positive and constructive way. The simplest method would probably be the provision by other central banks of a support facility, that is, a credit line, but there should be preconditions. Firstly, the conditions on which a balances agreement would depend should support the fulfilment of the conditions imposed by the IMF in connection with a UK drawing; secondly, the credit line should parallel efforts to reduce the reserve role of sterling; and thirdly, any arrangement should not encourage a further accumulation of sterling balances.[4]

McMahon spoke to Emminger, and a week later the Bank of England produced a three-page memorandum briefly setting out developments since September 1968, when the previous sterling balances agreement (the Second Basle Group Arrangement in 1968) had been signed (see Chapter 1).[5] Sterling balances have two components, the official balances and the private balances. Official balances are exchange reserves held by central monetary institutions, while private balances are held by companies and private individuals not resident in the UK. Private balances were much more stable than official balances, never falling significantly in total; indeed they had risen substantially since 1968. This reflected in large part an increased need by banks and trading companies for working balances (as well as reflecting the impact of inflation). Official balances were more volatile. They had reached their peak in March 1975, when they had totalled £4.9 billion, but subsequently there had been a continuous

Table 2

The Sterling Balances, Official and Private, 1976–1979
(£ millions)

		Official Balances			Private Balances		
		Oil exporters	Other	Total	Oil exporters	Other	Total
1976	March	2623	1397	4020	473	2761	3234
	June	1964	1135	3099	444	2779	3223
	September	1541	1209	2750	449	2986	3435
	December	1421	1218	2639	497	2987	3484
1977	March	1443	1386	2829	532	3151	3683
	June	1197	1234	2431	828	3205	4033
	September	1288	1217	2505	787	3569	4356
	December	1360	1475	2835	747	4218	4965
1978	March	1404	1591	2995	789	4114	4903
	June	1212	1552	2764	790	3961	4751
	September	1169	1604	2773	861	4049	4910
	December	1006	1604	2610	984	4282	5266
1979	March	1072	1679	2751	1107	4633	5740
	June	1141	1702	2843	1235	4852	6087

Official balances = exchange reserves in sterling (balances held for central monetary institutions)
Private balances = banking and money market liabilities to holders other than central monetary institutions (e.g. banks, multinational companies, private individuals)

Numbers date from end of each month.

Source: Bank of England, *Quarterly Bulletin*, various issues.

drawing down (see Table 2). Withdrawals had been particularly heavy during the period March-June 1976 – £900 million – when OPEC countries had reduced their balances. By the end of September 1976 the private balances totalled £3.4 billion, while the official balances totalled £2.8 billion. As the memorandum noted, the total of the sterling balances, £6.2 billion, was almost exactly twice the sum of the UK's official gold and foreign exchange reserves of £3.1 billion.

A crucial factor, the memorandum went on to imply, was the OPEC countries, who held over half of all the official balances. They had been engaged in diversification of their portfolios over the previous eighteen months, and by September 1976 no major holder any longer held a substantial part of their reserves in sterling.[6] (Indeed, the implication could be drawn that Callaghan's goal, the end of sterling's role as a reserve currency, was already well on its way to being achieved.) Private holdings were more widely dispersed, with only 13 per cent being held by OPEC countries. The Bank had found it difficult to establish the composition of the private holdings, but it estimated that two-thirds represented the working balances of companies and embassies and the holdings of individuals, 'the last of which would appear to be larger than might be expected'. One-third represented the working balances of overseas commercial banks.[7]

It may have been that this memorandum also served to brief Harold Lever for his journey to Washington the following weekend. His attempt to get the Americans to take the problem of the sterling balances seriously worked, and once President Ford had agreed to support an agreement, preparatory work by the Federal Reserve and the US Treasury got under way. On 21 November Burns asked staff members about the size of the sterling balance problem, and the following day he requested an assessment of two approaches to the problem. With regard to the size, Burns was advised that the UK could probably manage in 1977–78 without a special funding operation if the UK could continue to borrow from the Eurocurrency market at the rate it was doing in 1976 (at an annual rate of $3 billion). On the other hand, such an operation, plus the appropriate domestic economic policies, would help to restore confidence in the pound and contribute to a final solution to the problem of sterling as a reserve currency.[8] The second memorandum was more dismissive of Britain's request, stating that 'it is . . . the judgement of the staff that under present circumstances a strong economic case cannot be made for international action on official sterling balances.'[9]

The preparatory work on the part of Federal Reserve Staff, then, was not of a type to discourage Yeo from approaching the problem in his own manner. According to Fay and Young, once President Ford had decided in principle to support a sterling balances agreement, Yeo was given the task of drafting it. The British side of the talks in Washington was now conducted 'with consummate skill' by the Ambassador, Sir Peter Ramsbottom, who was, according to Yeo, '"working them over in the White House, especially Brent Scowcroft. He used to have Scowcroft practically in tears"'. Yeo, on the other hand, was prepared to be tough, and in his first draft he tied the sterling balances tightly to the IMF loan conditions, including a clause that would terminate the agreement whenever the British failed to fulfil any of the conditions.

Burns was even tougher. By early December, backed by the opinions of his staff, he was intractable. 'He not only refused to discuss the agreement, he attacked Ford and Kissinger for meddling in a technical matter, and was furious at Callaghan's consistent pressure. "They tried to corrupt the whole world. It was shameful manipulation, quite shocking. I had an astonishing conversation with Denis Healey about that time when he called me interfering and unfriendly," Burns [said] in a sorrowful tone.'[10]

By the end of the first week in December there were at least three draft agreements in Washington (and there may have been others in London): the US Treasury Plan, the Volcker Plan, drawn up by Paul A. Volcker, President of the New York Federal Reserve Bank, and the Bank for International Settlements (BIS) plan. There was apparently no Bank of England or UK plan, in spite of the fact that the Bank had been working on one for several weeks. McMahon, however, has emphasised that the BIS were keen to play a role in any agreement,[11] and this, plus the fact that the BIS plan shared a number of points with the UK Treasury memorandum, allows the possibility that the BIS incorporated British wishes in their proposal.

There is no need to look at these drafts in detail, since the final agreement differed from all three – though bearing the closest resemblance to the Treasury plan – but there were significant differences between them. The Treasury and Volcker plans, for example, dealt only with the official balances, while the BIS plan wanted to cover both official and private ones (as the British wished). All three provided temporary rather than permanent protection, but only the Treasury plan included phasing out of the official balances and ensuring IMF conditionality amongst its objectives. Volcker, interestingly, believed that a new facility needed to deal only with the balances held by OPEC central banks, totalling some £1.6 billion or $2.7 billion, and therefore the size needed to be only $2 billion. The US Treasury proposed $5.2 billion (SDR 4.5 billion), while the BIS did not specify a size.[12]

The real difference between the US Treasury plan and the other two was the insistence on tying continued access to a sterling balances agreement to fulfilment of the IMF conditions for its loan. The continuing theme of US negotiations over financial aid to Britain was tying it as tightly as possible – and by all means possible – to IMF control. As will be seen, the question of who was to judge whether or not the UK was fulfilling the necessary conditions for the balances facility was to be answered by giving the Managing Director of the IMF new responsibilities.

The US Treasury plan was presumably circulated to the central banks of the Group of Ten in mid-December. It may have been that it was soon taken as the draft to which the negotiators would work; certainly the files of the Bundesbank do not appear to contain copies of the Volcker or BIS plans (unless they were weeded out as unnecessary some time later). The main points were as noted, with the additional points that (1) there would be direct UK funding of the balances into dollar debt with no assured liquidity, or only limited liquidity with a stand-by facility; and (2) conditionality for the UK would be tightened by making access to the mechanisms conditional upon *quarterly* satisfaction of IMF conditions.[13] Direct negotiations on the balances would not begin, however, until the IMF loan was in place. The main reason for this was Burns's outright refusal to send his international expert, Henry Wallich, to Basle to discuss the details, since he feared being outflanked at the last moment by the British government.[14]

Messages had certainly gone from Callaghan to Ford and from Healey to Simon, and these presumably helped to convince the Fed and US Treasury that talks at least were necessary. Late on the night of 9 December Yeo made a telephone call to Mitchell: if he would like to discuss the sterling balances and possible swap arrangements with Simon and Burns, they would be ready to do so any time the following week in Washington. This was to be taken as their response to Callaghan's and Healey's messages.[15] Callaghan kept up the pressure, asking Kissinger on 11 December, at a farewell party in his honour at Downing Street, to intervene once more with the President to get the sterling balances agreement through. 'Kissinger obliged by sending a message that weekend reporting the British anxiety at the bloody-mindedness of Yeo and Burns, and told [Callaghan] that he would do what he personally could on his return.'[16]

The following day Mitchell met with Yeo and Burns. Both of them continued to insist that there was no real problem, and if there was, there was nothing that the Fed or the US Treasury could do about it, since they were now lame ducks (Yeo would leave office when the Carter administration took power on 20 January 1977). In addition, Yeo disliked the idea of setting a precedent of giving special help to the UK. Were there to be an arrangement, however, one made through the IMF and subject to its conditionality would be more likely to be viewed favourably by Congress. They also discussed the possible size of a credit facility, Mitchell proposing $5 billion and Yeo countering with $2 billion or less (a much smaller figure than the $5.2 billion mooted in the US Treasury plan). Mitchell expected discussions to continue that evening over dinner with William Rogers, Kissinger's predecessor as Secretary of State and then in private law practice, but the occasion turned out to be wholly social. His final meeting with Burns and Yeo took place at breakfast the following morning (13 December), when Burns's attempts to check Yeo from pushing his own scheme pointed up the split between the two Americans.

Yeo's version of the meetings was given to Fay and Young:

Yeo first suggested that the British should borrow a vast sum to pay them off entirely; the Treasury replied that this would be too expensive; all they wanted was an insurance policy – money in the bank in Switzerland – to call on when the markets began a run on sterling. Yeo was intensely suspicious. 'What I was afraid of,' he [said], 'was sabotaging the IMF agreement by having a sterling balances deal which just provided a lot of unconditional money by the back door. We had sweated blood, and believed it was absolutely essential that the market perceived that the centrepiece was the IMF deal and not a sterling balances agreement that looked like a crock of gold in disguise. With that we would have been finessed at the last moment.'[17]

Meanwhile, according to Fay and Young, the Germans, believing that the British had fulfilled their part of the bargain, sent Emminger of the Bundesbank and Pöhl of the Finance Ministry 'to soften up Burns. They said there was no reason why the agreement should not be put through at the pre-Christmas meeting of the Bank for International Settlements in Basle. Burns, crustier than ever, told them that Chancellor Schmidt had no business interfering, and that he would not accept the dictates of anybody, PM, Chancellor, even President.' He then refused to send Wallich to Basle.[18]

Mitchell and Pöhl met on the 14th. Pöhl insisted that Yeo's scheme, which was an IMF-only scheme, was not feasible, since it would not be possible to restrict it to the UK – what about Mexico, for example? He told Mitchell quite frankly that the only reason that Germany was supporting the idea of a safety net was because the UK wanted it so badly, although he himself was not at all clear why they did want it: after all, it would turn away capital inflows which were good business for the City of London. Pöhl then told Mitchell that he was going to talk to Witteveen; was there anything Mitchell would like him to say? Mitchell asked him to keep up the pressure to allow the UK a large initial drawing from the IMF. Mitchell also told

him of the IMF mission's pressure for an agreed downward path for
the sterling exchange rate, at which Pöhl became 'positively indig-
nant' (he believed that it was low enough). Finally, Pöhl said that
Schmidt was very relieved that the British were not to adopt import
controls: they would have touched off the French, alienated German
business and seriously affected Schmidt's ability to help the UK in
other ways, including pressing for a safety net for the sterling
balances.[19]

In a sense, Yeo and Burns were about to be finessed by the White
House. President Ford, probably encouraged by Kissinger, decided
that the matter had to be settled, and he called a meeting for that
purpose. Everyone who counted was there: Kissinger, Burns, Yeo,
Scowcroft.

'The seriousness of the crisis can be judged from the fact that the President,
who was watching the Washington–Minnesota football match, switched
down the sound,' [said] one of the participants in heavily accented English
. . . . Burns delivered a vigorous attack on the way the White House had
handled the affair: if the politicians had kept out of it, he and the technical
people could have fixed it all in a couple of weeks. But, Kissinger replied, it
was a political problem, and the sterling balances were a key decision: they
would help end the sterling crisis.

As Kissinger later explained, '"I thought [Britain] should be able
to get out of this without any major public crisis. To have failed to
do that might have destroyed Britain's ability to go on playing a
major role in world affairs."' As Yeo later remembered the tone of
the meeting, '"Oh well, everything's done," they said. "Come on
Yeo, the battle's over."' Nevertheless argument raged during the
football match over what kind of agreement there would be. 'Kissinger wanted a broad, generous agreement which would be a political bonus to Callaghan, while the money men wanted something
more limited. Kissinger scored some points, because Yeo was told to
stop being bloody-minded, but the President gave him the vital job
of drafting the deal.'[20]

This had, of course, been under way for some time, so there was
little more for Yeo to do in Washington. Attention would now shift
to the Continent, where the IMF agreement was to be considered
first by Working Party 3 and then by the Group of Ten deputies,
since the financing of the IMF loan through the General Arrangement to Borrow (GAB) depended upon their agreement. (According
to McMahon, once the UK and the IMF had come to an agreement,
the Group of Ten financing was assured: what followed was

shadow-boxing.[21]) The stand-by requested was for $3.9 billion or SDR 3,360 million, the largest ever. Out of that, the liquid resources of the IMF itself would only extend to a drawing of SDR 500 million; the remaining SDR 2,860 million would have to come from the reserves of the Group of Ten plus Switzerland.[22] In formal terms, the Managing Director of the IMF, Witteveen, had requested the Group of Ten to finance partially the stand-by on the Fund, through letters of credit in the context of the GAB. Before agreeing to this, the Group of Ten needed expert economic advice as to whether the proposed IMF agreement was likely to accomplish what it was meant to do, and this was the task of Working Party 3.

Working Party 3 was part of the Organisation for Economic Cooperation and Development (OECD), and as such had no direct institutional link with the Group of Ten. (The Group of Ten itself had developed from 1961, when the GAB had been set up, as the mechanism by which the largest western industrial countries plus Japan funnelled money to the IMF for the Fund to extend to other countries.) Two representatives from each country normally attended Working Party 3, one each from the finance ministry and the central bank, although the US also sent a third from the Council of Economic Advisers. Its reputation for economic expertise and judgement – perhaps even extending to political judgement when necessary – was very high, and it was customary for the Group of Ten (G10) to turn to it for its judgement.[23]

On 21 December 1976 Working Party 3 met in Paris under the chairmanship of Emminger to consider the UK situation and the IMF agreement. Those who attended included Mitchell and Peter Middleton from the UK Treasury and McMahon from the Bank of England, Whittome for the IMF, Yeo and Wallich from the US Treasury and the Fed, John Fay, the Assistant Secretary-General of the OECD and his colleague Stephen Marris, and representatives from other G10 countries. They had before them various documents, including the IMF's analysis of the agreement, the Chancellor's Letter of Intent to the IMF and a copy of his speech on 15 December to the House of Commons. Mitchell opened the discussion by explaining why the stand-by was necessary, followed by Whittome's explanation of the IMF's view: there was then 'fairly thorough' discussion by all those attending.

Emminger tried to bring the discussion to a point. What, he wanted to know, should be said to the G10 deputies (who were meeting the following day)? They had been asked in particular to express themselves on the balance of payments prospects. He thought that they agreed that through stabilisation of the economy it (the economy) would come back into balance; to ensure this, stabilisation probably had to extend over two years. As Marris of the OECD had said, this was necessary because of the seriousness of the problem. Secondly, should they associate themselves with the judgement of the IMF staff appraisal? Yes, they should, and it would be Emminger who would report to the G10 deputies over the following days.[24]

The deputies of the Group of Ten met on 22 December under de Larosière to consider the IMF agreement and the activities of the GAB. (Central bank representatives met separately the same day to consider the modalities of a swap arrangement for the sterling balances.) Emminger reported the discussion and favourable conclusion of Working Party 3, and the representative of the IMF explained the reasons why it would be necessary to activate the GAB. The deputies raised a number of problems about the GAB programme, and Emminger regretted that because of their own balance of payments problems a number of countries in G10 would participate only with small amounts or not at all. It seemed that Italy would contribute nothing, Canada just a bit and France only $50 million, while Germany would be providing $785 million.[25]

The G10 deputies then had to return to their own central banks and Treasuries where they reported on the discussions and secured final agreement to taking part in the GAB procedures for the IMF. Emminger, for example, wrote to the Central Bank Council of the Bundesbank on the following day, 23 December. After explaining to them that the IMF did not itself have the liquid resources to finance such a big stand-by, he reported that Working Party 3 had looked closely at the British programme for putting the economy back on its feet and that the G10 deputies had agreed after this consultation to the refinancing proposal of the IMF. He reported that the negotiations about a safety net of the Basle central bank group for the sterling balances were proceeding separately, and it was likely – although not certain – that in January central bank governors would have before them a paper setting out the basis for such an agreement.[26]

The uncertainty about whether a sterling balances paper would appear reflected uncertainty about how Washington was going to act. Certainly Mitchell had remained apprehensive in the days following his visit to Washington. He and McMahon were due to meet with Pöhl and Emminger, Yeo and a representative from the Fed, and he was convinced that negotiations over the balances were in a mess because of so much publicity. The position in Washington was still uncertain, with Burns seeing difficulties with Congress. Mitchell decided that he should warn London not to be surprised if there was coverage of the official balances only, with a facility much smaller than London wanted, perhaps only $2.5 billion. The British negotiating position was very weak: their apparent desperation to get an agreement had encouraged potential negotiators to increase conditionality in one form or another.[27]

On the same day that Emminger met with the G10 deputies about the IMF stand-by, there was also a meeting of central bank officials to discuss the problem of the balances. It may be that this was the meeting which Burns had forbidden Wallich to attend, although at least one participant was certainly pushing the hard line of the Fed and the US Treasury. The agreement that was beginning to take shape had two main components: sufficient reserves to resist any renewed pressure on the pound – the safety net – and arrangements to phase out the balances. Clearly they were worried about possible British plans to impose import controls, since the minutes emphasised that the safety net arrangement would ensure that the British government would not be obliged by the decline of the balances to take such measures. The suggestion was that the balances be funded into medium-term obligations; that is, holders of the balances would receive in exchange bonds repayable over a five-to-ten-year period, thereby removing the element of volatility. There was agreement that Britain had 'to take steps designed to avoid the need for rebuilding of sterling balances'; presumably they remembered the early 1970s, when the OPEC surpluses held in sterling helped to finance the deficit. However, there was no desire that the British be precipitate in running down the balances, since too quick a rundown might trigger a crisis. There was to be a link between 'the use of the facility and the continuing appropriateness in relation to the IMF programme', and use of the facility was to be subject to periodic certification by the IMF that the UK was continuing to fulfil the conditions. It is worth noting that some members objected to the latter, since they did not want the Bank for International Settlements to be tied to an IMF approval. The US representatives thought that their government would be able to accept an agreement such as had been outlined – perhaps this is not surprising, since it contained many of the elements of the US Treasury Plan circulated in mid-December.[28]

After a Christmas and New Year break, attention returned to Washington and the meeting on 3 January 1977 of the Executive

Directors of the IMF. At a day-long meeting, they thrashed over all the elements of the draft agreement. Interestingly, they noted some of the same problems as had members of the British Cabinet. One director asked whether the considerable fall in real wages implicit in the current agreement with the trade unions would be tolerable? Did the policy give due regard to wage differentials? Noting that it was difficult to promote social justice and a redistribution of income without at the same time increasing total national income, another director congratulated the UK authorities for not taking the easy way out by introducing import controls, since these would have adversely affected developing countries. In the end, they unanimously supported the UK request.[29] A few days later the UK drew down its first tranche of SDR 1 billion.

The way was now clear for an agreement on the sterling balances. The governors of the central banks of the major industrial countries, including Richardson and Burns, met at the BIS in Basle on 10 January to sort out the final draft. The meeting was chaired by Jelle Zijlstra, President of the Netherlands Bank, who was also chairman of the BIS; he had invited Witteveen to be present. The main elements of the agreement were as follows: (1) the facility would be for $3 billion, to be furnished by the participating central banks and the BIS;[30] (2) the facility was to cover only the official balances – not both official and private, as the Bank of England had wished – and the official balances should not be allowed to exceed $3.75 billion (£2.165 billion), their level on 8 December 1976. If they did increase while the drawings were still outstanding, repayment equal to the amount of the increase had to be made within ninety days; (3) the facility would last for two years with possible extension for a third; and (4) repayments would begin at the end of the borrowing period and be completed within four years.

The UK had had to agree to certain undertakings: (1) eligibility to draw on the facility was conditional on continuing eligibility to draw on the IMF stand-by; (2) to reduce the official balances to working levels only, by the sale of foreign currency bonds and other appropriate means if necessary; (3) this would be done by offering foreign currency 'funding' securities in exchange for official holdings of sterling. These would have a maturity of five to ten years, would be negotiable, and not more than 75 per cent should be denominated in dollars; and (4) to exercise restraint with respect to future increases in private balances. The US Treasury feared that Britain might in future turn to private balances to help finance a deficit, since they had not been forced to forswear this as they had with official balances. This would create volatile short-term debt, as well as loosen the constraints on public spending. It would be the duty of the Managing Director of the IMF to monitor the agreement: the UK would 'review regularly' with Witteveen and with the central bank governors the progress made in meeting the undertakings; if, in Witteveen's opinion, the UK was not making reasonable efforts, he would notify the BIS and they could suspend the facility.[31]

On 11 January 1977 the Chancellor announced the agreement in the House of Commons, affirming that it would enable the government 'to achieve an orderly reduction in the role of sterling as a reserve currency',[32] and on 8 February the agreement came into force. Once the agreement had been announced, the government was able to return to the markets. On 24 January the Bank of England arranged a $1.5 billion, seven-year Eurodollar loan with thirteen commerical banks on quite good terms. The Chancellor was later to emphasise that the loan provided evidence of their firm intention to finance any future deficits through fixed-term borrowing, rather than by volatile, short-term flows.[33]

Indeed, the reaction of the markets had been immediately favourable. Confidence in the pound was restored, and huge inflows of capital took place both into sterling and into the gilt-edged securities offered for sale by the government in accordance with the sterling balances agreement. In January 1977 short-term capital inflows amounted to $2 billion, some $500 million more than even the most optimistic forecasts. On 21 January Richardson was able to write to Burns that 'the welcome improvement in sentiment which we have experienced in recent weeks has meant that we have not had to draw on your swap line'.[34]

The only hiccup was political. On 20 January Barnett, as the Chief Secretary to the Treasury, won final Cabinet approval of the Public Expenditure White Paper containing all that had been agreed in the December Cabinet discussions. Relations between the Cabinet and the Parliamentary Labour Party worsened, and the nadir was reached on 17 March during the debate on the Public Expenditure White Paper. There was a motion before the House to adjourn. As Barnett described it,

we could not risk a motion to 'take note' of the White Paper, which covered the controversial plans agreed in the 1976 IMF Year of the Many Cuts, as the motion would then be amended, and we would undoubtedly lose the vote. When it came to 10 p.m., after I had wound up the debate in a noisy

noisy half-hour, it had become clear we would lose a vote even on the Adjournment. Some of our backbenchers were definitely abstaining, despite the serious consequences for the Government. The Prime Minister decided, after consulting Michael Cocks, the Chief Whip, that we should all abstain, and just allow the House to adjourn. It seemed a simple enough ploy, but it backfired badly when the Scottish Nationalists forced a Division and we lost the vote by 293 to nil. There was an uproar and Margaret Thatcher put down the customary Motion of 'No Confidence'. If we lost the vote, there would be a General Election.

The upshot was that the Prime Minister came to an agreement with David Steel, the leader of the Liberal Party, and the so-called Lib-Lab Pact was born.[35]

The economy took all this in its stride, and continued to improve. Between 1 January and mid-April 1977 the pound appreciated some 1.5 per cent on a trade-weighted basis, and the UK exchange reserves increased from $4.1 billion at the end of December to $9.6 billion at the end of March. In May the UK drew its second tranche of SDR 320 million from the IMF and in August its third and last, this also of SDR 320 million. Altogether the UK drew less than half of the IMF stand-by.

In July 1977 the Executive Board of the Fund was scheduled to review the performance of the UK economy. Ryrie told the other executive directors that in the second half of fiscal 1976–77 public sector borrowing was £2.4 billion below the limit agreed under the stand-by arrangement, and that domestic credit had actually contracted by £0.4 billion, rather than expanding by £4.5 billion. Cash limits had kept down public expenditure, and incomes policy was also a success, reflecting a fall in the increase in average earnings from 26.5 per cent in July 1975 to 8.5 per cent in July 1977. The Chancellor continued to consult with the Fund over the life of the agreement – according to one account he 'found it useful to retain the Fund as a bogeyman against extremist ministers and the unions'[36] – but there was no tension between the UK Treasury and the Fund: during 1978 both public spending and domestic credit expansion were under target, and the economy continued to improve. By January 1978 the reserves totalled $20.6 billion.[37]

The attempts to wind down the sterling balances were considerably less successful: the attractiveness of holding sterling increased as the economy improved, and the Federal Reserve staff noted in September 1977 that by mid-August the official balances were some £150 million above the limit set in the 1968 Basle Arrangement.[38]

Nevertheless the Managing Director judged in September 1977, March and September 1978 that the UK authorities were making reasonable efforts to reduce the official balances to working balances; however, as shown in Table 2, the official balances were, by the end of September 1978, £600 million above the limit.

The private balances fared even worse. The Bank of England had been somewhat unhappy about the agreement, partly because of the humiliating insistence on IMF surveillance, and partly, according to one Bank official, because they had wished the agreement to cover the private as well as the official balances (as had the 1968 Arrangement).[39] McMahon, however, has taken the opposite view: the private balances were not a problem, since they were stable and even increasing. At the end of December 1976 the private balances had totalled £3,484 million; by the end of September 1978 they were £4,910 million; and by the end of June 1979 they were £6,087 million – nearly double their total in December 1976 (see Table 2). In any event, if the Bank had wanted to run down the private balances in the same manner as the official ones, there would have been little the Bank could have done to coerce their holders.[40]

Yet there seem to have been few complaints about the balances; apparently not from the Fund and certainly not from Callaghan.[41] Indeed there was satisfaction all round, particularly about the IMF stand-by and, perhaps, particularly in the Fund. As their historian has concluded, 'as of the end of 1978, the stand-by arrangement had to be termed a success. Some members of the Executive Board went so far as to label it "the most successful ever implemented".'[42]

PART II

The Economics

CHAPTER 5

The Movement of Opinion

In one way 1976 was a year of crisis not unlike those earlier years – too many to enumerate – when the balance of payments was under severe pressure. It was, so to speak, a year of devaluation with all the attendant excitement. But it was also something more, and it is the something more that distinguishes it from other earlier crises. It was a turning point in the philosophical basis of economic policy and in the thinking of the Treasury about economic management.

For the first two decades after the war there had been a broad consensus on the need to maintain employment and output even at the cost of a continuing increase in prices. But as inflation accelerated in the early 1970s the consensus was shattered. The ideas that had previously governed policy came under challenge and the aims and instruments of policy became the subject of bitter debate. New prescriptions for the management of the economy were advanced from many different quarters. There could be no doubt about the need to contain inflation; but how it should be done and at what sacrifice of other objectives was very much in dispute.

The change in opinion in the 1970s is vividly illustrated in public addresses delivered by successive heads of the Treasury: William Armstrong in 1968, Douglas Wass in 1978 and Peter Middleton in 1988.[1] The first of these was written at a time when the world economy was expanding rapidly and the anxieties of national economic management were overborne by a universal 'mood of almost Victorian optimism'.[2] Demand management was still regarded with confidence as a guarantee of economic stability, and fiscal policy – in practice, tax changes – as the prime instrument of control. Monetary policy, on the other hand, took a subordinate and supplementary place, as is evident in the absence of any reference to it in Armstrong's lecture until almost the final paragraph. So far as it was an object of policy to limit inflation it was to incomes policy, not monetary policy, that Armstrong and his contemporaries looked.

Things looked very different ten years later when Douglas Wass felt unable to echo Armstrong's conclusion that 'modern economic policy has been a success'. He was conscious of 'major uncertainties and controversies in fundamental issues' and emphasised the difficulties facing any single country in an increasingly integrated world if it tried to solve its problems unilaterally. The rapid growth in financial flows within and between countries gave increased importance to monetary factors and to the reactions of financial markets to changes and expected changes in monetary conditions. Wass accepted the usefulness of monetary targets so long as they were consistent with the fiscal stance and went on to describe the Treasury's efforts to build up a forecasting model of the monetary sector of the economy. He continued to lay stress on fiscal policy but took a cautious view of tax changes because of the disruption they might cause to the private sector; he recognised that in practice it had been necessary to attach more weight to changes in public sector programmes and make adjustments 'more frequently and more substantially than was earlier thought desirable'. Wass took a somewhat agnostic view of incomes policy but agreed that it had on occasion been successful, given sufficient public understanding and an absence of strong demand pressures in the labour market. With his stress on international integration and financial flows, and with six years of floating rates behind him, Wass was conscious of increased limitations on the freedom of governments to influence the rate of exchange but hesitated to accept that they had no influence at all.

Ten years later still, Peter Middleton echoed some of these points (especially the growing power of foreign exchange markets over exchange rates) but put a very different construction on events and particularly on the changes in ideas that accompanied the IMF crisis in 1976. He attacked what he took to be the attempt in the 1950s and 1960s to make the economy grow faster by expanding demand and leaving it to incomes policy to control the resulting inflation. Incomes policy he dismissed as ineffective, the only real financial discipline coming from rates of exchange fixed under Bretton Woods arrangements. The abandonment of these arrangements 'simply let inflation loose'. Middleton's was hardly a convincing explanation of British proneness to inflation, given that demand pressures were at least as high in other countries such as Germany and inflation more rapid in countries like Italy and Japan. He represented the crisis of 1976 *both* as the culmination of longer-term trends and as the consequence of a mistaken response to the oil shock of 1973. Other countries, he argued, applied restrictive policies to prevent higher oil prices feeding into prices in general while the United Kingdom preferred to borrow through the nationalised industries until it could borrow no more.

Not surprisingly, Middleton's exposition mirrors the thinking of the Conservative government in office in the 1980s. He questioned the power of fiscal and monetary policy to alter the level of output or employment more than temporarily and alleged a breakdown in the belief in a long-run trade-off between unemployment and inflation – a belief which, if it was ever entertained in the Treasury, was not to blame for the policies followed. He then cited as decisive changes associated with the IMF agreement three major departures in policy-making.

The first of these was 'the explicit embracing of monetary policy' and the establishment of monetary targets, in common with other countries, as a way of imposing financial discipline. He did not explain why targets that are regularly missed should have such a powerful effect. Secondly, he pointed to ceilings for public borrowing as well as for monetary expansion. These he claimed made it possible to introduce an effective system of cash control of public expenditure (although in fact the sequence was the other way round) after public expenditure had been 'out of control for a decade and a half'. The only evidence offered of this was a rise in the proportion of GDP taken in public expenditure from 36 per cent in the mid-1960s to a peak of 48 per cent in the mid-1970s – a rise paralleled in many other European countries (see Table 18).

A third change was the introduction of a medium-term financial strategy. Middleton set out the advantages of this but had nothing to say about the success of governments in adhering to the medium-term strategy they enunciated.

One cannot help feeling that in 1998 the then head of the Treasury will find it necessary to review the ideas so firmly held by his predecessors and put yet another complexion on the events of 1976. Nothing can change the conclusion that resort to the IMF symbolised the triumph of the market over a government in deficit. But the market can be mistaken, even at times foolishly so; it changes its mind, tends to take a short view, and neglects many things that matter greatly. It has its theories just as governments do, including theories about what governments will do, and since its theories are often superficial it is given to suddenly embracing new theories. Above all it can respond to a government lead or be brought to take a different view of government policy; what governments can do and what they ought to do in the face of market opinion is not fixed and unalterable but may change and be made to change.

We shall not attempt to trace in detail the progress of the debate between the various schools of thought over the years between the first and last of these lectures. We shall instead try to convey the gist of the conflicting economic doctrines and to indicate the reasons for their appeal as well as the criticisms to which they can be subjected. It can be assumed that most of these criticisms were advanced by the mid-1970s; but rather than rehearse the succession of arguments between economists in a long series of controversies it seems preferable to look back on the debate from the perspective of the 1990s.

DEMAND MANAGEMENT

We can begin by summarising the orthodoxy of the period up to the 1970s. This took as the prime object of policy 'a high and stable level of employment' and, under the influence of Keynes, regarded the management of demand as the means of achieving this aim.

Keynes's starting point was that employment and output were a function of effective demand. Of the various elements in aggregate demand, he regarded investment or capital expenditure as peculiarly unstable while the habits of consumers in spending or saving were remarkably stable. Investment was the active element, responding to expectations that were inevitably volatile, while savings were passive and influenced mainly by changes in income levels. The two could be kept in step only if the fluctuations in investment were paralleled by similar fluctuations in savings; and these would occur only if incomes, and the employment giving rise to them, were driven up or down until savings were supplemented or reduced to the required extent. A fall in investment, for example, would throw workers out of a job in the engineering and construction industries; their impoverishment would reduce the demand for consumer goods and cause more unemployment there; and these workers in turn would spend less and deprive other workers of their jobs. At each stage the fall in spending would fall short of the earlier fall in the income of the spenders as they drew on their savings; and the process of contraction would come to a halt (unless renewed by a further fall in investment as was only too likely) only when the total drop in savings overtook the reduction in investment.

In the Keynesian scheme of things there was always, or nearly always, underemployment and the pace of expansion or contraction was set by investment. It was investment that dictated the level of savings (and hence the level of income and employment) rather than the other way round. Once investment increased, it would generate additional income through the multiplier process just discussed and out of that higher income would come the savings necessary to finance the investment. Once the process began, other investment was also likely to be affected, creating a still bigger swing in output, employment and income. These swings were not inevitable if action was taken promptly to offset the initial change. If, however, action was not taken, there was a danger that things would get out of hand, leaving the economy in a deep depression or suffering from galloping inflation.

These ideas pointed to an overriding need to stabilise demand, with the emphasis on domestic demand, and comparatively little consideration of supply side problems or of difficulties in balancing the international accounts (although neither of these was by any means neglected). Stabilising employment required stabilisation of effective demand. But how was this to be accomplished? Keynes concentrated on the need to stabilise investment and hoped to achieve this by varying the rate of interest and using state-financed public works, preferably in conjunction with a capital budget separate from the annual revenue budget. He did not, however, approve of trying to mop up excess savings in the private sector by deliberately running a budget deficit on revenue account. This, he thought, would encourage profligacy. Nor did he expect to see unemployment fall below an average of, at best, 5 per cent.

Demand management after the war followed a rather different pattern. Little use was made of the rate of interest and Keynes himself had urged in 1946 that expectations of a continuing long-term rate of about 3 per cent should not be disturbed. So far as monetary policy was used, it was at first largely confined to requests to the banks to be selective in their lending. When revived in 1952 by Butler, monetary policy was thought, probably mistakenly, to have played an important part in moderating demand in that year. When used again to cut bank lending in 1955–6 it proved slow and ineffective. Then in 1957 came Thorneycroft's attempt to master inflation by appealing to the quantity theory of money. Thorneycroft is often represented as a forerunner of Mrs Thatcher but in fact when he talked about money he usually meant spending, and it was over government expenditure, not monetary policy, that he resigned.

For most of the postwar period the rate of interest was used to influence international capital flows and the balance of payments, not the level of demand, and tight money meant restrictions on bank lending, not a cut in the stock of money. Indeed in 1959 Professor Harry Johnson complained that there were no adequate figures of the money supply. It was not until the mid-1960s that attempts were made to put together a long run of figures on the stock of money in the United Kingdom.[3] What was not in doubt was that the stock of money, measured against the growth of GNP, was a steadily diminishing proportion of it, while the long-term rate of interest, measuring income forgone on cash holdings, was a steadily mounting quantity.

So far as monetary factors were brought to bear on demand, the most obviously effective weapon was hire purchase controls, first used in 1951 and often renewed during the next two decades. These had the great disadvantage of affecting only a limited range of industries that were in the course of rapid expansion all over the world. These controls produced an instability of demand in those crucial industries that had to be set against any contribution to the stabilisation of aggregate demand. Although frequently condemned, hire purchase controls continued to be used in the 1950s and 1960s and were revived for the last time in December 1973.

Thus monetary factors were thought of in terms of interest rates and restrictions on credit. Their influence was judged to be rather limited. As Blackaby put it in 1977, discussing the preparation of economic forecasts by the National Institute:

The main areas that were found to have some sensitivity to interest rates were private housing and capital inflows from abroad. Changes in hire-purchase terms were also found to have effects. Private industrial investment appeared to depend heavily on the degree of capacity working, and did not appear to respond much to interest-rate changes. Prices were not forecast from the money-supply, but from the movement of labour costs, import prices and indirect taxes. Wage-costs, in turn, which in the earlier years were assumed to respond to unemployment, in the later period were forecast on the basis of an *ad hoc* assessment of the situation. Altogether, monetary factors were peripheral rather than central to the forecast – mainly because examination of past relationships suggested that their influence was not strong.[4]

If demand management made little use of monetary policy it relied correspondingly heavily on fiscal policy. While this meant some attempt to vary public investment, the main impact was on taxation and to a lesser extent public expenditure. At first there had been the idea of a shelf of projects that could be taken down, dusted, and put into operation in a depression. But once there were regular programmes stretching over several years it was obviously more sensible to think in terms of advancing or retarding some part of the programmes. Even this was found to be not very effective, since it took a long time to get new work started and it was hard to abandon projects already under way. There was apt to be a rise in public investment two years or so after it was approved. By that time recovery was usually already far advanced and the brakes were about to be put on again.

This left current expenditure and taxation as the leading instruments of demand management. The margin between the two – the budget surplus or deficit – seemed an obvious means of operating on demand and had been suggested by Evan Durbin as early as 1940. The idea was strongly opposed by the Treasury in 1944 as contrary to all principles of expenditure control, received no support from Keynes, was omitted from the wartime White Paper on Employment Policy, and was never fully accepted by senior officials, even in the 1950s, whenever what was in prospect was a budget deficit rather than a surplus. A system was, however, developed within the Treasury under which forecasts of demand and output over the next 18–24 months were prepared about three times a year, assessments were made of the economic situation and prospects on the basis of these forecasts, and recommendations were submitted to the Chancellor in advance of the Budget on the scale of action required in order to stabilise employment. The Budget judgement, as it came to be called, was a judgement on the change in taxation required for that purpose, not about the budget surplus or deficit. But since the Treasury's forecasts and calculations were not made public, while budget surpluses or deficits – particularly deficits – were highly publicised, it was on the latter that debate usually focused.

This was unfortunate for a number of reasons. First of all, the budget outcome is the resultant of all the influences on government revenue and expenditure, not itself an instrument of management. Estimates of the outcome are subject to error, like all estimates, and the error can be a large one. Moreover the estimate is the product of different calculations, made by different people, from those relating to the impact of the change in taxation on economic activity. The two estimates may point in quite different directions, especially if the Budget estimate takes no account of the change in the level of activity that the tax change is intended to procure. In 1954, for example, Butler hesitated to introduce a Budget that might yield a deficit (officials had provided him with estimates showing a surplus of no more than £10 million). But at the end of the financial year the surplus turned out to be £433 million with no change in policy, the difference reflecting a misjudgement of the reaction of an expanding economy on tax revenue. The change in the level of activity, on the other hand, was in accord with the pre-Budget estimate.

A further difficulty was that a Budget surplus was not what it seemed. It was not, as most people imagined, a revenue surplus measuring government saving, as a glance at the Annual White Paper on National Income and Expenditure, which *did* estimate the government's contribution to saving, immediately made clear. Both revenue and expenditure included capital as well as current items; and different components of either total had quite different impacts on demand and economic activity. A cut in social security benefits, for example, reduced demand more powerfully than higher rates of income tax on the very wealthy.

The Budget surplus of those days was confined to central government transactions and omitted other parts of the public sector: the nationalised industries and the local authorities. Once these were added in, a surplus could be calculated for the whole public sector: a surplus showing for all transactions, capital and current, the net surplus of funds made available to the rest of the economy or, in the case of a deficit, the financial deficit of the public sector. This was significant, not as a measure of the impact of the public sector on the level of economic activity but as a measure of the impact of public sector borrowing on financial markets. For some purposes it was the *gross* amount of the public sector's borrowing (the public sector borrowing requirement, or PSBR) that mattered, for others the net balance between what was borrowed and what was lent (the public sector financial deficit, or PSFD). When reference is made to budget deficits nowadays it is usually the PSBR that is in mind.

The transition to the PSBR as the test of budgetary propriety was part of a general shift in opinion laying increasing emphasis on money and finance. From the point of view of a Keynesian, there was no greater economic logic in using one measure of the Budget deficit than another. Just as there had been no simple connection between the expansionary impact of a Budget deficit and the size of the deficit under the old measure so there was little reason to expect any close relationship under the new one. Different items of expenditure (and revenue) have very different effects on the generation of income, so that, if one is trying to assess the impact of the Budget on the level of activity in the economy, one needs to study the make-up of total revenue and expenditure as well as the totals themselves and cannot stop at subtracting one total from another unless one thinks the amount of government borrowing involved all that matters.

The practice of including the capital expenditure of nationalised industries in the calculation was peculiar to the United Kingdom and inflated both public expenditure and the borrowing requirement. There is a difference between borrowing to finance a government deficit and borrowing to finance capital expenditure in the highly capital-intensive industries under public ownership, even if both make calls on the limited savings of the private sector. Similarly, there is a difference between a Budget surplus and selling off a publicly owned industry, even if both affect the borrowing requirement in the same way.

In using fiscal and monetary policy to manage demand, the Treasury recognised that rising demand would weaken the balance of payments and if carried too far would push up prices by causing 'overheating', that is, pressure on capacity, shortages and bottlenecks. It associated inflation with excess demand, or alternatively with cost-push, rather than with 'too much money' in the sense of too much cash. There was undoubtedly a link between money and demand and a second link between demand and prices, but these links were not such as to point to control of the money supply as offering an obvious and certain way of controlling prices. In the long run, as the quantity theory of money maintained, the value of money might keep pace with the supply but in the short run the association between the two was complex and uncertain.

In the 1960s monetary policy was seen, as in the Radcliffe Report, as capable of playing a helpful but strictly subordinate part in economic policy. It featured in the periodic packages of measures taken by the government to regulate demand but was added almost as an afterthought, usually with an eye on the balance of payments, never as a weapon with almost magical powers for overcoming inflation. Nobody in the Treasury, with one or two possible exceptions, would have thought of an expansion in the money supply as the driving force behind inflation although there would have been sympathy for the view that such an expansion was necessary in order to 'validate' inflation. If pressed, government economists would have argued that tightening the money supply would be more likely to re-act on output than on prices; and that until other influences on the price level, such as the rate of wages and the cost of imported food-stuffs and materials, were held steady, inflation would not yield, or yield very little, to changes in the money supply. This did not imply a denial of the influence of the rate of interest on aggregate demand and of demand on prices. What it indicated was first an insistence that demand inflation could not be explained in simple monetary terms and secondly a belief in the importance of cost-inflation as a more or less independent element in the inflationary process.

The limitations of the Keynesian approach became increasingly evident as inflation mounted towards the end of the 1960s. It was attacked on various grounds: for its neglect of the supply side of the economy; for its emphasis on 'fine tuning' and the short-term out-look; for its concentration on the domestic economy in face of the in-creasing importance of international influences; and most of all for its inability to offer a satisfactory solution to the problem of inflation.

MONETARISM

The attack on the latter score was led by a school of economists labelled 'monetarists' because they attached special significance to changes in the money supply or, as others prefer to call it, the money stock: not spending or money expenditure or money GDP but *money* in the sense of cash and bank deposits. Looking for the causes of in-flation, which they took to be the primary problem of economic management, they found it in the quantity theory of money, which traced an increase in the price level to a prior increase in the quantity of money. Budget deficits financed by borrowing from the banks were blamed for most of the increase in the money supply and were at all costs to be avoided. They did nothing but add to inflation; any short-term boost to output and employment would rapidly dis-appear once prices had time to respond, as they inevitably would. While the Keynesians thought that governments could do very little about inflation except through incomes policy so long as the pressure of demand was kept within limits, the monetarists thought that governments could do very little about employment except by con-trolling the money supply and removing market imperfections that allowed trade unions to exercise monopoly powers.

Monetarist ideas developed sooner and more widely in the United States than in the United Kingdom and indeed before 1970 it would have been difficult to find more than one or two followers of Milton Friedman in academic life in Britain. In America the monetarist debate went well back and intensified in the 1960s. After Friedman's famous presidential address to the American Economic Association in December 1967,[5] the flow of articles on the subject in newspapers, pamphlets and journals was greatly swollen. In Britain, however, monetarist thinking in 1967 was still far from widespread. It remained generally accepted that wage-push was a more obstinate threat than excess demand, that fiscal policy was a more effective and satisfactory instrument of demand management than monetary policy and that to use monetary rather than fiscal policy to curb inflation was to run unnecessary risks with full employment since it took a very strong dose of monetary policy to make it work on demand.

What brought monetarism to the fore was not academic research but the inflation of the early 1970s. Only then did people begin to look round for new theories as a guide to policy. With inflation roaring away at over 30 per cent, the balance of payments in record deficit, and unemployment rising from a level unprecedented in postwar experience, it was hard to see how any Keynesian prescription could provide a cure. Confidence in the government's ability to restore full employment by increased spending was evaporating. On the other hand, the monetarists exuded confidence that they, and only they, had the answer, not perhaps to unemployment, but at least to inflation and so to a more stable economic environment.

Monetarism appeared to offer a convenient and convincing explanation of the inflation that followed the Barber boom in 1971–73, if one assumed that there was a lag of a couple of years between the explosion in the money supply and the explosion in wages and prices. If one accepted the monetarist view, one could conclude that all that was necessary to cure inflation was to restrain the growth in the money supply – an apparently impersonal process not involving confrontation with the trade unions or any form of government intervention. On Milton Friedman's view of the world, inflation could be mastered without interference of any kind with collective bargaining and without any direct limitation on the freedom of the government to borrow. It might be wise on other grounds to deny trade unions monopolistic powers or to prevent governments from overspending: but control of the money supply was a sufficient as well as a necessary means of stabilising prices.

The monetarists started from apparently simple and intellectually appealing propositions. Inflation, they claimed, is 'always and everywhere a monetary phenomenon'. It could occur only if the money supply expanded as prices rose. If the money supply did not increase and 'validate' the rise in the price level, inflation would be brought to a halt. This seemed axiomatic; but it was not in fact in accord with British experience. If the money supply was restricted by the only means available to the authorities, namely higher interest rates or a credit squeeze, business would no doubt be depressed and profit margins would contract. To that extent there would be some check to rising prices. But unless business costs were affected – and especially wages, which represented on the average something like 70 per cent of domestic costs – there would be no further check to prices. Wage-earners, however, might go on pressing for higher wages – as they did in 1975 and again in 1980–81 and 1990–91 – even when business was making losses and unemployment increasing. No doubt in the end rising unemployment would begin to moderate wage demands. But rising unemployment was a much less attractive cure for inflation than an apparently innocuous – indeed desirable – slowing down of monetary expansion.

A central proposition of monetarism is that there is a stable demand for money at any given level of income: that is, that over time the public will hold a predictable proportion of their income in cash. Sometimes, but not invariably, account is taken of the rate of interest (that is, the cost of holding money) so that the link is between the money supply on the one side and money income *and* the rate of interest on the other. The implication of this is taken to be that monetary policy, operating on the money supply, has predictable results, and can ensure stability in its value. If this is true, earlier views on the ineffectiveness of monetary policy can be dismissed.

CRITICISMS OF MONETARISM

But can stability of the demand function be counted upon? It may be possible to demonstrate that the demand for money changes little over time. If this is so over long periods it lacks significance and could be pure coincidence: all kinds of financial innovation, such as cheques and credit cards, the introduction of new facilities and new types of institution, impinge on monetary habits in the long run, some in one direction, some in another, and may or may not cancel one another out. In any event, what matters is the very short run, not the long. It is the immediate impact of monetary policy that dictates the subsequent course of events, and in the short run there can be no question that the velocity of circulation of money, far from being stable, is often highly unstable. We need only observe what happens in a prolonged bank strike, such as occurred a few years ago in Eire, to see how readily other forms of credit take the place of bank credit and how the business of the country can be transacted with limited access to money.

Monetarists took for granted the power of the monetary authorities to control the money supply. This may seem an easy task in which central banks have engaged for at least a century; but experience shows that when they set themselves monetary targets they are rarely able to hit them. In the days when commercial banks maintained fixed reserve ratios, and their reserves could be acted upon by open market operations, some precision was possible in control of the money supply – although the monetary authorities took little interest in it and had no adequate statistics of its amount. Once banks were no longer limited in their lending to some multiple of their balances at the Bank of England and could, at will, add to their reserves by reducing their take-up of Treasury bills, the old machinery of control no longer functioned. Indeed, there was some danger that once the authorities started to raise interest rates and the banks paid correspondingly higher rates on deposits, money might become a more attractive asset and expand in supply in response to measures designed to restrict it.

The views developed by the monetarists were also open to the objections, urged, for example; by Kaldor in 1970 (and later by Hicks and Dow) that the stock of money is an endogenous element in the economy, co-determined with other elements such as the price level and the level of output, and not something fixed independently by the monetary authorities. If prices rise for reasons unconnected with monetary changes, the public will want to hold more money and it would then be quite wrong to attribute the rise in prices to the additional money created. Moreover since the power of the Bank of England to control bank lending is severely limited, its control over bank liabilities is equally limited and these liabilities constitute the bulk of the stock of money. This is not to dispute that a large Budget deficit may add to the money supply and that the process of absorption of the additional money can be inflationary. It is going too far to regard the authorities as unable to influence the money supply except through interest rates.

A further difficulty is to decide what measure of the money supply to use. It is simply not true, as is sometimes suggested, except perhaps over periods of time too long to be operationally relevant, that all measures move together. An extreme example is provided by the experience of 1971–74. In the two and a half years between the third quarter of 1971 and the first quarter of 1974, when retail prices rose by 25 per cent, the money supply rose by 70 per cent if one uses a broad definition (£M3) but by only 20 per cent on a narrow definition (M1). The spread between the two is some indication of the ambiguities of monetary explanations of events. On one measure the public had less cash in relation to the expenditure in which they engaged by 1974 while on the other they were a great deal more liquid.

Some monetarists try to meet this difficulty by distinguishing between money and credit, arguing as Alan Walters has done that 'money is used to pay bills; credit is used to delay paying them.'[6] The distinction is valid in relation to commercial credit but not to bank lending, since every increase in bank lending is matched by an equal increase in bank deposits, which are most certainly money. Alternatively, a distinction is drawn between money held for transactions and money held as savings, the one including sight bank deposits held by the private sector (M1) and the other time deposits and certificates of deposit as well (M3).[7] But the distinction is increasingly hard to draw when interest is paid on sight deposits and banks make transfers automatically between time and sight deposits to cover transactions exhausting the balance in sight deposits. The fact that the banks perform two analytically distinct functions, as creators of money and investment intermediaries, does not provide us with separate totals of money held for transaction purposes and as savings.

Another element in monetarism was its insistence on the need to take a long view and avoid fine tuning. This has been a very popular theme, especially once unemployment rose to a high level. There is always room for debate over the time perspective that should govern policy and the attraction of long-term plans never seems to diminish. But, as Keynes always argued, once the balance of the economy is disturbed, delay in responding makes the restoration of balance far more difficult. It is easy to deride interventions in one year that were reversed the next and point to action that merely aggravated the cyclical swings in activity. On the other hand, there have been other occasions when reliance on monetary policy for whatever purpose – slowing down inflation, reviving activity, checking a boom – proved much too slow to do what was needed.

The long view recommended by the monetarists – in practice, refraining from responding to signs of mounting unemployment – goes with another prescription: to abide by fixed rules rather than leave things to the discretion of the authorities. Some monetarists regard a fixed annual increase in the money supply as preferable to attempts to vary the pace of money creation to match current developments in the economy. That is, they want to reduce monetary management to obedience to a fixed set of instructions and make the process as automatic as possible.

The difficulty with this prescription is that it assumes that the growth of the money supply is within the control of the authorities and that they can regulate it within fixed limits – a proposition already discussed. When the money supply increases fourfold between 1979 and 1989 under a government strongly opposed to monetary laxness it is hard to see how a fixed annual increase could be procured.

Whatever the academic merits of monetarist doctrine, what counted far more was its claim to have the only credible cure for inflation. It had a plausibility for the average man who had been taught long ago to associate inflation with 'too much money'. It attracted politicians and journalists disillusioned with other remedies. Incomes policy was believed to have been a failure and to offer no hope of stemming the rise in wages and prices. Deficit spending simply pumped in more money and increased the risk of inflation. Above all, no one could doubt that there had been an abnormal increase in the stock of money after 1971 and it was not surprising that people associated it with the great inflation that followed.

Monetarism was part of a wider movement of opinion that came to a head in the 1980s: a reaction against the state, against controls, against high taxation and in favour of market forces, individual freedom of choice and the enjoyment of the full fruit of one's labours. It was part of a return to the principles of nineteenth-century liberalism. And it developed into an ideological crusade.

The crusade at first did not involve any political figures. It had begun in the academic world and then moved to the publicists and commentators. Amongst academic economists, Harry Johnson, Alan Walters and Victor Morgan lent weight to monetarist views. An important part was played by the Institute of Economic Affairs, which was not originally a monetarist body but was a strong believer in allowing market forces freer play. This made it suspicious of the state, opposed to controls interfering with the market, and increasingly doubtful of the achievements claimed for the state, including demand management. Its publications came to include pamphlets by leading monetarists – it was, for example, the first to publish a popular account of Friedman's views in Britain – and it continued to comment on monetary policy with a predominantly monetarist slant.

The first attempt to convert the Treasury to a different view of the significance of the money supply was made in 1968 by the IMF, which, although never really monetarist, believed wholeheartedly in control of the money supply. After the devaluation in November, the Letter of Intent contained an undertaking to limit the growth in the money supply in 1968 to its estimated growth in 1967. A second Letter of Intent in May 1968 set a target for a growth of domestic credit expansion (DCE) – that is, the money supply adjusted for changes in the balance of payments. Later in the year a seminar was arranged at the Treasury to allow the IMF an opportunity of expounding their views on DCE. There was a large attendance, including Jacques Polak as leader of the IMF mission, Nicholas Kaldor, defending Treasury views at inordinate length, John Fforde from the Bank of England, and among the Treasury representatives one or two younger officials already sympathetic to IMF views.

The 'Seminar' may have started new trains of thought; but it did little to change Treasury thinking at the top, especially as the IMF could give no comprehensible account of how changes in the money supply, as distinct from demand, affected spending. If the public felt that it had too much cash, it seemed more likely to use it to repay debt or for the purchase of other assets rather than spend the surplus on consumer goods. The surplus could be eliminated just as easily through the purchase by the public of government paper previously held by the banks or by non-residents as by increased spending followed by a rise in prices that made people reassess how much cash they required. Nobody doubted that lower interest rates or additional bank credit would produce some expansion in demand that could impinge on prices. But that an expansion in the money supply would of itself, divorced from changes in demand and without any accompanying change in interest rates, lead to a rise in prices was far from self-evident.

Perhaps the biggest single influence on popular thinking was that of the financial journalists. Both Samuel Brittan and Peter Jay, for example, went overboard in support of ideas which they later came to view more critically. Sam Brittan, probably the most widely read commentator on economic affairs in Fleet Street, had been disenchanted with Keynesian ideas and followed a monetarist line in *The Financial Times*. So also did Peter Jay in *The Times*. These two alone had tremendous influence on City opinion (which was never much in sympathy anyway with Budget deficits). But they were by no means alone. William Rees-Mogg, Editor of *The Times*, Alfred Sherman, the editor of the studies issued by the newly founded Centre for Policy Studies and a frequent contributor to *The Daily Telegraph*, and other writers, gave publicity to monetarist ideas far beyond the importance attached to them by academic and government economists.

While events of 1972–74 heightened fears of inflation and strengthened the conviction of the monetarist school that they had the one certain answer to those fears, most academic economists were unconvinced that inflation had invariably a monetary origin. It seemed much more natural after 1973 to point to the rise in import prices as the key, supplemented by the very high pressure of demand occasioned by the expansionist policies of the government. Except perhaps in 1972–73 the increase in the money supply could be regarded as a response to over-expansion and rising prices rather than a prime cause.

From this period, however, a more willing ear was lent to monetarist doctrines, a growing number of academic economists embraced these doctrines and the press carried a succession of articles that made the money supply the centrepiece of anti-inflationary policy. Whatever else this accomplished, it made for a greater readiness to make use of monetary policy.

While different views were urged on the Chancellor it became common ground in the Treasury that something must be done to slow down the alarming pace of inflation. It was difficult for the government to use fiscal policy for this purpose since this would be interpreted as reducing the pressure of demand and deliberately allowing unemployment to increase as a check to the bargaining power of labour. Unemployment from 1974 onwards was steadily increasing and the government felt bound to exert itself to limit the increase, not aggravate it. The natural recourse of a Labour government was to incomes policy and a pact with the trade unions. But given the state of feeling about inflation and the insistence in the press and elsewhere on the key role of the money supply, an insurance policy limiting the growth of the money supply provided a useful supplement. This took the form of monetary targets, at first not disclosed, but from the summer of 1976 publicly announced.

To strict Keynesians, the adoption of monetary targets was a masquerade that might do little harm if the targets did not aim at an immediate cure but were designed to bring inflation down gradually. Inflation was due either to excess demand, not excess cash, or to wage-push, or to higher import prices, and so far as money played any part it must be through its effect on one or other of these. Monetarists, however, pointed to the influence on market opinion of official targets that by limiting the supply of money limited also the financial backing for any rise in prices. This line of argument did not require the monetarist view of inflation to be theoretically sound: it merely relied on the adoption by the market of the monetarist credo. If the market thought that an increase in the money supply would cause prices to rise in another six months or a year or even two years then it could compel the monetary authorities to act as if that were necessarily true; and if the government pandered to such views it might in fact enjoy more success in combating inflation. The expectation of inflation would depress the market in gilts and in foreign exchange and could oblige the government to take deflationary action; while the setting of monetary targets, if it reassured market opinion, might allow the government more latitude in its fiscal policy and in an attack on inflation that required heavier spending.

THE ATTACK ON GOVERNMENT SPENDING

A second line of attack on Keynesian doctrine, not confined to the monetarists, was on increased public spending as an instrument of economic management. In December 1968, for example, Harold Wincott, a well-known financial journalist, outlined the damaging effects of heavy spending resulting in a large PSBR, in an article immediately following an exposition by Milton Friedman of the importance of limiting the money supply.[8] Samuel Brittan in March 1972 had challenged (in *The Financial Times*) the idea of 'spending ourselves into prosperity' when the Heath government planned to increase public expenditure as a means of reducing unemployment. Brittan's contention was that a fiscal stimulus in 1972 would 'run into the sand' of higher prices without affecting output and employment. The subsequent recovery in employment did little to bear him out – in the short run at least.[9]

The attack on deficit spending was continued in October 1975 by Tim Congdon in *The Times*. His argument was rather different from Brittan's and rested on the danger of 'crowding out' private investment through the rise in interest rates necessary to raise funds to cover the deficit. The same argument had been used by the Treasury in the 1920s and dismissed by economists in the depression of the 1930s when, as Congdon agreed, there was no competition for resources between the public and the private sector amid the high unemployment of those days. It would have been justifiable to print money, he admitted, in those circumstances. But government commitment to a fixed money supply target would neutralise fiscal policy: the money spent by the government would simply take the place of private spending and investment. More government expenditure would be like pumping air into a tyre with a puncture.[10]

These were not convincing arguments to anyone who had observed the impact on economic activity of changes in the fiscal stance of policy. They implied an inelasticity in the use of money as if it was impossible to change the flow of expenditure without a corresponding change in the money supply. Indeed it was difficult to see how, on the 'crowding out' hypothesis, there could ever be any change in the level of activity with a given amount of money; and yet large changes did occur.

Economists have put forward other grounds for doubting whether higher budget deficits add to employment. Alan Walters, for example, has argued that when the deficit is already large a further increase may so damage confidence and create fears of higher taxes and interest rates to come that no net increase, or even a decrease, in aggregate spending results.[11] There have undoubtedly been episodes in British economic history when a more restrictive fiscal policy was accompanied by an expansion in output and employment, sometimes associated with a consistent policy of cheap money, as in the 1930s. There have been other periods when fiscal policy had very marked effects on demand and monetary policy was relatively ineffective, as in the 1950s and 1960s. We shall see later how demand responded to large changes in both in the mid-1970s.[12]

A more ingenious attempt to show how increased government spending could be deflationary came from the the London Business School in a letter to *The Times* in October 1976 by R.J. Ball and Terry Burns. They argued that more government spending would add to inflation by causing a fall in the exchange rate and that this in turn would make people save more and so, by reducing demand, would create more unemployment.[13] A letter from Lord Kaldor poured scorn on the 'absurd' assumption that inflation would stimulate saving for investment in depreciating assets and later argued that an increase in the savings ratio in a depression was the product of uncertainty, not inflation. He also pointed out that since the import

Table 3

Inflation and savings, 1970–76

	Increase in consumer prices (%)	Personal saving ratio as published in	
		1981	1990
1970	5.9	9.3	9.0
1971	8.2	7.6	7.3
1972	6.7	9.7	9.1
1973	8.6	11.7	10.1
1974	16.4	13.5	10.7
1975	23.6	12.7	11.6
1976	11.5	11.8	10.9

Sources: Economic Trends Annual Supplement 1981 and 1990; National Institute *Economic Review*, 1977.

content of government spending was lower than that of spending by private consumers, the substitution of government spending for an equal amount of consumer spending would strengthen the exchange rate and produce less, not more, inflation.

At the time, the Ball/Burns argument derived a plausibility, which has since largely disappeared, from estimates of the household savings ratio in the early 1970s. As is evident from Table 3, the increase in the savings ratio after the acceleration in inflation in the early 1970s is much less dramatic after revision of the estimates. On this revised evidence a Chancellor might hesitate to pursue the converse of the Ball/Burns argument and cut £1 billion in government spending in the hope that it would stimulate a larger fall in personal saving and a reduction in unemployment.

The most celebrated attack on public spending was made in 1976 at the Labour Party Conference by Prime Minister Callaghan himself (above p.55–6); but when it came to negotiations with the IMF he made plain his distaste for further cuts. He might find it necessary to impress market opinion (and particularly opinion in the leading creditor countries, the United States and Germany) with evidence of a change of heart in his approach to public spending. But he showed no sign of translating his views into cuts that to his supporters would have meant an unmistakable loss of jobs.

THE VIEWS OF BACON AND ELTIS

Doubts about the efficacy of public spending as an instrument of economic management were supported from another angle by two Oxford economists, Robert Bacon and Walter Eltis, who argued that the growth of public expenditure represented a denial of resources to the market and their pre-emption by the state.[14] The additional taxation required to finance higher expenditure in the 1970s held down the after-tax incomes of wage-earners and underlay their efforts to restore the previous rate of improvement by demanding higher money incomes. Increased public expenditure, in other words, operated to produce inflation, not just by expanding demand but by generating wage-push as well.

Bacon and Eltis made three important points. First of all, employment kept increasing in what they called the non-market sector of the economy, mainly the public sector, which did not sell its output on the market, while employment in the market sector was dropping steadily. For example, employment in health, education and public administration had increased in each three-year period between 1964 and 1973, with a net growth over those nine years of just under a million, while employment in the rest of the economy had fallen in each period and by well over a million during the nine years to 1973. Much the same point emerges from the change in the proportion of workers employed in the public sector or by a comparison of the growth in public expenditure with the growth in GNP. The number of local government employees in Great Britain, for example, increased by 54 per cent (nearly a million) between 1961 and 1974; and expenditure by central government and local authorities, excluding expenditure on financial assets, rose from 38 per cent of GNP to over 49 per cent between 1964 and 1974.[15]

Secondly, this cut in the share of GNP available to the rest of the economy was not in favour of uses with high or rapidly rising productivity. Figures for health and education seemed to substantiate the view that the use of resources in the public sector was very wasteful,[16] and that the real 'outputs' of the public services had grown much more slowly than the expenditure needed to produce them. If so, it was not surprising that workers should take little account of the increase in 'the social wage' in their wage bargaining.[17]

Thirdly, the rise in taxes to pay for 'the social wage' and other 'non-marketed output' left the average wage-earner with a disappointing share in the secular growth in output. In the ten years 1964–74, according to Bacon and Eltis, the real earnings of the average wage-earner, after paying rates and taxes, had risen only from £15 to £17.13 (at 1961 prices) while the taxes paid by the average family had risen from £2.65 to £10.25. Thus while taxes quadrupled, real disposable incomes rose by no more than a seventh.

It is not necessary to agree with the whole of the Bacon-Eltis thesis to appreciate the political impact of these arguments. Public expenditure had been absorbing an increasing share of total output without disposing wage-earners to rest content with the cash income this left them. Their demands for higher wages might do little to improve their real incomes but could be only too successful in forcing up money wages.

The implication of the Bacon-Eltis argument that cuts in public expenditure would produce an improvement in real wages, appears more doubtful. That result depended in part on what happened to output; and there was good reason to fear that, with unemployment already increasing, a fall in output would result. Whatever might have been true in the decade before 1974 – and even more true in the years 1974–76 – it could not be assumed that the private sector would quickly absorb the resources released by cuts in public expenditure in 1976. Indeed it could have been argued that some of the growth in public expenditure was a response to the failure of the manufacturing sector to maintain employment, not its cause.

'NEW CAMBRIDGE'

A third line of attack on government spending was that of a Cambridge group of economists led by Lord Kaldor and including Professors Wynne Godley and Robert Neild. This group regarded Budget deficits as the progenitors of trade deficits, the one being a kind of mirror image of the other. When the public sector was in deficit, they argued, funds to finance it had to come from one or other of the three elements making up the private sector – the business, household and overseas sectors – since the surpluses and deficits of all four sectors must sum to zero. In the absence of repercussions on the first two, which were represented as stable and unchanging, the overseas sector was bound to feel the impact and adjust to it by moving into deficit, so giving rise to foreign borrowing on a scale that covered the external deficit. The deficit could be removed only by greater budgetary discipline designed to cut the public sector deficit.

So far from looking to the government to spend its way out of the depression the Cambridge economists denounced the government's laxity and wanted, like Mrs Thatcher, a lower PSBR. Expansion should be fostered instead by protection of the domestic market, which would allow manufacturing industry to win a larger share, expand output and offer more jobs. As employment increased, more tax revenue would flow to the government and reduce the budget deficit and more money would be spent on imports out of a higher national income, until they might even come to exceed their previous level as expansion continued and absorbed the unemployed. The Cambridge group saw little hope of economic recovery if it were sought to achieve similar results by depreciation of the currency. This would, it is true, improve industry's competitive position, both in the home market and in export markets, but only if costs were unaffected, and that simply would not happen. On the contrary, a slide in the pound would first raise the sterling price of imports and the cost of living and would then have repercussions on wages. The net result would be more inflation and little or no change in competitive strength.

There were two main elements, not closely linked, in the 'New Cambridge' doctrine. One was the accounting identity showing that a deficit in the public sector must be covered either by a surplus in the private sector or by borrowing abroad to cover the external deficit. The other was the proposition that the private sector surplus rarely varied very much, so that any fluctuation in the public sector deficit *must* involve a corresponding fluctuation in the overseas deficit. But was it true that the private sector ran a more or less unchanging surplus? Whatever may have been true in times of milder fluctuations, there is little evidence of such a constancy in the 1970s. No doubt a larger public sector deficit tends to push the balance of payments in the direction of a deficit, whether it originates in a rise in public expenditure or a cut in taxation. But there can be no presumption that a change in the public sector deficit, however it is brought about, will impinge exclusively on the balance of payments and leave the private sector's surplus unaffected. It is only too easy to read into accounting identities causal sequences that oversimplify the full consequences of the forces at work.[18]

PROTECTION

The Cambridge group's advocacy of protection derived from a new-found pessimism about the uses of devaluation which was by no means confined to Cambridge. In the 1960s academic economists had mounted an attack on the government for its reluctance to devalue, and presented a picture of an economy held back by this reluctance from more rapid expansion under the stimulus of export-led growth. The slowness with which the balance of payments improved after 1967 did not discourage this view since the balance of payments did eventually improve quite strongly. But by 1974–5, when the inflationary impact of a slide in the exchange rate was more clearly visible, there were growing doubts about the benefits to be expected from a lower exchange rate.

Some went so far as to treat the long-term improvement in the balance of payments as negligible, while others concluded that import controls were to be preferred. Expansion, it was argued, could only be given a solid foundation if it was prevented from weakening the balance of payments by holding back the extra imports that would otherwise be drawn in. It was no use hoping to do this under cover of a falling exchange rate since this would raise, first sterling import prices, then the cost of living and finally money wages, leaving little or no net competitive gain. The deeper the depression into which the world sank in 1974–75 and the further the United Kingdom retreated from full employment, the more urgently the Cambridge economists developing the argument, called for protection, and the more political support they received from the left wing of the Labour Party.

One Labour MP, Bryan Sedgemore, tried to persuade the Expenditure Committee (of which he was a member) to approve a report he had drafted urging protection rather than the one they decided to publish. His draft warned against

the dangerous syllogism which says that the level of taxation is already too high to finance further public expenditure by raising it, and the only methods of borrowing the money are inflationary, therefore public expenditure should be cut. . . . If the Chancellor were prepared to reflate the economy behind widespread but selective import controls, cutting the import bill on manufactured and semi-manufactured goods by some £3 billion a year then we could expect economic growth of some 4 to 5 per cent per annum. . . . While public expenditure might decline slightly as a proportion of GDP in real terms it will nevertheless increase absolutely.[19]

The attraction of protection whether in the form of import quotas or tariffs lay not only in its supposed contribution to full employment but equally in the industrial regeneration it was expected to bring about. Opinion was sceptical on both scores. Like all protectionist measures, they might help to meet an emergency but how were they to be withdrawn? Did it make sense to look to protection to make British industry more efficient and restore its competitive power when the usual outcome of protection was the reverse and the weaknesses of British industry were of long standing? Might not protection push up prices just as much as devaluation, do nothing to help exports and little even to displace imports, given that British industry would not be able to take over markets without a struggle from importers whose products had proved themselves either cheaper or more acceptable?

Lord Kaldor, one of protection's strongest supporters, turned to it in desperation because all other remedies seemed to him to have failed. He believed that it had worked in the 1930s although this was largely a misconception. The rapid recovery of manufacturing in the 1930s followed in the wake of the housing boom and that in turn owed a great deal to the low rates of interest that were possible once the pound was allowed to float. So far as protection contributed to recovery it did so in conjunction with devaluation at a time when industry abroad was either prostrate or diverted by rearmament. But it was cheap money that was the biggest single agency – a demonstration that in some circumstances monetary policy can be remarkably powerful.

Protection in either form was an explosive issue internationally and open to serious political objections. Unless coupled with a call to withdraw from the European Community, how was it possible to restrict imports from the Community, which the United Kingdom had so recently joined? On the other hand, how could the Community be given exemption when most of the increase in imports of manufactures over the previous ten years were of Community origin? Measures that excluded Europe would not only be far more limited but would seem to single out the United States and Japan and might provoke protectionist reactions there, with consequences the United Kingdom would have cause to regret. Were imports from the developing countries to be restricted in the interests of the British balance of payments when many of these countries were themselves in acute balance of payments difficulties? Would quota restrictions once introduced be a short-term measure with correspondingly little effect on domestic production, or a long-term measure that was more difficult to withdraw the longer it continued? Tariffs raised even more awkward issues since the United Kingdom was bound to apply the Community common tariff. Without the Community's agreement, there could be no changes in tariffs nor, for that matter,

Table 4

Inflation and the burden of public debt

	Public sector debt held outside the public sector (£ billion)	Of which sterling debt (£ billion)	Increase in GDP deflator over previous year (%)	Depreciation of sterling debt over previous year (£ billion)	Public sector borrowing requirement in previous year (£ billion)	Adjusted borrowing requirement (£ billion)
31 March 1971	44.31	42.01	9.0	—	—	—
1972	47.54	45.47	8.8	4.77	+ 1.0	− 3.8
1973	48.51	46.28	8.1	3.68	+ 2.4	− 1.3
1974	52.79	49.16	7.5	3.47	+ 4.3	+ 0.8
1975	61.60	56.05	27.0	13.27	+ 8.0	− 5.3
1976	74.33	66.79	20.0	11.25	+ 10.3	− 0.9
1977	87.74	77.20	11.3	7.55	+ 8.3	+ 0.7
1978	98.53	87.36	11.3	8.72	+ 5.4	− 3.3
1979	107.35	98.15	11.1	9.70	+ 9.2	− 0.5

Sources: Annual Abstract of Statistics, 1981; Economic Trends Annual Supplement, 1990.

any qualitative import restrictions, even against non-members of the Community.

At the political level, the idea of protection made little headway. The Cabinet rejected comprehensive protective measures and was willing to approve only *selective* protection but this had little effect on the totality of production. In the battle over the Cambridge proposals, as indeed over monetarism, academic opinion was largely brushed aside. The commentators, the politicians and the business community formed their own conclusions in the light of their experience and were influenced more by what they judged could be done than by theory, old or new.

BORROWING

The controversy over public expenditure was also a controversy over borrowing. Those who attached more importance to expanding employment than to stabilising prices argued for maintaining or increasing public expenditure and borrowing for the purpose. There might, however, be difficulties in finding lenders and if debt accumulated it might be difficult to repay without a change for the better in economic performance.

In an inflationary world the problem of repayment was not a major one so long as the debt was contracted in sterling. As each year went by, the fresh debt incurred could be more than offset by the depreciation of all outstanding debt. Even the large borrowing requirements of the 1970s added less to the national debt, contracted in sterling, than was subtracted by the annual dose of inflation (see Table 4). With a national debt of about £60 billion a rise in prices of 20 per cent was sufficient to reduce the real value of the debt by £12 billion; and in 1975 prices rose at over 20 per cent per annum. Inflation raised the interest burden on the Budget; but it simultaneously reduced the burden of existing debt.

A more effective limit was set by lack of confidence among potential lenders and by the reluctance of the authorities to overcome that lack of confidence by offering a higher return. This reluctance derived partly from the cost to the Exchequer, partly from the discouragement to private investment of higher interest rates and partly from the prospective difficulty of bringing interest rates down again. A more powerful influence than any of these may have been doubts whether higher interest rates were the right response to a loss of confidence.

Other considerations limited borrowing abroad. Inflation in the United Kingdom might write off sterling debt but it added to the weight of external debt contracted in foreign currency by causing the exchange rate to slide and the burden of repayment to grow in consequence. Where the debt was denominated in sterling, foreign holders could not disregard the danger that when they wished to withdraw their money it would not be there or would be repaid at a much lower rate of exchange. That these were not negligible dangers was very apparent in 1976 when there was a fear that the reserves might run out and the effective rate of exchange fell by over 20 per cent in less than eight months – the most rapid devaluation of sterling ever to take place.

Borrowing is always the most politically attractive option to a country in balance of payments difficulties. It puts off the evil day and, more positively, it offers more time for the necessary adjustments to be made. In 1976 more novel arguments were used to justify borrowing. If the industrial world continued to buy oil at much higher prices after 1973 and the OPEC countries could not at once spend the proceeds on imports, then borrowing was the inevitable counterpart of the OPEC surplus. It was better, Denis Healey maintained, to accept this necessity and borrow than for all countries to deflate in an effort to wipe out the deficit. It is easy to ridicule Healey's efforts, as the Chancellor of an unsuccessful country, to preach this idea to heretic chancellors from stronger and more successful countries. But whether or not it lay with Healey to do the preaching, it was in the circumstances sound doctrine.

There were three difficulties about it. The first was that Britain was already in heavy deficit in the last quarter of 1973 *before* the rise in oil prices: on a seasonally adjusted basis, it was halfway to the peak in the deficit in 1974. There was therefore every justification for Britain to take urgent measures to reduce the deficit and limit the borrowing required, whatever it urged on its neighbours. There was *no* justification for putting additional pressure on the economy in 1974 through *increased* public expenditure, and so adding to the external deficit, not even the justification of relieving unemployment since unemployment was lower than in the boom of the previous year. Secondly, sterling was still a reserve currency and there were large external holdings of liquid sterling balances that could be withdrawn if the currency came under pressure. Reserve currency countries cannot lightly run a deficit, least of all if their past record is far from reassuring and their current economic performance is thought to be inadequate. A third difficulty was that it might not be possible to borrow enough. The oil-exporting countries might be obliged to lend, but they were under no obligation to lend to the countries in greatest difficulty with their balance of payments. This was a point lost on those who thought only of the borrower's need, not the lender's conditions.

As the limits of creditworthiness were approached, the whole argument about being driven to borrow in order to mop up the oil exporters' surplus became totally irrelevant. Once its credit was in doubt, the government had no option but to limit its borrowing abroad, limit the balance of payments deficit giving rise to the borrowing, and take action that could avoid being deflationary only if it involved limiting imports through quantitative restrictions. Since import restriction was anathema to creditor countries that line of action was unlikely to be a realistic, and probably also not an effective, option. In short, there was no question of unlimited borrowing: on the contrary there was a need to keep borrowing within limits and a need to reassure lenders if those limits were to be maintained.

There were of course different ways in which these two objectives could be pursued. Argument focused on the PSBR and the Budget; cuts in public expenditure were fought over as if they alone met the necessary conditions. But most of the cuts applied to some future year, had little immediate effect on the balance of payments and carried no guarantee that they would not later be reversed. Import restrictions were advocated as an alternative, with the advantage that they would raise, not lower, employment but on very doubtful assumptions about their acceptability. Devaluation was also considered as a way of mitigating the reduction in activity that deflationary measures would produce. But as experience proved, with a floating currency this was a dangerous expedient that might get out of hand; and if it was slow or ineffective in encouraging exports and checking imports it would cause a faster rise in prices, creating fresh problems and eating into the new competitive advantage. What was largely left aside until too late and hardly entered into the debate was the use of monetary weapons, including hire purchase restrictions, special deposits and high interest rates. It was these that halted the decline in sterling in October 1976, backed by the announcement of an approach to the IMF. They not only made it more attractive to lend to the United Kingdom but could be expected to have an early effect on the balance of payments.

OPINION AT THE POLITICAL LEVEL

Turning to opinion at the political level, the Conservative Party had for many years been strongly in favour of the resolute use of monetary weapons: not least because by tightening monetary policy they could compensate for reductions in income tax which they itched to make. They never became whole-hearted monetarists because they were never willing to let the rate of interest move freely to whatever level (if there was one) would hold down the money supply. They hoped to keep interest rates within limits by means of prudent Budgets involving little or no borrowing; and for this purpose, as well as for ideological reasons, they were anxious to cut public expenditure by at least as much as they hoped to cut taxation.

The key figure in the conversion of much of the Conservative Party to monetarism was Keith Joseph. He in turn, used his influence on Margaret Thatcher to get across to her at least some of the monetarist doctrines, although she was always willing to exercise control over interest rates in ways of which strict monetarists would have disapproved. By 1975, in a surprisingly short time, Mrs Thatcher had become the leader of the Conservative Party, which from then on gave voice more and more to monetarist views of economic policy.

The Conservatives, as one might expect, were all for fiscal 'discipline'. They were quick to appreciate the average man's fear of inflation which affected everyone, in contrast to unemployment, which affected only a small proportion of the electorate. They were also sceptical of the power of Budget deficits to sustain employment. Mrs Thatcher, backed by *The Times*, claimed in a radio interview in October 1976 that the Budget deficit could be cut in half without much harm and pressed for cuts of £5.5–6.5 billion.

Conservative views were echoed in *The Times* and *The Economist*. *The Times* on 20 September 1976 – just before the Party conferences – published a leading article spelling out the prescription becoming fashionable on the right of the Conservative Party. It began by arguing for a cut in the PSBR from an expected £9 billion in 1977–78 to £4 billion, followed by a further cut in 1978–79 to £1 billion and an approximate balance thereafter. This was to be brought about by substantial cuts in public expenditure aimed at subsidies of all kinds and recruitment of new workers. Any tax increases necessary should be concentrated on VAT, that is, on indirect taxes. At the same time the growth of the money supply should be limited to 9 per cent in 1976 (it had already grown by that amount), 6 per cent in 1977 and 4 per cent thereafter. These limits were to be 'institutionally entrenched'. Interest rates (presumably long-term rates) were to be held 3 per cent above the expected rate of inflation. Other proposals involved a 'clean' float for the pound, free bargaining on pay from mid-1977, an end to price and dividend controls, a requirement that nationalised industries should earn a sufficient surplus to cover most of their investment programme and should enjoy freedom to set their own prices, tougher anti-monopoly policies, and a campaign for higher industrial productivity, industry by industry, through the National Economic Development Council. There was no mention of unemployment.

These proposals were neither realistic nor consistent. For example, they took no account of the repercussions of a tighter monetary and fiscal policy on the level of activity, or of the implications of those re-percussions for government revenue. They assumed that the govern-ment had the means to control the money supply within narrow limits and yet could pursue interest rate objectives that were likely to prove incompatible; they contemplated a freedom in the labour mar-ket, the market in foreign exchange, in price-setting by nationalised industries (but not by other monopolists) that assumed some other restraint such as lower pressure and higher unemployment.[20] None-theless, these proposals were congenial to right-wing Conservatives, and many became the accepted policy of the party.

The Times claimed to be vindicated by later experience. That out-put continued to rise after it seemed that the PSBR had been cut by £5 billion between 1975–76 and 1977–78 demonstrated, they argued, that deficit financing was not the way to maintain employment. We consider below (pp.193–97) whether this is a claim that stands up.

The Economist was, if anything, to the right of *The Times*. It thought the reasons for Britain's difficulties 'simple and dog-eared'.[21] Public spending was far too high and should be cut drastically. 'All European countries should be cutting government expenditure like mad.'[22] The government should sack 15 per cent of the staffs of government departments and local authorities and set about cutting expenditure by another £5 billion.[23] It should also limit the growth of the money supply rather than keep pushing up interest rates and tightening credit. A limit to growth in the stock of money of 10 per cent in any year should be an absolute requirement on the Bank of England, because this was a sure recipe for sensible economic policy. 'Any nation', *The Economist* assured its readers, 'which keeps the annual expansion of its money supply between 4 per cent and 10 per cent is unlikely to run into a major depression or an intolerable deflation.'[24]

The Labour Party was divided. So far as inflation was concerned it put its faith in incomes policy but had difficulty in devising a policy acceptable not just to the trade unions but to their members and yet sufficiently restrictive of (money) wage increases to bring down inflation at a reasonable rate. There was no great dispute over monetary targets or even over a 15 per cent minimum lending rate. As described in Chapter 3 disagreement focused on cuts in public expenditure on the one hand and import restrictions on the other. The left wing of the party, led by Tony Benn, was strongly opposed to the cuts and pressed instead for a kind of siege economy. Yet the Chancellor insisted that without cuts he could not finance his Budget deficit and was willing to introduce selective import restrictions only. In the autumn of 1976 at the Labour Party conference the Prime Minister delivered a speech, (above, pp.55–56), much quoted by monetarists in later years, in which he seemed to repudiate resort to increased government spending as an antidote to depression and unemployment. The scepticism he expressed went further even than the pre-Keynesian doctrine of the 1920s, since in some versions at least that envisaged resort to public works as a way of reducing unemployment. What the Prime Minister urged on his bemused audience in 1976 was essentially the Treasury doctrine of 1929: that increased spending by the government would be offset by a withdrawal of spending intentions elsewhere in the economy. Just as in the 'crowding out' argument of the 1920s, financial markets would react to increased borrowing by the government by denying funds to other borrowers or making borrowing too costly for them.

In his memoirs, *Time and Chance*, Callaghan disclaims any intention in his speech to endorse monetarist opposition to all use of a Budget deficit to boost employment. His argument, he says, was confined to the circumstances of 1976. This can hardly apply to his contention that deficit spending had never worked except by injecting a bigger dose of inflation into the economy – a contention echoing Sir Keith Joseph's speech at Preston in September 1975 when he first unfurled the monetarist flag. But there can be no doubt that Callaghan's main aim was to appease the markets and re-establish a claim to financial rectitude so as to improve the chances of desperately needed financial support.[25] Callaghan was also trying to impress on his party and his colleagues the precarious state of the economy and the impossibility of taking expansionary measures while markets were in panic. His speech undoubtedly served his purpose in bringing reassurance to pro-British elements in the American administration and on the Continent. But it did not represent a conversion of the Prime Minister to monetarist dogma.

A similar judgement can be made of Healey's adoption of monetary targets. He had to decide how far to yield to the obsession of the financial markets and the press with the money supply. The Bank of England was under attack for failing to control the money supply and for being either indifferent to monetarist ideas or hostile to them. Officials in the Bank and in the Treasury, looking for a way in which to respond to this criticism, were attracted by the idea of a target for the growth of the money supply, even though the Bank was not amongst those who thought control of the money supply a relatively simple matter. The Bank also appreciated, as others did not, that it is not possible to combine control of the money supply and control of the exchange rate through the use of a single instrument – the rate of interest. Experience with monetary targets soon showed that they were not only very hard to hit but that they made it necessary to acquiesce in movements in the exchange rate that would otherwise have been resisted.

Thus it came about that when the Cabinet was faced with the IMF proposals at the end of 1976 there were representatives of various schools of thought urging very different responses to the proposed cuts in public expenditure. It is doubtful whether there were any out-and-out monetarists among them. But the Chancellor, although far from sharing the views of Milton Friedman, recognised that he could not run a deficit larger than he could finance and that to raise the finance he needed the support of market opinion. In his view he could hope to raise £9 billion, so that was the appropriate figure at which to aim.

A second group shied away from making the size of the deficit dependent on what the market thought, and still more from accepting the IMF as an arbiter. But unless it could point to some alternative source of funds that could be tapped without reducing the borrowing power of the government, there was no way of sustaining public spending on the scale proposed. Moreover, so long as the *external* deficit had to be financed and the exchange reserves remained inadequate, the borrowing would have to include borrowing from abroad. This might be obtained by letting the pound drop to bargain levels; but that was playing with fire, since every fall in the rate of exchange meant a rise in import prices that could easily set in motion powerful inflationary forces.

Where monetary policy in the 1960s had been regarded as of

limited help and budgetary policy exalted as the most reliable and comprehensive weapon at the government's disposal, now the situation was reversed. Monetary policy was seen as indispensable and powerful in the fight against inflation while fiscal policy was seen as ineffective, even from the point of view of employment policy. If government spending could not do anything to pull the economy out of a slump, it presumably mattered little to the level of economic activity whether the Budget was in heavy deficit or nearly in balance. It was a short step from the Callaghan speech of 1976 to Mrs Thatcher's conviction that a cut of £5 billion in the PSBR would do little harm to employment and Sir Geoffrey Howe's later decision to tighten fiscal policy when unemployment was rising fast. These views might find little favour with most academic economists. But of their influence on policy there could be no doubt.

Above all, the powers of individual governments were seen to be limited in a world that was increasingly integrated. The instruments of policy in use in the war and postwar years had narrowed down more and more and at the same time the links between national economies had expanded more and more so that even the instruments that survived exercised their influence under increasing restraint from abroad. Fiscal policy, which had been the instrument of national economic policy *par excellence*, was now confined by the limits of borrowing power – limits that were set by credibility in *international* markets. Monetary policy was constrained more closely than before by the movement of interest rates in foreign money markets. The role of government was increasingly suspect and the powers of government increasingly limited. But just as creditor countries had always enjoyed a liberty denied to debtor countries so, in the interational economy of the late twentieth century, governments that managed their affairs without recourse to extensive borrowing enjoyed a freedom of action denied to those with few assets and large borrowing requirements.

CHAPTER 6

The Loss of Control:
The Balance of Payments

In the years after 1945 it came to be widely accepted that governments should pursue an active policy of economic management and assume responsibility for a number of major economic objectives. These included a high rate of economic growth, a 'high and stable' level of employment, stability in the value of money and in the balance of payments, and greater economic equality. The relative importance attached to those objectives fluctuated and so, also, did the success of governments in achieving each of them.

Economic management implied powers of control. But the powers at the disposal of governments in a free economy were limited. The use of administrative controls was largely abandoned in the first decade after the war. In Britain many financial controls – over bank lending, new issues on the Stock Exchange, consumer credit (through hire purchase restrictions) – had been relaxed or removed by the mid-1970s. Exchange control remained for a few years more; but it was no longer thought to give the government a firm grip on outflows of capital. The rate of exchange had been allowed to float since 1972 and, although it could be influenced by official intervention and changes in bank rate, it was controlled more by market pressures than by the authorities. In its efforts to manage the economy the government relied primarily on its annual Budget, supplemented from time to time by changes in interest rates and various forms of incomes policy.

The limitations of economic management had been concealed until the 1970s by the apparent success of economic policy. Economic growth, though slower than in other industrial countries, was faster than ever before; unemployment hardly ever rose above 2 per cent –

a rate far below what had been expected in 1945; inflation, in spite of occasional surges in prices, had averaged about 4 per cent in the twenty-five years between 1948 and 1973 – a modest rate by the standards of later years, although enough to reduce the value of money by two-thirds where there had been little or no reduction in the hundred years after 1815; as for the distribution of income, the wage-earner had greatly improved his/her position and welfare benefits of all kinds relieved the pressures on the poor. Only the balance of payments was a perennial source of anxiety, moving from one crisis to another with no end in sight.

It was gradually appreciated how much these achievements owed to international influences beyond the power of national governments to control. The secular boom from 1945 to the 1970s had been worldwide, accounting for high employment and contributing to rapid growth wherever the beneficent influence of expanding demand had been felt. The efforts of governments in industrial countries had been directed quite as much to checking excess demand and avoiding its inflationary consequences as to reviving demand when it appeared to be flagging. Although governments were given credit for the successful management of demand, it was never necessary for them to take really drastic expansionary measures so long as the world economy remained buoyant under the stimulus of high investment and rapid technical progress. The short-term oscillations which preoccupied the policy-makers were little more than ripples on an international groundswell of expanding demand.

In a world where international economic forces were so important it was not possible to assume that these forces would remain as benign as they had been up to the 1970s. Demand pressures might become deflationary or world prices might become inflationary, or both things might happen at once. Given adequate reserves and a flexible and competitive economy no great harm might follow. But these preconditions did not apply to the United Kingdom. There was a danger that the government might be largely helpless to exercise control and that it would discover that the powers on which it had relied for economic management in favourable circumstances would prove ineffective when they became unfavourable.

The ability of national governments to pursue a policy of their own choosing was being steadily narrowed by the increased integration of the world economy. International trade in the postwar period had expanded fast and outstripped the growth of domestic economies so that the international content of the goods on sale to con sumers was higher than ever before. By 1976 nearly 30 per cent of total expenditure in the United Kingdom was on imported goods and services – a proportion some 50 per cent higher than ten years previously. International investment had greatly increased and at least a quarter of the profits earned by British companies were made abroad. Above all, the movement of funds across the exchanges was on a scale far outdistancing the movement of goods. The money markets of the world were joined together by currency flows that governments could not hope to control.

The trend towards international integration was singled out in 1978 by Sir Douglas Wass, then Permanent Secretary of the Treasury, as 'the single most important structural change in the world economy in the second half of the twentieth century. Its implications for the independence of national economic management,' he suggested, 'are still not fully grasped.'[1] Not only did it limit the freedom of action of individual governments. It also brought monetary factors into far greater prominence as influences on economic activity. Short-term flows of funds between international financial centres, reflecting in part differences in monetary conditions in those centres, could exercise a compelling influence on exchange rates, and through exchange rate changes, on inflation. At the same time, flows of funds were themselves influenced by inflationary expectations that were often based on an assessment of trends in the quantity of money. Financial markets had always attached importance to changes in the stock of money as a portent of economic conditions; now these changes began to dominate their thinking and reactions.

An inevitable consequence of economic and financial integration was to increase the pressure on countries to keep in line with one another and not allow demand to grow faster than accorded with their circumstances. They had also to remain internationally competitive by preventing costs and prices from rising too fast or, if they failed to do so, would have to acquiesce in seeing their currency depreciate. These were conditions of equilibrium when capital movements were relatively insignificant. Once monetary flows came to dominate exchange rates it was less the state of the current account that provided a test of equilibrium than the view taken by financial markets of a country's economic prospects. The trade balance could be in serious deficit without disturbing the markets or, as in 1957, an exchange crisis could develop even when trade and services yielded a substantial surplus, depending on the fears and expectations of market operators.

It had seemed to some economists that once exchange rates were allowed to float, as sterling floated after June 1972, there would be no need to exercise control over the balance of payments: the exchange rate would move, more or less instantaneously, to preserve equilibrium. This soon proved an illusion. It was of course axiomatic that total payments in one direction must always equal total payments in the other. But if this result required a continuing fall in the rate of exchange, the position remained one of deficit, not of equilibrium. A falling rate, by raising import prices, could produce a general inflation of costs and prices, weaken the country's competitive position and prolong the deficit in the balance of payments. If the authorities sought instead to deal with the deficit by raising interest rates this might attract funds from abroad to the necessary amount but, again, borrowing in itself did not restore equilibrium, and higher interest rates could have undesirable effects on the domestic economy.

However they were handled, balance of payments pressures were always unwelcome. In its power to withstand such pressures, the British economy was in a particularly weak position. A quarter of a century earlier British industrial production had exceeded that of France and Germany combined. Britain had accounted for nearly one-fifth of world trade in manufactures, and half the world's trade had been financed in sterling. But while the continental economies had raced ahead shortly after 1945, Britain had jogged along at about half their pace, with periodic 'stops' associated with balance of payments crises that brought expansion to a complete halt for a year or more. In consequence, the standard of living on the Continent had crept up to, and by 1970 was moving well ahead of, that of the British. As the country dropped down the international league table, it accounted for a dwindling proportion of world production, supplied a dwindling proportion of world trade in manufactures and exerted a dwindling influence in international affairs.

The British public, at first oblivious to the divergence between the country's record and that of their European competitors, began in the 1960s to look to the government to find the key to faster growth, blaming slow growth on errors of government policy rather than on their own attitudes and institutions, and dreaming of a British 'miracle' to match the succession of 'miracles' with which they credited France, Germany, Italy and, latterly, Japan. When the government's efforts to meet these aspirations produced little except more inflation and a balance of payments deficit, the inevitable result was a devaluation in 1967 that seriously damaged the government's

credit abroad and reinforced the impression of a laggard and mis-
managed economy.

Balance of payments difficulties almost invariably are taken as
proof of mistaken policies, often with little justification, and tend to
be regarded as the one sure test of the strength or weakness of an
economy. A country in deficit is, almost *ipso facto*, open to criticism
while a country in surplus is usually immune. No doubt there is
some justification for this since debtors are made vulnerable by their
need to borrow while creditors are correspondingly in a position of
power. But markets may lay quite disproportionate emphasis on
short-term current account deficits, unless they are seen as transient,
to the neglect of other equally important aspects of economic performance. British balance of payments crises damaged the country's
image abroad and its self-confidence domestically, all the more
because of their frequency. Many foreign observers, particularly
Americans, tended to see Britain as a country staggering from one
balance of payments crisis to another and needing to be bailed out
again and again. It was not a view calculated to stabilise the exchange
rate or relieve the uneasiness of countries holding large balances in
sterling.

The weakness of the British balance of payments position was
twofold. First there was a chronic insufficiency of reserves in relation
to enormous short-term liabilities. Up to 1970 the reserves of gold
and dollars had never exceeded $4 billion while sterling balances held
in London, mainly by foreign monetary authorities, had for many
years after the war run at $20 billion or more, sustained by the use of
sterling as an international currency. In the early 1970s the position
improved a little and the reserves had risen to $7 billion by the spring
of 1972. From then until the last quarter of 1976 they remained between $5 billion and $7 billion, a level that was not only inadequate
in relation to liquid liabilities in the form of sterling balances, but
which would have paid for only two months' imports. It was largely
the absence of an adequate buffer stock of gold and dollars that made
the foreign exchanges so volatile.

If a foreign central bank decided to sell its sterling or there was a
sharp rise in import prices such as occurred in 1973–74, it was enough
to threaten a crisis. After the 1967 devaluation exchange guarantees
had been provided to official holders of sterling, but such guarantees
had lapsed while the risk of withdrawals soon revived.

A second weakness was that Britain's competitive position was
steadily deteriorating for a variety of reasons. One was the decline of

empire and the protection afforded to British exports in Commonwealth markets by Imperial Preference. These were the traditional
markets to which in 1950 51 per cent of British exports went. By 1970
this was down to 29 per cent, partly because of increased competition
from other countries and local producers, and partly because Commonwealth markets for manufactures grew less fast than markets
elsewhere, especially those in Europe. By 1970 Britain had succeeded
in extending sales in West European markets till they absorbed 40 per
cent of exports compared with 26 per cent ten years earlier and the
same percentage in 1950. But to effect the change was an uphill struggle, even after entry into the European Community in 1973, since it
meant competing with strong industrial competitors in their home
market, not supplying developing countries with the help of pre-
ferential advantages.

British reliance on imports was also increasing. Consumers
showed a preference for imported manufactures and their appetite
for these imports grew more rapidly than foreigners' appetite for
British goods. In the 1950s and 1960s it was possible to explain some
of this trend by pointing to the removal of restrictions on imports of
manufactures. But by 1970 this was ancient history and it was clear
that the rapid rise in imports of manufactures was simply a more reliable measure of declining competitive power than the more gradual
fall in Britain's share of foreign markets.

Competitive power was reduced both by a higher rate of inflation
and by a lower rate of productivity growth than in other industrial
countries. Until the 1970s, the lower rate of productivity growth was
probably the more important of the two. British managers were
slow to improve their products, enter new markets and meet the requirements of their foreign customers with the punctiliousness of
their chief competitors. Workers were less ready to accept changes in
productive methods. As a result, productivity grew more slowly and
so too did the domestic market, while, as explained above, the
British share of it, like the British share of foreign markets, continued to decline. The process appears to have been self-reinforcing
since the more slowly the domestic market expanded the more it
tended to dampen enterprise and innovation. Equally, in foreign
markets, the more rapid advance of other countries improved their
image and made it easier for them to gain share. On the other hand,
once the pound started to slide, the apparent restoration of competitive advantage that this might be expected to bring was partly
offset by customers' scruples about placing orders in an apparently

Figure 5

Balance of payments on current account (half-years 1971–77)
(seasonally adjusted)

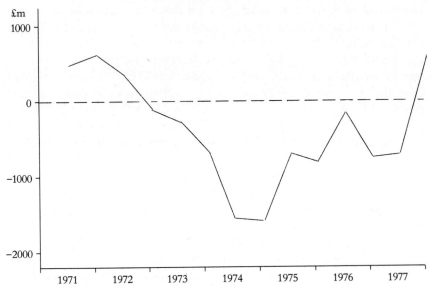

Source: *Economic Trends Annual Supplement 1990*

unsuccessful economy.

These two weaknesses – in reserves and in competitive power – meant that the government was not in a strong position to maintain a stable rate of exchange. First it was necessary to devalue in November 1967, then it was decided to abandon the defence of a fixed rate of exchange in June 1972. By letting the pound float the government was leaving control over the rate to the market. It did not, it is true, completely abandon control since it could, when it chose, intervene. Moreover, it was by no means alone in moving to a floating rate in the early 1970s. But it soon proved that leaving things to the market did not put an end to exchange crises. With a floating rate the loss of control in such a crisis was, if anything, more widely advertised in the shape of a falling rate of exchange.

Yet although in 1976 the balance of payments once again proved to be the Achilles' heel of the British economy, the picture was never wholly black. The balance on current account which had deteriorated year by year between 1971 and 1974 improved year by year between 1974 and 1977 when it finally moved into surplus in the second half of the year (Figure 5). The biggest setback was in the first half of 1977 when, paradoxically, money was pouring in from abroad and the reserves mounting to a record total.

Already, well before 1976, arrangements had been set on foot to exploit the large supplies of oil under the North Sea and it was recognised that within a few years Britain would be self-sufficient, and more than self-sufficient, in oil. Thanks to North Sea oil, after 1976 it was to be many years before Britain was again in balance of payments difficulties. But for some reason the market in 1976 paid little regard to the prospective oil bonanza, while in 1977, when other anxieties had been quietened, it seemed to have become almost obsessed by it.

The underlying position of the balance of payments was never easy to assess. As the 1970s opened, it appeared to be gathering strength with a series of surpluses on both current and capital account. In the three years 1969–71 the current account had been in ever-increasing surplus, the net outflow of long-term capital had been relatively small and short-term funds had begun to pour in on an unprecedented scale. The official reserves increased over those three years from $2.4 billion to $6.6 billion while the IMF and other monetary authorities were repaid $3.8 billion.

In the next three years there was a rapid deterioration. The current account swung from a surplus of £1.1 billion in 1971 to a deficit of £3.4 billion in 1974. The capital balance swung from a surplus of £2.1 billion in 1971 to a deficit of £1.4 billion in 1972 but then recovered in the next two years, partly under the influence of increasing investment from abroad (for example, in North Sea oil) and partly because of the deposit in London by oil producers of their swollen revenues (Table 5). These inflows made it possible to finance the heavy deficit on current account in 1974. This was also assisted by heavy borrowing on the part of public bodies in foreign capital markets with exchange cover from the government, the central government joining in with large borrowings in the final quarter of 1974. By the end of 1974 a foreign debt had been incurred in this way of £2,750 million in nominal terms although as the pound depreciated the sterling burden of the debt increased considerably.

When the Labour government took office in March 1974 the external deficit on current account had already reached £1.5 billion a year in the last quarter of 1973. The rise in oil prices then added to the deficit at an annual rate estimated at £2.5 billion. With a GDP of about £75 billion, an external deficit totalling £4 billion per annum represented a gap of over 5 per cent between what the country was producing and what it was using for consumption and investment.

Table 5

The movement of funds, 1971–78
(£ million)

	Current account	Long-term capital movements[1]	Short-term capital movements[2]	Balance for official financing	Financed by		
					IMF and other monetary authorities[3]	Foreign currency borrowing	Official reserves
1971	+1076	+ 26	+2044	+3146	−1692	+ 82	−1536
1972	+ 176	− 738	− 703	−1265	+ 573	–	+ 692
1973	−1056	− 238	+ 523	− 771	–	+ 999	− 228
1974	−3379	+1046	+ 687	−1646	–	+1751	− 105
1975	−1674	+ 161	+ 48	−1465	–	+ 810	+ 655
1976	−1116	− 119	−2393	−3628	+ 984	+1791	+ 853
1977	− 284	+2829	+4817	+7362	+1113	+1113	−9588
1978	+ 620	−2209	+ 463	−1126	− 1016	− 187	+2329

1. Including special grants and capital transfers to or from the UK government.
2. Including the balancing item.
3. Including in 1971 and 1972 allocations of SDRs.

Source: Economic Trends Annual Supplement, 1981 (later issues do not show the same detail). There have been a number of changes in the 1980s in the estimates but it is unlikely that these seriously affect the picture given. One clear change is a re-duction in the deficit on current account: for example, in the years 1975, 1976 and 1977 by £170 m., £175 m. and £134 m. respectively. The inflow of capital in those years must accordingly be adjusted downwards.

The deficit in 1974 was not in fact quite as large as £4 billion but even the actual deficit of £3.2 billion implied an excess of at least 4 per cent in current levels of utilisation of supplies over what was available domestically. The excess, however, was possible only so long as it was financed out of borrowings from foreigners or the realisation of assets owned by British residents. If no such borrowing or realisation of assets was possible and the deficit persisted, an abrupt adjustment would be necessary to bring imports and exports into balance.

It was important to decide, therefore, how much of the deficit represented a change in the underlying balance of payments requiring action to restore a sustainable balance and how much would eventually right itself. Some of the deficit arose out of circumstances likely to be transitory: the inability of the oil producers to make immediate use of their much larger foreign earnings; the inability or unwillingness of other industrial countries to prevent a contraction in their markets; the sharp turn in the terms of trade against importers of primary products of all kinds. Also in prospect was the early availability of North Sea oil, bringing in foreign exchange on a scale comparable with the deficit. On the other hand, the United Kingdom's competitive position had been weakening since 1971 and might continue to weaken as costs shot up with an acceleration in wage inflation and little improvement in productivity.

Even if the underlying situation was likely to improve, there remained the question of how much it was possible or prudent to borrow abroad. If money flowed in from the oil producers, as it did in 1974, there was the further question of whether it might not flow out again at an awkward moment. If it was used to finance overspending on imports instead of to add to reserves, this would then precipitate an exchange crisis. As things turned out, it was withdrawals of deposits made in 1974 at least as much as the continuing imbalance on current account that caused the trouble in 1976.

The current account did in fact improve greatly in 1975–76 and the deficit appeared to be close to vanishing point by the end of that period. First of all, there had been an improvement in the terms of trade of about 4 per cent by the end of 1976 as commodity prices moved closer to their earlier relationship to the price of manufactured goods. This by itself was equivalent to a reduction in the external deficit by over £1.5 billion at 1976 prices. There was also an improvement in the balance of trade. Thanks largely to the fall in the exchange rate, exports expanded in volume between the end of 1973 and the end of 1976 while imports contracted a little. Had there been no change in the terms of trade over those years and an improvement in invisible exports similar to the improvement in visible exports, the current account would have ended in substantial surplus.

The change in the balance of trade was assisted by the reduction in pressure on resources reflected in the doubling of unemployment since 1974. This and the slide in the value of the pound contributed both to the rise in exports and the check to imports.

Some of the improvement in the balance of payments after 1974 could also be put down to a higher savings ratio. The change between 1974 and 1976 was very small but the personal savings ratio in both years was appreciably higher than in the early 1970s and continued to rise in the later years of the decade. The higher savings ratio and the doubling of unemployment help to explain why in spite of a sharp rise in real wages in the second half of 1974 consumer spending *fell* in 1974 and remained below the 1973 level until 1978. There was no fall in real wages until late in 1976 but the level of consumption was cut nonetheless throughout the four years after 1973 – an experience unique in postwar years. In the much deeper and longer recession of the early 1980s there was no year in which consumer spending fell and throughout that depression real wages went on rising.

So the necessary adjustments turned out to be less than looked likely in 1974 and some of the most important changes were not the result of deliberate government action. At the end of 1976 the balance of payments was still in deficit, employment and investment were still depressed and the profits needed to encourage higher investment were still not being made. But most of the underlying imbalance had gone.

Not much of this could have been foreseen at the beginning of 1974 when a strategy for dealing with the external deficit had to be devised. At that stage unemployment was down to about 500,000 and even at the end of the year was not a great deal higher: it was not until 1975 that the big increase took place. There was therefore no need for deficit spending in order to sustain employment; and in any event borrowing abroad for the purpose would never have been countenanced by Keynes. What the external deficit reflected was overspending in relation to a GNP reduced by less favourable terms of trade; and common prudence pointed to a need to reduce real expenditure, if not correspondingly at least part of the way. This might come about without government intervention as higher import prices bit into consumer incomes. But it would not come about if the government increased its spending as in fact it did in 1974, when public expenditure in real terms grew by 8 per cent. Nor would it come about without faster inflation if wage-earners tried to protect their current level of real earnings by pressing for high increases in pay; or even succeeded, as they did in 1974, in raising real wages with the help of the thresholds.[2] Profits had already fallen a long way by the mid-1970s as inflation accelerated and manufacturers continued to price on historical costs. There was little possibility of squeezing them much further. It was real wages that would have to bear the brunt of any reduction in real incomes. But would wage-earners who were exacting 20 per cent increases in their nominal incomes agree to abstain and let rising prices outstrip money wages? If they turned militant would that not alarm foreign lenders and make matters worse?

There was, as Denis Healey urged, a case for acquiescing for the time being in a deficit corresponding to a share in the oil producers' almost inevitable surplus. But the 'share' could not be a large one for a country with such limited reserves. The United Kingdom was in no position to outdo other industrial countries in contracting short-term debts in order to save the world from an unnecessary depression.

Much of the adjustment in Labour's first year was deferred by the redeposit in London of some of the oil revenues of the oil producers (Table 6). Although the lion's share of their surpluses was deposited elsewhere, the £2,200 million that they deposited in sterling in 1974 covered over two-thirds of the current account deficit in that year and more than offset the additional cost of imported oil. As the current account improved in 1975–76, however, the central monetary institutions of the oil producers, who owned most of the deposits, began to withdraw them. In 1975 the net amount withdrawn was comparatively modest. An initial deposit of £350 million in the first quarter was followed by a withdrawal of £600 million in the next three quarters so that the net reduction over the year was only £250 million. The effective, or trade-weighted, exchange rate,[3] which had been steady in 1974 in spite of the enormous current account deficit, fell in 1975 by 11.5 per cent.

Distrust in sterling increased in 1976 as the outflow reached a peak comparable with the inflow in 1974 (see Table 5). It was at its height in the second and third quarters of 1976 when the exchange rate was falling rapidly and it was both a response to the fall and a principal cause of it. It is doubtful whether these withdrawals were much affected by the size of the Budget deficit or the growth of the money

Table 6

Changes in exchange reserves of sterling of central monetary institutions, 1974–76[1]
(£ million)

		Oil-exporting countries	Others	Total
1974	Q1–Q4	+2224	−814	+1410
1975	Q1	+ 348	−120	+ 228
	Q2	− 210	− 93	− 303
	Q3	− 296	− 84	− 380
	Q4	− 105	+ 26	− 162
1976	Q1	− 215	+135	− 80
	Q2	− 659	−262	− 921
	Q3	− 423	+ 74	− 349
	Q4	− 120	+ 9	− 57

1. The figures for fourth quarters are affected by revaluations of the hold-ings of government bonds. This added £83 million to the total for Decem-ber 1975 and reduced the total for December 1976 by £54 million. The figures given for the fourth quarter in cols 1 and 2 are after revaluation, while the figures in col. 3 are for the cash flow.

Source: Bank of England *Quarterly Bulletin*, Statistical Annex, various issues.

supply except in so far as these affected market sentiment and the stability of the exchange rate. But the withdrawal of over £2 billion by the central monetary institutions of the oil-producing countries between the spring of 1975 and the end of 1976 was bound by itself, once it got going for whatever reason, to force down the rate as the withdrawal fed on itself.

Other central monetary institutions were using up their sterling holdings in 1974, presumably in order to meet deficits occasioned by the rise in oil prices. They continued to do so in 1975, but in 1976 they added to their holdings except in the second quarter, when the pressure was at its height and all groups of sterling holders were sell-ing sterling.

Other short-term capital movements (including the balancing item) were at first into sterling, both in 1974 and in the first three quarters of 1975, but by the final quarter of 1975 the movement was reversed and in the first half of 1976 the drain of funds out of sterling was running at an annual rate of £4,000 million, half of it exchange reserves and half other movements of short-term capital (Table 7).

The pressure was at its height in the spring of 1976 when the rate

Table 7

The movement of funds, 1975–77
(£ million)

	Current account	Long-term investment (net)	Changes in exchange reserves held in sterling	Other capital movements[1]	Total officially financed	Financed by		
						IMF and other monetary authorities	Foreign currency borrowing	Official reserves[2]
1975 Q1	−625	− 33	+228	+ 104	− 326	—	+468	− 142
2	−391	− 317	−303	+ 439	− 572	—	+162	+ 410
3	−572	+ 468	−380	+ 271	− 213	—	+ 43	+ 170
4	− 86	+ 43	−162	− 149	− 354	—	+137	+ 217
1976 Q1	−125	+ 137	− 80	− 610	− 678	+ 580	+276	− 178
2	−375	− 153	−921	− 506	−1955	+1019	+582	+ 354
3	−341	− 56	−349	− 115	− 861	+ 309	+491	+ 61
4	−275	− 47	− 57	+ 245	− 134	− 924	+442	+ 616
1977 Q1	−675	+ 921	+190	+1478	+1914	+ 682	+601	−3197
2	−499	+1003	−398	+ 802	+ 908	+ 217	+ 33	−1158
3	+495	+ 627	+ 74	+1412	+2608	+ 214	+405	−3227
4	+395	+ 278	+115	+1144	+1932	—	+ 74	−2006

1. Including the balancing item.
2. Including changes in reserve position in the IMF.

Source: as Table 5.

of exchange dropped sharply. In the second quarter of the year the authorities found themselves faced with a deficit on current and capital account now estimated at £2 billion for that quarter alone (Table 7). This came on top of a deficit of nearly £700,000 in the previous quarter and deficits of about £1.5 billion in each of the two preceding years. Foreign currency borrowing had more than covered the deficit in 1974 and more than half of the deficit in 1975, the rest coming from the reserves. But in the first half of 1976 foreign currency borrowing met less than a third of a much larger total.

What saved the day in the first half of 1976 was heavy borrowing (£1 billion) from the IMF in January (under the oil facility) and May (the first credit tranche) and from other monetary authorities in June. By mid-year all these IMF funds had been used together with £580 million from the stand-by. There was every cause for alarm. The June loan offered only temporary respite and would have to be repaid in December. Foreign central banks and monetary authorities still held £3 billion in sterling and might continue withdrawals on a scale as large as in the second quarter. The current account had ceased to improve and appeared to be in even heavier deficit than in the winter months. The domestic situation with a Cabinet deeply divided, and wages still rising fast, was far from reassuring to holders of sterling.

Matters were not made any better in 1976 by gloomy unofficial forecasts of the balance of payments and estimates of the deficit that have since been revised downwards. In November 1975 the forecasts showed the current account in heavier deficit in 1976 than in 1975 and registering little improvement in 1977.[4] Three months later, in February 1976, the next set of forecasts conveyed a slightly more favourable picture. In May the fall in the exchange rate and improved prospects for world trade suggested a further improvement in 1976 and a larger one in 1977. By August, however, the forecast deficit for mid-1976 to mid-1977 was back up again to about where it had been in November 1975. It was not until November 1976 that a major change occurred; a surplus was forecast from the second quarter of 1977 onwards. These forecasts were far removed from the eventual outturn. For the year 1976 deficits were forecast in successive estimates of £2.03 billion, £1.65 billion, £1.94 billion and £1.67 billion while the recorded deficit, at first estimated at £1.55 billion has since been revised downwards to £0.96 billion. For 1977 the deficits forecast ran £1.93 billion, £0.90 billion, £1.50 billion, and a surplus of £1.12 billion compared with an initial estimate of a deficit of £35 million since revised to one of £175 million. That the forecasts were wrong is of little significance. They are, however, an indication of the state of professional opinion during the year and help to explain the consistent pessimism of the market. The Treasury offered no forecasts to the market but they, too, seem to have erred on the side of pessimism.[5]

When the market completely changed its mind about sterling in 1977 after the agreement with the IMF it was not because of any change in forecasts and figures. North Sea oil is sometimes credited with changing the outlook. But the National Institute in November 1976 was already forecasting an expansion in the output of North Sea oil from a negligible total in 1975 to £2.8 billion in 1977 as *part* of its forecast of the current account. The oil was there all along and had no rational association with the change in sentiment.[6]

The exchange market remained throughout in trepidation and fearful of fresh shocks. Having plunged once in March–April 1976, as described in Chapter 2, the exchange rate collapsed again in September–October to a low point in October nearly 25 per cent lower against the dollar than at the end of 1975 (see Figure 4, p. 56).

In spite of all the alarms in October further withdrawals by central monetary authorities fell away, and in the fourth quarter of 1976 capital movements were already inwards rather than outwards. The reserves took most of the strain of the December repayment and by the end of the year, indeed even before the agreement with the IMF, the exchange rate had pulled back from its lowest point. Nevertheless the effective exchange rate was nearly 40 per cent down on the rate before the float in June 1972.

By the first quarter of 1977 everything was in reverse. The exchange rate held steady while funds, long term and short term, poured in. The reserves increased rapidly and continued to increase at a record rate unimaginable a year previously. By the end of the year the balance of payments on current account had at last moved into surplus, the reserves had risen by £9.5 billion and the government had been obliged to let the pound appreciate for fear the inflow of funds would overexpand the money supply.

CHAPTER 7

The Loss of Control:
Domestic Economic Policy

While Britain's balance of payments difficulties were greatly exacerbated by the rapid increase in commodity prices in 1972–74 and the marked shift in the terms of trade that this occasioned, the pressure on sterling in 1975–76 reflected a more general loss of confidence in Britain's prospects and policies. The fact that the external account had so often been out of balance was taken to be the fruit of feeble and irresolute domestic policies. Inflation had got out of hand, it was alleged, because of failure to control the Budget deficit, the money supply and the level of wages. The fall in the value of money at home was echoed in the fall in the value of the currency on the foreign exchanges, and once the fall was under way it gathered speed without further prompting.

In the next three sections we shall examine each of these three factors separately – the Budget deficit, the money supply, and wages – concentrating on the question of control.

FISCAL POLICY

There have always been those who regard it as the government's plain duty to keep the Budget in balance and limit revenue expenditure to what can be covered by taxation: except of course in wartime when borrowing on the grand scale is justifiable. During the Second World War a different conception of fiscal policy took shape based on the ideas of Keynes, although Keynes himself actively opposed the new approach.[1] The Budget was now regarded as an instrument for the stabilisation of employment. An increase in the Budget surplus was thought appropriate when effective demand was too high and putting a strain on productive capacity, and a Budget deficit when there was a danger of underemployment and stagnation.

By the 1960s it was generally assumed that this view of policy had triumphed. In fact, however, there had never been occasion to run a large Budget deficit, so the idea of boosting public spending or remitting taxation in a slump had not been fully tested. Apart from that, there was plenty of room for disagreement over what constituted a Budget surplus. What people were talking about in the 1950s and 1960s was the surplus (or deficit) in the Budget of the central government, and this was very different from the public sector borrowing requirement that people talked about in the 1980s. The PSBR included the borrowing of local authorities and nationalised industries, much of which was for capital expenditure. To get the PSBR (alternatively, the public sector financial deficit which excludes public lending) down to zero is a more demanding (and deflationary) objective than to avoid a deficit in the Budget of the central government. Both kinds of deficit can be measured in different ways depending on which items of revenue or expenditure are included, and the objective of Budget balance is consequently much more ambiguous than it seems. While some people use balance as a test of Budget discipline, others regard it as a quite inappropriate aim of policy.

To make matters worse, governments do not go in for inflation accounting. A deficit is a deficit if the government has to borrow even when it is being enriched and its bond-holders impoverished as inflation eats into outstanding debt. As we saw in Chapter 5, the amount of debt wiped out by inflation exceeded in every year in the 1970s the total of the government's *net* borrowing. As the 'profligate' 1970s progressed, public sector debt fell steadily as a proportion of national income. Between 1971 and 1979 the proportion shrank from 76 per cent to 56 per cent – no mean capital levy. If we narrow the period to 1970 to 1976 and confine the comparison to long-term government debt and the guaranteed debt of the nationalised industries, we find that a near-doubling of the nominal amount was accompanied by a reduction at constant 1970 prices of over 25 per cent.[2]

Of course, the government's need to borrow was unaffected; but its power to borrow was enlarged because the holders of depreciating government bonds tended to save more in order to replenish their wealth. In an inflationary world it was not possible, in measuring savings, to disregard capital gains and losses from the resulting transfer of wealth from lenders to borrowers. If in such a world the state continued to aim at balancing its accounts unadjusted for inflation it would throw the economy out of balance just as surely as if it opted for a surplus in a non-inflationary world.

There are also serious intrinsic difficulties, particularly under inflationary conditions, in keeping to the exact Budget limits laid down a year or more in advance. This applies particularly to the PSBR, which covers a wide range of spending agencies. As Denis Healey learned, 'it is impossible to get the PSBR right.'[3] The timing of expenditure, the level of prices and employment during the year, the flow of revenue at levels of pay and profit yet to be decided, make estimation in advance a hazardous business; and it is not at all surprising if quite wide divergences occur, without any change of policy, between what appears in the Budget at the beginning of the financial year and the outturn recorded a year later in the next Budget. Such forecasting errors do not by themselves demonstrate a loss of control; but they do underline some of the difficulties of control.

If we go back to 1969–70 the Budget was for two years in surplus, whichever of the measures referred to above is applied. From 1971 on, however, the PSBR was in steadily increasing deficit (see Table 8). By the financial year 1972–73 it was already higher, at £2.5 billion, than at any time in the 1960s. It nearly doubled in 1973–74, rose to £8 billion in 1974–75, went on rising in 1975–76 to £10.6 billion, and was expected to reach £12 billion in 1976–77 – nearly 12 per cent of GDP in that year and more than enough to absorb the whole of personal savings. The rise in the borrowing requirement over those years was not only enormous in relation to previous experience: it far outstripped Budget plans and expectations.

In Denis Healey's first Budget in March 1974, for example, he aimed to reduce the PSBR to £2.7 billion from the £4.3 billion then recorded as the outturn for the previous financial year. In intention the Budget was 'broadly neutral', not expansionary.[4] But by November 1974 he had re-estimated the PSBR at £6.3 billion. Even if one leaves out the £800 million that can be imputed to new budgetary measures between March and November that still represents a doubling of the original estimate. At the end of the financial year the scale of underestimation was found to be still higher, the PSBR for 1974–75 being put at £7.6 billion (later revised upwards to £8 billion). In this as in other respects, the conduct of policy in 1974 contributed powerfully to the difficulties of 1975–76.

There can be no doubt that in 1974 the Treasury greatly under-

Table 8

Public sector borrowing requirement and financial deficit, 1971–79[1](£000 million)

Financial year	PSBR			PSFD		
	Budget forecast	Provi-sional outturn	Latest estimate	Budget forecast	Provi-sional estimate	Latest estimate
1971–72	1.2	1.3	1.0	0.3	−0.7	0.7
1972–73	3.4	2.9	2.1	2.4	2.1	2.0
1973–74	4.4	4.3	4.3	2.9	3.1	3.5
1974–75[2]	2.7/6.3	7.6	8.0	1.2/4.8	5.9	6.0
1975–76	9.1	10.8	10.3	7.6	8.2	8.1
1976–77	12.0	8.8	8.3	10.6	7.7	7.4
1977–78	8.5	5.7	5.4	7.6	5.8	6.6
1978–79	8.5	9.2	9.2	7.4	7.5	8.3

1. The financial deficit differs from the PSBR by the net amounts lent by the public sector.
2. The forecasts relate to the March and November Budgets.

Source: Annual *Financial Statements; Financial Statistics; C.S.O.*

estimated the impact on the Budget of the oil shock, the threshold wage agreements and the inflation that accompanied them. The mis-calculation mainly affected public expenditure. In March the Budget had provided for a total of £37.9 billion; in November this was raised to £41.3 billion; the outturn in April 1975 was still higher at £42.4 billion. Only a part of the excess can be attributed to deliberate changes in the volume of expenditure. The greater part was due to the rise in costs, which was more pronounced in the public than in the private sector.

In 1975–76 it looked as if the same process was being repeated. As in March 1974, the Chancellor aimed to reduce the prospective bor-rowing requirement, now £10 billion, by a substantial amount – on this occasion by £1 billion. But public expenditure continued to rise faster than planned, largely because the rate of inflation had again been underestimated, and the PSBR turned out to be £10.8 billion, an excess of £1.7 billion over the Budget forecast: £10.8 billion was a far cry from the forecast of £2.7 billion for the year before.

It was not unnatural, therefore, that when the Budget for 1976–77 was introduced it should be greeted with some scepticism. The pros-pective borrowing requirement continued to increase and the feeling was spreading that public expenditure was out of control. Cash limits had been in preparation since the previous autumn and were introduced in April in an endeavour to set firmer bounds to public expenditure. In his Budget speech, the Chancellor agreed that there had been an underestimation in the previous year of the effect of inflation on the borrowing requirement but was optimistic about the future. Inflation was diminishing and was moving towards the government's target of 'single figures by the end of the year'. The steep fall in economic activity in other industrial countries in the first half of 1975 had largely been reversed in the second half of the year. It was too early to point to any significant recovery in the United Kingdom but there were signs of improvement in the economic situation. The picture presented by the Chancellor was one of resumed expansion, falling inflation, an improving balance of payments and confidence in the financial outlook.[5] Nothing in the Budget speech heralded the disastrous experiences of the following months.

The Chancellor's reputation was now one of inveterate optimism – a matter of some importance in a year when market confidence in government policy was evaporating. When he estimated the prospective PSBR in 1976–77 at £12 billion he was at once challenged by Mrs Thatcher, who asked what faith could be put in such an estimate when the previous year's figures were so badly out.

Such scepticism proved unjustified. After the cuts in July, Healey revised his estimate of the PSBR downwards to £9 billion. In the negotiations with the IMF at the end of the year, it was revised upwards again to £11.2 billion. This soon proved to be much too high: the figure announced at the end of the financial year was £8.8 billion (now revised to £8.3 billion). In a year of acute crisis, the PSBR was overestimated by more than it had been underestimated in the previous year. If the PSBR was not under control, neither did it always exceed expectations. As the Expenditure Committee commented on a similar experience in 1977–78, 'Shortfall has proved more significant in amount than the Government's expenditure cuts which were so widely debated when they were proposed.'[6]

The Treasury seems to have been unaware of the shortfall during the negotiations with the IMF, to whom an estimate of £11.2 billion for 1976–77 was submitted. According to Sir Leo Pliatzky, 'the estimate of the prospective PSBR [for 1976–77] had moved up again' in the autumn and was presumably at least £11 billion in November.[7] 'Unknown to us at the time, unplanned shortfall was much bigger than the planned reductions which had brought the government of the country to crisis point.'[8] It was not until January that 'the estimates suggested that there had been some moderate underspending.' Even in February 1977 the National Institute expected the PSBR for 1976–77 to reach £10.4 billion.[9]

Yet there were indications well before the end of 1976 of a downward trend in the PSBR. Some forecasts were well below the Treasury's.[10] From the second quarter of 1976 onwards the quarterly figures fell below the figures for the corresponding quarter in 1975 with a particularly large dip in the final quarter of the year. As Tim Congdon pointed out in *The Times* on 4 September 1976, the seasonally adjusted figures showed the PSBR hovering at an annual rate of about £10 billion after reaching a peak rate of £11.5 billion in the third quarter of 1975.[11] While tax concessions and higher social security benefits and pensions had yet to come into operation, the nationalised industries would have smaller deficits and would not require further compensation from the central government for price restraint. It was increasingly apparent that the government could neither control nor forecast its borrowing requirements with the precision that its critics were apt to assume.

The shortfall in 1976–77 was plainly associated with the introduction of cash limits. Since the issue of the Plowden Report in 1961 the system of expenditure control by the Public Expenditure Survey Committee (PESC) had been in terms of volume and stretched over a period four years ahead. The proposed expenditures were translated into volume terms, not by applying a single price deflator such as the Retail Price Index or the GDP deflator but by repricing each item at survey prices, that is, correcting for the rise in price *of that item*. There were thus three measures of expenditure: the cash disbursement, the cash value adjusted for inflation in general and the cash value adjusted for the rise in price of what was bought by the government (that is, applying both an index of inflation and of the relative price deflator).

A difficulty with volume control was that there was no reconsideration by departments of how much they should spent when things rose in price. They could recost existing policies each year and fight for their continuation regardless of price changes. They had also less incentive to contest higher prices when these did not affect authorisations. Indeed it was the need to reinforce counter-inflationary policies more than the need for stricter control of public expenditure that first attracted ministers to cash limits.[12]

The system of cash limits meant that control was over Exchequer issues of cash, as authorised by the supply estimates approved by Parliament. This did not mean – in the late 1970s at least – the abandonment of the annual public expenditure surveys at constant prices but the superimposition of cash limits on volume control. It did mean that specific allowance was made in advance for inflation in the year ahead with no automatic adjustment if the rise in prices proved to exceed the allowance. There was no 're-costing of existing policies' annually such as had previously taken place: programmes in volume terms were carried forward from one year to the next, unchanged in volume apart from additions and reductions specifically approved. These additions and reductions in the course of the year represented a loss of control which the Treasury had tried unsuccessfully to end. With cash limits a procedure was devised for containing additions. The Contingency Reserve which had hitherto been a purely statistical allowance, was converted into an operational control by requiring all new commitments to be contained within the White Paper total. In addition, after the rules of procedure were allowed to prevent Treasury Ministers from being overruled on financial matters in Cabinet Committees, any proposal for additional expenditure opposed by Treasury Ministers had to go to full Cabinet. This added materially to the ability of the Treasury to resist the pressure of spending ministers. The Cabinet was also supplied for a time with regular Progress Reports on the Contingency Reserve so that they could see what remained to meet further expenditure proposals.[13]

Arrangements for the introduction of cash limits (or 'cash control' as they were called initially) were first made in the public sector. In 1974–75 and 1975–76 these covered the main building programmes for public services (but not dwelling houses and roads). In July 1975 the government announced that work was in hand to extend their use in 1976–77 to expenditures where they 'can impose greater financial discipline and precision'. They were to be applied to about three-quarters of the voted expenditure of the central government (social security cash payments being excluded). In November 1975 it was announced that they were also to apply to most local authority capital expenditure excluding new dwellings and to the rate support grant.

For public expenditure, a rate of inflation of 9 per cent had been projected in the 1976 White Paper and was applied to expenditure subject to cash limits.[14] Public sector prices, however, rose by 17 per cent in 1976–77. Had cash limits applied throughout the year and remained unaltered, this in itself would account for most, if not all of the divergence from plan. In addition, two other factors seem to have operated. One was a shortfall of nearly two-thirds (£600,000) in government lending to the nationalised industries. The other was the caution natural to programme managers when cash limits were first applied.[15] As Denis Healey tells us, departments were so frightened of exceeding their limits that they tended to underspend, sometimes dramatically so.[16]

What had caused the PSBR to reach such alarming dimensions was the rapid growth of public expenditure and it was this that made people like Arthur Burns talk of 'profligacy' and others like Stuart Pardee insist on the need for 'discipline'. Likewise in Britain it was over public expenditure that the battle lines were drawn in the autumn of 1976.

It happened that the Expenditure Committee of the House of Commons was enquiring in 1975–76 into the financing of public expenditure.[17] Its General Sub-Committee heard evidence on 3 November 1975 from Wynne Godley attacking root and branch the system of control over public expenditure.[18] Godley had served in the Treasury for many years, had been a pioneer in the preparation of official economic forecasts, and had spent a good deal of time as a Treasury official enquiring into the way in which departments monitored their expenditure over the financial year. His strictures were widely publicised and must have done much to strengthen the impression that the growth of expenditure was getting out of hand because of the inadequacy and sloppiness of the system of control.

Some of Godley's evidence related to inadequacies in the planning system and the information available for planning purposes. These were matters of long-term organisation and needed careful consideration. But they were not what caught the attention of the public. The really striking points in Godley's evidence were (1) that public expenditure had absorbed two-thirds of the increase in gross domestic product over the four years 1970–71 to 1974–75 and (2) that, out of an increase of 28.6 per cent in the volume of public expenditure up to September 1975 only 15 per cent had been planned in 1971 or represented policy changes between then and 1975. Nearly £5 billion at current prices was unaccounted for.

The first of these points was not altogether surprising since public expenditure (as then measured) was already half GDP in 1971 and the proportion that public expenditure bore to GDP was known to have increased perceptibly. It was obvious, therefore, that as a proportion of the *increment* in GDP, public expenditure must have been well above 50 per cent. What excited comment was not this point but the implied accusation of unaccountability. Although the Treasury responded at once with an explanation of the difference of £5 billion – on the Treasury's arithmetic £5.5 billion – between the actual and planned totals, the impression remained widespread that there was no adequate control over public expenditure.[19]

How did the difference between planned and actual totals arise? First of all, the Treasury pointed out that what was planned for the fourth year of an expenditure survey (1975 was four years away in 1971) was bound to be affected by later review of the way in which policies were working out, particularly if, as in 1974, there was a change of government. Policy changes by the incoming Labour government accounted for £1.5 billion of the difference. Secondly, forward plans were expressed in volume terms and any comparison with the outturn had to be in volume terms. Actual expenditure, however, depended not just on the change in volume but also on the change that occurred in the price of goods and services purchased. This change might diverge from the *average* change in prices for the whole economy, including private and public sectors, and for this change in relative prices only a broad allowance, based on past trends, could be made. In the period 1970–71 to 1974–75 the 'relative price effect' had exceeded the trend allowance made in 1971 by £1.75 billion. The excess was not because of a faster rise in pay in the public services. That accounted for only a little. Most of the excess, about three-quarters of it, was attributable to the sharp rise in land and house prices and construction costs that began in 1972 – a rise that led to the imposition of cash limits on some construction programmes in 1974–75.[20]

Of the remaining £2.25 billion, £0.75 billion was accounted for by higher interest payments – partly higher interest rates, partly more borrowing – and £1.5 billion by other changes, of which the most important was one of £1 billion as a result of a deliberate change of policy on housing. All changes, announced or hidden in the total for 'other changes', were, of course, approved by the government.[21]

The Expenditure Committee, commenting on this evidence, argued that on the Treasury's own admission nearly 70 per cent of the £5.5 billion excess over plan was not the result of announced policy changes and concluded that: 'even allowing for unannounced policy changes the Treasury's methods of controlling public expenditure are inadequate in the sense that money can be spent on a scale which was not contemplated when the relevant policies were decided upon'.[22]

The nub of the matter was that expenditure was sanctioned without regard to subsequent changes in pay and prices. The calculations, as Sam Brittan kept insisting in *The Financial Times*, were done at constant prices (in 'funny money'), not at current prices. The institution of cash limits was intended as an answer to this criticism and it did appear to put an end to charges of inadequate control.

It may be doubted, however, whether it was the new system of control over expenditure rather than the dip in the volume of expenditure that silenced the critics. In cash terms public expenditure had doubled between 1972 and 1975 and was set to go on increasing in 1976. In volume terms the position was very different. Allowing for the fall in the value of money, public expenditure had reached a peak in 1975–76 after climbing by about 22 per cent over the previous three years. Over the next two years it fell back by 9 per cent to a level not much higher than in 1973–74 under the Heath government. Making a further allowance for the relative price effect (that is if one uses constant – 1977 – survey prices), the peak in 1975–76 works out at only 13 per cent above the level in 1972–73 and the subsequent fall becomes one of only 4.5 per cent (see Table 9). The general rise in prices, reinforced by the faster rise in survey prices, accounted for the bulk of the growth in public expenditure up to 1975–76 and for nearly all the growth between 1973–74 and 1977–78. The charges of 'profligacy' come down quite largely to failure to react to rising prices by greater economy.

One factor which excited disquiet was the high and rising proportion of the national income that went in public spending. Denis Healey in his memoirs laments the statement in his White Paper on the government's expenditure plans of February 1976 (Cmnd 6393) that 'the ratio of total public expenditure to GDP at factor cost has grown from 50 per cent in 1971/2 to about 60 per cent in 1975/6'.[23] This proportion, he argues, was completely misleading since it included expenditures that no other country included in its total. 'When we defined public spending in the same way as did other countries,' he tells us, 'our spending was reduced by some £7.7 billion at a stroke. And when we costed GDP, like public spending, at market prices, the ratio of public spending to GDP fell from sixty per cent to forty-six per cent.' This is perfectly true. But what he does not say is that the proportion, even on the revised basis, had risen

Table 9

Public expenditure, 1972–77
(£ billion)

| | Cash total[1] | At 1977 'cost'[2] | At 1977 survey prices[3] | Ratio to GDP at market prices[4] (%) | |
				(a)	(b)
1972–73	26.1		51.1	52.5	38.5	41
1973–74	31.5		55.1	54.2	39.9	42.25
1974–75	42.2	42.9	62.2	58.6	45.0	48
1975–76		53.4	62.5	59.5	45.4	48.5
1976–77		60.0	61.0	57.9	43.0	46
1977–78		63.3	56.8	56.8	39.3	42.75

1. As in Pliatzky, *Getting and Spending*, p. 219: i.e., using for 1972–73 and 1973–74 the definition of public expenditure as in Cmnd 9143, but excluding market and overseas borrowing by public corporations; using for later years definition in Cmnd 9143. Debt interest has been added to make the figures comparable with these in the other columns.
2. Deflated by the GDP deflator, as in Pliatzky, *Getting and Spending*, p. 218, but at 1977 prices, not 1981–82 prices.
3. As given in Cmnd 7049–I, Table 9 but adding back proceeds of sale of BP shares. This includes foreign and market borrowing by public corporations.
4. *Col. a:* Planning total plus debt interest and imputed consumption of non-trading government capital less market and overseas borrowing of nationalised industries, as given by Pliatzky, *Getting and Spending*, p. 218.

   Col. b: Ratio of General Government expenditure to GDP as given in *The Government's Expenditure Plans 1990–91 to 1992–93*, ch. 21 (Cm 1021 January 1990).

   It will be evident that the estimates in col. b show a steeper upward trend than those in col. a.

steeply in the early 1970s. On the definition used by Pliatzky, the rise was from 37.6 per cent in 1971–72 to 45.4 per cent in 1975–76, the big rise being in 1974–75, and it was this trend almost as much as the size of the deficit that was causing concern.

The passage in the White Paper that Healey regrets gave a more balanced picture of the consequences of rising public expenditure than he appears to imply. It pointed out that in three years public expenditure had risen in real terms by over 20 per cent while output was up by less than 2 per cent. Taxation had risen to the point at which a married man on average earnings was paying a quarter of his income in income tax whereas in 1961 he would have paid only a tenth. A married man on two-thirds average earnings was paying a fifth compared with a twentieth of his income in tax. A quarter of the yield of income tax came from workers earning below the average. The tax burden would have been much larger if the government had not been prepared to run a high public sector deficit. But it was a deficit that had to be reduced as output recovered. While rising public expenditure had helped to sustain employment in the middle of a world depression, it could not be allowed to go on expanding and it was intended that after a small rise in 1976–77 the level of re-sources absorbed by the public sector should be stabilised.

The cuts that took place in public expenditure under the Labour government have no parallel in any other period in the postwar years. The Thatcher government did not succeed in reducing public expenditure in real terms until after 1986–87 and the drop to the low point two years later was no more than 2.5 per cent whereas between 1975–76 and 1977–78 there was a drop of nearly 8 per cent.[24] The cuts in the 1970s, moreover, were made not in a buoyant economy like that in the late 1980s but in the middle of a prolonged depression in which unemployment never ceased to rise. Ministers kept hoping for a recovery and accompanied their expenditure plans by forecasts of rapid expansion at rates of up to 5 per cent per annum while output remained depressed and lagging further and further behind what had once seemed easily attainable.

PUBLIC EXPENDITURE CUTS

Efforts to cut the growth in public expenditure went back to 1973 when a mini-Budget included among other deflationary measures a cut in expenditure programmes for 1974–75 of £1.2 billion. The annual public expenditure review in December 1973 (Cmnd 5519) showed a rate of expansion in cost terms of 2 per cent per annum be-tween 1973–74 and 1977–78 whereas a year before the rate contem-plated over the following four years was 2.5 per cent. In terms of the implied increase in the demand on resources the contrast was even greater, a contraction from 3.4 per cent per annum to 2.5 per cent.

In normal circumstances such a rate of expansion would have left public expenditure in much the same ratio to GNP at the end of the four years as at the beginning. Two factors, however, increased the ratio. On the one hand, GNP rose at a very slow rate over those four years and on the other, prices in the public sector (for the things on which the government spent its money) went up relatively steeply. Both factors made for a rise in the proportion of the nation's resources disposed of by public authorities quite independently of any spending decisions taken by those authorities.

If we look at the succession of spending programmes in the White Papers, beginning in December 1972, we find that a typical pattern is a big jump in the current year followed by a planned expansion at a much slower rate over the next four years. It is not until the (February) 1976 White Paper that both these phenomena disappear. Only a small increase by volume was expected in 1975–76 and thereafter the planned course of expenditure was gently downwards over the following three years.[25] This was the position *before* the cuts in July and December 1976, that is before there was any question of further borrowing from the IMF.

What seems to have happened was that in 1972–74 expenditure began by outrunning plans and the gap between the two was further widened by the relative price effect. In addition, the incoming Labour government made substantial increases in expenditure in 1974 so that by the first half of 1975 the flow of expenditure was far above what had been contemplated at the end of 1972 or 1973. In proportion to GDP, public expenditure (as defined by Pliatzky, not as measured in the comparisons above) rose from 38.5 per cent in 1972–73 to 45.4 per cent in 1975–76 but then fell to 39.3 per cent in 1977–78.[26] The brake was put on in 1975 although it did not do much to check expenditure in that year. The cuts in 1976 were an amplification of changes already in progress.

The changes in expenditure made in the first two years of Labour government are listed in the White Papers of 1975 and 1976. They cover a large number of Budget-type statements as well as frequent announcements of fresh expenditures for particular purposes: industrial regeneration, temporary employment subsidies, additional welfare payments, food and other subsidies, and so on.

Reductions of £1.36 billion in the programmes for 1974–75 by the Conservative government in December 1973 were swamped by increases by the Labour government totalling £4 billion. These included about £1.3 billion on housing, and £500 million or more each on food subsidies, trade, industry and employment and debt interest.

In November 1974, when the government had had time to reconsider its spending plans, it was still proposing a 2.75 per cent per

annum increase for the next four years above the level it had envisaged for 1974–75 when it took office. This was repeated in the
White Paper on Public Expenditure that appeared in January 1975,
and was taken to be equivalent to a 2.25 per cent per annum increase
above the level that had in fact been reached in 1974–75. At the same
time the government was counting on a 3 per cent per annum increase in GDP between 1973 and 1979 (the central case, midway between possible rates of 2.5 and 3.5 per cent).[27] Unfortunately there
was no increase at all between 1973 and 1976 and for the six-year
period the annual rate of growth was under 1.5 per cent.

These plans were revised in the course of the financial year. By the
time the 1976 White Paper appeared it was recognised that public expenditure in 1975–76 was some 3 per cent higher in volume than had
been planned a year before and was likely to grow by a further 2.5
per cent in 1976–77. Unemployment was rising rapidly and GDP
was falling. In these circumstances the Chancellor had succeeded in
obtaining agreement in the expenditure review to holding public expenditure (excluding debt interest) at about the 1976–77 level for the
three succeeding years from 1976 to 1979. This meant that the programmes for 1977–78 and 1978–79 would be cut by £1 billion and
£2.4 billion respectively.[28]

These first major cuts were accompanied by highly optimistic
forecasts of output, which was expected to grow at 3.5 per cent per
annum between 1974 and 1979 and at 4.75 per cent per annum in the
immediate future, drawing on unemployed labour and unused capacity.[29] Developments in the first half of 1976 were altogether less
satisfactory and a fresh round of cuts took place in July after long
argument in Cabinet. Another £1 billion was knocked off spending
plans for 1977–78 and a second £1 billion added to National Insurance
contributions.

The cuts insisted on by the IMF were thus the third in a single year
and brought the total reduction in the 1977–78 programme to £3 billion and in the 1978–79 programme to over £5 billion. The cuts were
particularly heavy on capital expenditure; this apart, they can be
assumed to have been selected so as to keep down, as far as possible,
the impact on employment. Expenditure associated with industrial
regeneration was largely untouched and additional funds were provided to deal with unemployment, such as the Temporary Employment Subsidy.

On any showing it was reasonable to refrain from cutting expenditure when revenue was curtailed by industrial depression,

rather than make the depression worse by cuts. On a so-called 'Keynesian' view, one could justify going further and spending more heavily in order to maintain employment. There is little evidence that this played much part in Healey's spending plans in 1974–75. But when the monetarists and others clamoured for cuts in 1976 there was a natural reaction, all the more powerful because unemployment was still rising. The clash of opinion is discussed in Chapter 5. The Chancellor hesitated between the need to avoid measures that would be seen as creating unemployment and the need to reduce borrowing to a manageable level, given the views of lenders. It was a dilemma that was to recur. Healey, in some doubt about the power of increased government spending to create jobs under inflationary conditions, opted for cuts but sought to keep them to a minimum. The Prime Minister took a similar stand at the Party conference in September 1976.

But was it right to discount the effect on unemployment? There were many, including Mrs Thatcher, who thought that cuts of £5–6 billion would do no great harm in the short run and were likely to accelerate growth in the longer run. The lesson they drew from the experience of 1976 was that large cuts could be made in public expenditure without all the terrible consequences predicted by Keynesian economists. It is certainly hard to detect in the unemployment figures the impact of a rapidly rising PSBR in 1972–75 or of a falling PSBR over the next two years. Was it really possible to cut the PSBR by £5 billion without any apparent effect on the level of employment? And if so, what happened to offset the fall in government expenditure?

First of all, it is necessary to take account of the changes in the Budget that are a *consequence*, not a cause, of changes in employment and economic activity. In 1973–75, for example, output was falling and unemployment rising so that government revenue fell off and more had to be spent on unemployment benefit. Part of the increased deficit in 1975 reflected these influences and was not available to boost economic acativity. In 1975–77 we have the opposite situation, with output expanding, revenue more buoyant and expenditure in response to additional unemployment little changed. When we adjust for these developments the fiscal stance of the government would seem to be little different in 1975 from what it was in 1973 – if anything a little more *deflationary* – and in 1977 the adjusted deficit had been cut by about £1.5 billion rather than £5 billion. On this showing, the increase in the PSBR between 1973 and 1975 was attributable to cyclical changes which impinged on the Budget and were little affected by it; while more than half the fall in the PSBR between 1975 and 1977 was a product of economic expansion.[30]

A second approach is to make use of a model of the economy to simulate reactions to changes in the level of the PSBR. A model by M.J. Artis and R.C. Bladen-Hovell indicates a rise in activity of about 3.5 per cent between 1973 and 1975 and a fall of the same order between 1975 and 1977 in response to the fiscal policies actually adopted.[31] That is, quite powerful effects on employment, first in one direction, then in the other, are implied of just the kind traditionally assumed. But this result holds only if the model can be trusted as an accurate representation of the real economy; and the assumptions built into the model may assume the very relationships it is designed to test. So far as it goes, it corroborates the view that cuts in public expenditure, like cuts in private expenditure, tend to reduce output and employment.

A third approach is to look more closely at the actual changes that took place. It is significant that while the PSBR fell by £4.9 billion between 1975–76 and 1977–78 the fall in the financial deficit, which relates to current transactions only and excludes lending operations, fell by only £1.6 billion over that period. The big reduction was in net lending and it is open to question whether such cuts are translated into equal changes in capital expenditures. Between 1975 and 1977 public investment at current prices rose from £10.85 billion to £11.78 billion and at 1975 prices fell by £1.34 billion. If net lending was reduced by £3.3 (£4.9–£1.6) billion it is hard to see in these figures a cut in capital expenditure of that magnitude. It is of course possible that public corporations raised money abroad or drew on their reserves. The point is that reductions in public lending are a poor guide to the consequent change in public investment.

In 1973–75 the PSBR rose by more than the PSFD, the one by £6.1 billion, the other by £4.8 billion. In both periods a substantial part of the change was in lending transactions whose effect on the labour market is hard to trace. In the first period fiscal policy operated to sustain economic activity and in the second to contract it. There is, however, no sign that the trend changed for the worse as the second period succeeded the first. On the contrary, unemployment rose much more steeply in the first period and GDP, which hardly changed then, grew at a fairly satisfactory rate in the second (see Table 10). How was this possible?

The answer is that other elements in GDP changed to offset the

Table 10

Changes in public expenditure, unemployment and
national income, 1973–77

	Public sector financial deficit (£ billion)	Public expenditure in 1975 cost terms[1] (£ billion)	Un- employment[2] (000s)	GDP at 1975 market prices (£ billion)
1973–74	3.5	44.6	525	105.3
1974–75	6.0	50.3	654	105.2
1975–76	8.1	50.6	1128	105.6
1976–77	7.4	49.4	1307	108.7
1977–78	6.6	46.0	1423	110.9

1. Adjusted from Pliatzky's estimates at 1981–82 prices by deflation to 1975 prices using the GDP deflator.
2. In final quarter of calendar year (i.e. lagged by 1–2 quarters) and seasonally adjusted.

Sources: Pliatzky, *Getting and Spending*, p. 218; *Economic Trends Annual Supplement, 1981.*

changes in public expenditure and the question is, therefore, what were those offsetting changes and were they in some way connected with the simultaneous change in the PSBR or in public expenditure? Was there, for example, a crowding-out effect so that cuts in public expenditure allowed other spending to proceed? Or was there some psychological repercussion, with cuts in public expenditure encouraging more confident spending or less precautionary saving?

In the first two years the main contractionary element was stock-building, which was heavily negative (see Table 11). This was reinforced by reductions both in consumer spending and in investment. The fall in GDP was much smaller than these various influences would have produced had there been no counterweight. But what counterweight was there? The official statistics assign a major role to the balance of payments, which shows an increase in the volume of exports of goods and services and a fall in the volume of imports of goods and services between 1973 and 1975, the net expansionary effect amounting to £3.07 billion at 1975 prices. But since the balance of payments, far from improving by £3 billion, deteriorated by £0.62 billion, it operated to deflate, not expand, the economy.[32]

Table 11

Changes in demand, 1973–77
(£ billion at 1975 prices)

	GDP at market prices	Consumers'. expenditure	Gross domestic fixed capital formation	Increase in stock-building	Other (balance of payments, public expenditure, etc)
1973–75	−2.01	−1.91	−0.78	−4.02	+4.70
1975–77	+5.45	−0.18	−0.33	+2.86	+3.20

Source: Economic Trends Annual Supplement, 1981.

This leaves government operations as the only element sustaining demand in the first period. Some of the increased financial deficit of £4.8 billion impinged on consumers' expenditure and fixed capital formation and presumably helped to limit the reduction under these headings. There was, for example, a small increase in public investment (as now estimated) which partially offset the fall in private investment. The large reduction in consumer spending would presumably have been even bigger but for the net addition to consumers' disposable incomes through additional welfare and other transfer payments. A substantial part of the increased deficit went to offset the change in the terms of trade in its impact on consumer incomes. Another large part went to meet the swing in the relative price factor against the public sector. The higher deficit, therefore, did not mean a corresponding rise in output and employment; but in its absence, demand and output would have fallen further.

In the second period the main deflationary force, the running down of stocks, had finally halted and given way to some replenishment of stocks, an expansionary force. Exports were also growing relatively fast, and for once faster than imports without any change in the terms of trade. So there were two independent but powerful expansionary influences. Taken together, stockbuilding and the balance of payments added more than twice as much to demand (£4.2 billion) as the financial deficit removed (£1.9 billion). This meant that the economy could expand and carry with it other elements in demand. Private fixed investment grew by £900 million (at 1975 prices) to a record level. Public investment, however, seems to have taken the brunt of the reduction in the financial deficit and fell by £1.23 billion (at 1975 prices) so that investment in total was reduced. Consumer spending, also checked by government cuts, was more or less flat in spite of a 5.5 per cent increase in GDP. The only element depressing demand was government spending.

It is also of some importance that the profits of British industrial and commercial companies arising in the United Kingdom fell heavily in real terms between 1973 and 1975 and grew substantially in the next two years. As a proportion of GDP, profits (deducting stock appreciation) fell by 27 per cent and then recovered by 33 per cent. This was a much more tangible influence on private fixed investment in those years than the supposed dampening effect of an increasing Budget deficit in 1973–75 or any possible encouragement offered by cuts in the PSBR in 1975–77.

The picture that emerges is clear enough. Public expenditure moderated the fall in activity after 1973 and checked the quite rapid recovery after 1975. There was no magic by which changes in public spending took effect without *any* repercussions on national income. The only question is whether the 'offsetting' changes taking place in 1973–75 and 1975–77 were themselves attributable to the changing level of public expenditure. So far as this was so, it cannot have amounted to much.

MONETARY POLICY

Controversy over monetary policy in the 1970s was far more acute than in the previous decade. With the rise of monetarism there was a strong body of opinion that looked to monetary policy as the cure for inflation and regarded control of the money supply as the prime object of policy. This contrasted with the view of other economists that monetary policy had only a limited part to play in mastering inflation and that the rate of interest was a more appropriate focus of attention than the stock of money as the key instrument of monetary policy, especially as it was not possible to operate directly on the money supply and it was liable to fluctuate as an endogenous part of the economic system. Monetarists believed that a sharp increase in the money supply would be followed with a lag of about two years by an equally sharp increase in prices. Other economists were sceptical.

The controversy was not confined to the United Kingdom but it was given particular urgency by the surge in the money supply after the publication by the Bank of England of *Competition and Credit Control* in 1971. This freed the banks from the restraints that had previously limited their lending just before an international boom was about to develop in 1972–73. The money supply (£M3) which had been increasing at about 12 per cent per annum increased about twice as fast in 1972 and 1973. There are monetarists who claim that they were able to forecast at the end of 1971, when this acceleration was first apparent, that the rate of inflation in 1974 would also accelerate and would be 'over 10 per cent and perhaps as high as 15 per cent'.[33] That the rate of inflation turned out to be almost exactly 15 per cent may seem impressive. But money wages were already increasing by 12.5 per cent a year in 1971. Remembering how much of the rise in prices in 1974 reflected the movement of import prices in the boom (including oil prices) and the rise in wages after the miners' strike, most economists would dismiss it as a coincidence.[34]

A rather similar claim was made in *The Times* on 14 July 1976 by a former editor of the paper, William Rees-Mogg. In his eagerness to find a simple explanation of inflation he advanced one of the most preposterous arguments for monetarism ever published. By way of proof that monetarist theory 'can be tested scientifically', and is therefore superior to all other monetary theory, he cited, as his sole piece of evidence, the fact that what he called 'excess money supply' increased over the period 1965–73 in exactly the same proportion as the rise in prices over the period 1967–75, that is with the two-year lag beloved of Milton Friedman.[35] This coincidence so struck him that he saw no need to consider other influences on the price level and concluded that it was sufficient in itself to establish the futility of incomes policy. It did not occur to him that it might be the rise in prices that produced the 'excess money supply', that is the (proportionate) increase in the money supply less the (proportionate) increase in GDP. Still less did it occur to him to test whether the coincidence extended to other periods. But as Wynne Godley pointed out next day in *The Times*, in the period selected prices as often as not moved from year to year in the opposite direction to the corresponding change in 'excess money supply'. The most elementary statistical tests deprived the theory of its alleged predictive value.

That prices and the money supply tend to move together has never been much in dispute. What *is* disputed is just how close the connection is, and which exercises a causal influence on the other. On one view an increase in the money supply raises prices after a lag while on the other a rise in prices disposes business and the public to

Table 12

Increase in incomes, prices and money, 1971–78
(at 1975 prices)

	1971 Q1 –1973 Q1	1973 Q1 –1976 Q1	1976 Q1 –1978 Q1	1971 Q1 –1978 Q1
Earnings	125.7	173.6	124.1	270.7
Real personal disposable income	115.6	100.3	100.6	116.6
Retail prices	116.6	166.3	127.5	247.2
Import prices	120.7	210.5	129.0	327.9
Export prices	116.1	180.9	136.0	285.8
Money stock				
M1	119.8	138.9	135.6	247.5
M3	143.5	143.4	124.0	255.2

Source: Economic Trends Annual Supplement, 1981.

hold larger balances in cash. If, as in 1971, the banks actively seek to expand credit, the sequence is likely to be an expansion in bank lending and, as the money is spent, in demand, some of which will operate on prices and some on output, with a gradual restoration at higher prices and incomes of the earlier ratio between money and national income. In this and in other ways an increase in bank lending can add to the supply of money and produce inflation. On the other hand, if prices are pushed up by some external factor, such as the oil shock at the end of 1973, there will be an increased *demand* for money and higher prices will be *followed* by an expansion in the money supply.

Compare, for example, the two periods 1971–73 and 1973–76 using the first quarters of each year as a basis of comparison (Table 12). In the first period M3 increased by 43.5 per cent while M1 increased by only 20 per cent. The divergence corresponds to the larger flow of additional credit on to the market while requirements of cash for ordinary transactions were growing more slowly. Although some of the extra money was absorbed by a 14 per cent rise in output, the expansion of credit was clearly excessive and inflationary. But the rise in retail prices by 17 per cent over those two years did not hang at all closely on either measure of the money supply. It was affected more directly by the rise in international commodity prices. In dollar terms, the export price of manufactures (worldwide) rose by 18 per cent and primary produce rose by 38 per cent. British import prices (in sterling) rose by 21 per cent, partly because of the fall in sterling.

The general impression left by these figures is that the main influence on prices over those two years was not the expansion in credit but the more rapid rise in world prices. It is, however, arguable that a full adjustment to the expansion in M3 had not yet been made in 1973 and that some of the inflation that followed had its origin in an earlier over-expansion of credit.

In the next three years retail prices rose by 66 per cent while the money supply increased by 43 per cent (M3) or 39 per cent (M1). This time money was not out in front but lagging behind. The really dramatic change was in oil prices and it is not easy to find an index that does justice to the impact on the price structure of the fourfold increase in the price of this one commodity. The index cited previously for the price of exports from primary producers shows a rise of 40 per cent but this takes no account of side effects in importing countries such as a weakening of the exchange rate. Import average values in sterling more than doubled. Even allowing for an 18 per cent fall in the effective exchange rate (some part of which was a consequence of higher import prices) there can be no doubt that the main inflationary impulse in this period came from the rise in import prices.

This conclusion emerges with more precision from Table 13, which attempts to assign a magnitude to the different factors contributing to price inflation between 1972 and 1976. Throughout 1973 and during the first half of 1974 the biggest contributor was the rise in import prices. Import prices were again the major contributor in 1976, especially in the second half of the year. On the other hand, the rise in labour costs dominated the inflationary process from the middle of 1974 to the end of 1975 and it was the slower rise in labour costs that was the most powerful factor in the falling-off of inflation in 1976. Money does not feature in Table 13 as a factor contributing to inflation; but then neither does excess demand. The arithmetic does not establish the ultimate causes of inflation; it shows the relative importance of different channels of influence at a given time without revealing the source of all the pressures operating through those channels.

There is a second question about the money supply to be addressed. Was it the public sector or the private sector which, by its borrowing, inflated the money supply? Table 14 helps to provide an answer.

Table 13

Factors contributing to price inflation
(percentage increase on previous period)

	Prices	Labour costs	Import costs	Net taxes on expen-diture	Other factor incomes
Share of total final expenditure in 1976	100	49.5	23.1	8.4	19.1
1972 First half	2.8	1.8	0.9	−0.2	0.2
Second half	4.3	2.4	1.4	0.3	0.2
1973 First half	4.5	0.6	2.2	−0.4	2.1
Second half	6.6	3.1	4.1	0.2	0.9
1974 First half	10.2	3.9	6.1	−0.1	0.4
Second half	10.6	7.8	1.5	−0.6	1.7
1975 First half	12.0	8.9	0.3	0.9	2.0
Second half	11.4	5.4	2.0	1.8	2.2
1976 First half	6.2	2.2	2.1	0.7	1.2
Second half	7.6	1.7	3.3	0.8	1.9

Source: Bank of England *Quarterly Bulletin*, June 1977, p. 144.

Table 14

Contribution to domestic credit expansion of public and private sectors
(£ billion)

	Domestic credit expansion	Sterling lending to private and overseas sectors	Net contribution of public sector[1]
1971	1.18	1.92	−0.74
1972	6.69	5.65	1.04
1973	8.07	6.16	1.91
1974	6.93	3.73	3.20
1975	4.53	−0.41	4.94
1976	7.48	4.11	3.37
1977	1.13	3.60	−2.47

1. PSBR less sales of public sector debt to the UK non-bank private sector.

Source: Bank of England *Quarterly Bulletin*, 1978.

If we work in terms of domestic credit expansion instead of money supply we can easily show how much resulted from bank lending to the private sector or (to a much smaller extent) to the overseas sector and what resulted from the financing of public sector borrowing (that is, what, out of the borrowing requirement, was not met by sales of public sector debt to the non-bank public).

In 1972–73 the private sector made the running and the public sector's contribution was relatively small. In 1974 the two were more nearly equal but the big change came in 1975 when the private sector was paying off debt to the banks and unable to absorb the massive amount of public debt coming on the market (although sales of central government debt to the UK non-bank private sector leapt from an average of £1 billion in 1972–74 to £5.3 billion in 1975). In 1976 the private sector, recovering from the depression of the previous year, was again in the lead as a borrower. The public sector's resort to the banks fell back and in 1977 became negative for the first time since 1971. Domestic credit expansion was at its peak in 1973 and at its lowest in 1977.

Except in those two years the resort of the public sector to bank finance was a stabilising factor, offsetting to some extent, but never completely, the fluctuations in bank credit to the private sector.

Whatever the connection between money and prices, there is not much doubt that when the banks make credit available freely and cheaply they may help to fuel inflation. The image of too much money chasing too few goods still encapsulates a common view of the inflationary process and one that monetarism endorses. The big expansion in the money supply in 1972–74 was widely blamed in political and banking circles, if not for causing the high rates of inflation that followed, at least for making them worse. The lesson drawn from that experience in those circles was that the money supply must be kept under strict control.

The difficulty was to find a way of doing so short of outright deflation of money incomes. As Christopher Dow has shown, it is an illusion to suppose that there is some simple way in which central banks can arrange for the stock of money to increase at some predetermined rate.[36] Not that the Heath government made no attempt to limit monetary expansion. Bank rate was raised in stages from 5 per cent in September 1971 to 9 per cent in December 1972 and after a slight drop in the first half of 1973 had been hoisted again to 13 per cent by November and stood at 12.5 per cent when Labour took office in March 1974.[37] In addition, the Bank of England had devised and applied in December 1973 the Supplementary Special Deposits Scheme (the so-called 'corset') which obliged the clearing banks to deposit with the Bank of England a rising proportion of any increase in interest-bearing deposits beyond a stated rate of growth. On such deposits no interest was paid. Whether as a result of this measure or (more probably) because demand for credit was already slackening, there was a much slower growth in the money supply in 1974 – at only 10 per cent per annum compared with nearly 28 per cent in 1973.

The corset remained in place throughout 1974 until February 1975, by which time there was little demand for bank credit and monetary policy was easing. Bank rate had been falling slowly from the time when the corset was imposed, and had reached 10.5 per cent by mid-February 1975. With the removal of the corset it soon began to rise again, climbing from 9.75 per cent in April to 11.75 per cent in November. Once again the Bank set about lowering interest rates gradually and once again it did not get very far before it had to go into reverse. On 25 April 1976, faced with intense pressure on the pound, the Bank put the rate up sharply from 9 to 10.5 per cent and a month later by another full point to 11.5 per cent. No further rise took place until September, when there was a second rise of 1.5 per cent followed again within a month by a further two-point increase, bringing the rate on 7 October to 15 per cent.

No doubt larger increases were dismissed as counterproductive. But it is rather surprising in view of market reactions and the scale of the Bank's support operations in March that the rate was left at 9 per cent until near the end of April and that a rise of 1.5 rather than 2 points was judged to be appropriate. We do not know the scale of Bank intervention in April. But in the second quarter as a whole the Bank supplied the market with nearly £2 billion – no small amount when reserves were under £3 billion.

In the autumn the action taken was much more vigorous: not because the exchange losses were greater but because the need to avoid further losses was more urgent, with repayment of the June 1976 loan due in December. On 16 September there was a call for special deposits, raising the proportion that had to be deposited with the Bank of England from 3 per cent to 4 per cent. On 7 October a further call raised the 4 per cent to 6 per cent. On 18 November the corset was reintroduced and in token of such draconic measures a small reduction was made in Bank Rate.

18 November also saw the revival of a familiar method of tightening exchange control. Banks and merchants were banned from

financing trade between foreign countries in sterling although they could continue to do so in Eurosterling or in foreign currency. Restrictions were also imposed later on the finance of the trade of Commonwealth countries. The measures taken on 18 November were interpreted by the Federal Reserve Board as reflecting difficulties in selling sufficient government bonds to stay within the monetary target area.[38] But it is more plausible to associate the move with the Bank's expectations of a once-for-all gain to the reserves of 'hundreds of millions of pounds'.[39]

Monetary targets had been in use since 1975 or earlier. They were at first not made public but in his Letter of Intent to the IMF in January 1976 the Chancellor set a limit to domestic credit expansion (which the IMF preferred as an indicator to the money supply)[40] of £9 billion in the twelve months ending 20 April 1977. This was a remarkably high figure to offer to the IMF. It was higher than in any previous year and twice the rate of expansion in 1975.

In his April Budget the Chancellor reiterated his determination to control the money supply but offered a rather vague and elastic target. The growth of the money supply, he said, must be consistent with the growth of demand at current prices, that is with money GDP. This is a formula that has since become quite fashionable but in April 1976 it would have meant, on the experience of the previous six months, a target in excess of 20 per cent. In fact the money supply (M3), as the Chancellor recognised, was growing at about half that rate; and since he expected inflation to be in single figures by the end of the year he probably had in mind a target rate of growth of about 12 per cent in 1976–77.

It was this rate that he first announced as a target in July.[41] He coupled it with a warning that fluctuations in the government's borrowing needs and sales of gilts meant that there would be periods when the target was exceeded, so no one should interpret the target as applying month by month. But he repeated his determination not 'to allow the growth of the money supply to fuel inflation'.

But was the government in a position to exert the control required? Were monetary targets more than an illusion? If the target was hit, did that mean only that the Bank had made a lucky guess? And if it was not hit, what difference had been made by anything the Bank did? Experience with targets showed that even when they were broadened to a wide range, the money supply frequently ended outside the range altogether. When it was sought to control one version of the money supply, other versions could expand and substitute for it. For that matter if the money supply, however defined, was controlled, the credit structure might still expand or contract on an unchanged monetary base.

No doubt one can carry scepticism too far. The power of control over the monetary system in any country varies with the set of institutions and practices in the country, the strain put on the system, and the understandings and informal arrangements that can be made to work. One important element is the strain imposed by government borrowing. In nineteenth-century Britain fresh borrowing by the government was a relatively small part of the market. But in the mid-1970s the government's borrowing requirement was large enough to dominate the growth of the money supply. Unless the non-bank public had an elastic appetite for gilts, the banks would have to be enabled to take up any abnormal increase in government debt and the money supply would expand correspondingly. Lord Kaldor might be wrong in arguing, on the basis of experience in the 1960s, that the money supply 'increases almost £1 for £1 in the line with the PSBR'.[42] Indeed, the connection between the two seems to have become a good deal less close in the 1970s.[43] But the fear that a high borrowing requirement would inflate the money supply was widespread and shared by the Chancellor himself.

'The most important objective now,' he argued in June 1976, 'is to continue financing a large part of the borrowing requirement by sales of gilts outside the banking system.'[44]

The use of monetary targets, as the Federal Reserve Board put it, elevated sales of government bonds to non-bank purchasers 'to a position of extreme importance'. But was it possible to count on such sales when a very large government deficit had to be financed? The Bank of England took a pessimistic view. Sales could not be made on a falling market. Besides, it would be regarded as a breach of faith to offer bonds at one price one day and a lower price the next. The Bank preferred to operate indirectly on bond prices by putting up Bank Rate or offering more Treasury Bills until prices fell to a bargain level at which there was a general expectation that they would go no lower and would shortly begin to rise again. Manoeuvres of this kind to pave the way for sales on a rising market – the so-called Grand Old Duke of York technique – could only be successful if repeated, and to be repeated might require a progressively higher rate of interest on the bonds.

But if it was difficult to increase sales of gilts to non-banks, or to do so without disruptive effects on financial markets, the moral was that control over the money supply would have to rest heavily on control over the PSBR. This was something the Bank of England had maintained for a generation or more. In the 1920s it had preached that 'an uncorrected budget deficit is the root of forced increase in the supply of money and depreciation of the currency'.[45] After the Second World War it had looked to Budget surpluses to remove excess liquidity from the economy. Later it had turned invariably to cuts in government expenditure (ruling out increases in taxation) as an indispensable reinforcement of tighter money.

As a means of controlling the money supply the only other instruments at the disposal of the Bank were changes in interest rates, a call for special deposits, and the so-called 'corset'. Raising short-term interest rates, however, might have perverse short-term effects, bringing in money from abroad and *increasing* the demand for interest-bearing deposits. Special deposits had not proved very effective in the past and had a distorting influence on the financial system by penalising the clearing banks but not other financial agencies. The use of the 'corset' was effective in an emergency but was not an acceptable long-term instrument of control. The only sure way of keeping down the money supply was to limit the growth of money incomes.[46]

The way in which things worked out in 1975–76 is illustrated in Table 15. Sales of central government debt reached a peak in the last quarter of 1975, leaving only a small balance to come from other sources to cover the central government's borrowing requirement. As a result, the expansion in the money supply, which had been rapid in the third quarter of the year, dropped sharply in the final quarter. Thereafter the expansion in the money supply grew faster as sales of gilt-edged fell off. By the third quarter of 1976 the growth of M3 had mounted to 17 per cent per annum, was causing general alarm and was throwing doubt on the ability of the government to hold its target of 12 per cent. The papers of the Federal Reserve Board express considerable anxiety on this score.[47]

Denis Healey had to admit to the IMF that bank lending had grown faster than expected and that this had added to pressure on the pound. However he claimed, rightly, that the Bank of England had taken action to bring the growth of money and credit under control. The measures taken helped to revive the gilt-edged market, sales in October being particularly heavy at the high rates of interest then ruling. In the final quarter of the year the growth of the money supply was completely arrested.

Table 15

The money supply and the borrowing requirement, 1975–77[1]

	Percentage increase in £M3 from quarter to quarter (%)	Sales of central govt. debt to non-bank public in UK (£m.)	Central govt. borrowing requirement (£m.)	Borrowing requirement not covered by sales of government debt (£m.)
1975 Q1	1.59	1660	1330	− 330
2	1.45	496	1894	1298
3	3.32	1227	2686	1459
4	0.22	1961	2435	474
1976 Q1	1.89	1419	1807	388
2	2.68	1048	1734	686
3	4.21	665	1980	1315
4	−0.01	2338	1265	−1073
1977 Q1	1.32	2366	1583	− 783
2	2.79	1180	1094	− 86

1. All figures are seasonally adjusted.

Source: Economic Trends Annual Supplement, 1981.

When it came to the Letter of Intent in December Healey offered no new monetary target for 1976–77 but repeated his earlier objective of keeping domestic credit expansion within the limit of £9 billion. For the following year he submitted a target of £7.7 billion, undertaking to review that figure after the Budget. When the financial year ended in April 1977 the increase in £M3 was no more than 8.3 per cent, well below the 12 per cent set as a target in the previous July. Throughout 1977 the central government sold its debt to non-banks on a scale exceeding its borrowing requirement, the excess for the year reaching £3.5 billion. Nevertheless the money supply (£M3) increased by 10 per cent (that is, faster than in the previous year) because of the large inflow of funds into sterling that continued throughout the year.

The experience of 1976 may suggest that in the end, if sufficiently tough measures are taken, the money supply can be brought under control. But the events of the final quarter of 1976 included more than the measures taken by the Bank of England. At the very beginning of the quarter the Chancellor had announced his intention of seeking assistance from the IMF, and it was generally accepted that the IMF would only agree to such a loan if it were satisfied that government policies met its conditions. Sales of gilt-edged reached over £1 billion in the month ending 20 October – a total only once exceeded in the previous five years and then, too, after an approach to the IMF in January 1976. While the rise in Bank Rate no doubt contributed, resort to the IMF would seem to have been the more powerful factor. The flood of money from abroad and into government debt in 1977 can hardly be assigned to the tightening of monetary policy. As we have seen, the money supply expanded *faster*. Bank Rate fell progressively from 15 per cent to 5 per cent between one October and the next. The main influences on the money supply would appear to have been the degree of confidence that the government could and would control the PSBR, the inflow of funds responding more to renewed confidence than to high interest rates.

INCOMES POLICY

Ever since 1961 there had been a constant debate over the possibility of reducing inflation by operating directly on money wages. This usually meant either a wage freeze or some attempt to influence wage settlements by taking statutory powers or by securing the voluntary cooperation of the trade unions. Such attempts had usually been made at times when wages were accelerating under boom conditions, that is at times when the unions were in a strong position and under most pressure from their members. Incomes policy might then be particularly desirable but it was also least likely to be successful.

The Conservative Party oscillated in its attitude between hesitation to interfere in collective bargaining, reinforced by doubts about the likely fruits of such interference, and the adoption of measures, limiting the powers of trade unions, that risked making matters worse. The Labour Party was in a cleft stick. Its leanings towards expansionist policies made it peculiarly dependent on a successful incomes policy. On the other hand, its commitments to the trade unions severely reduced its room for manoeuvre in securing agreement to such a policy. The Labour government had sought to legislate in the late 1960s for a more orderly procedure in wage bargaining but had been obliged to desist; and its failure then put it in a weak position when it was again in office in 1974.

It was the pace set by the rise in money wages that was the undoing of efforts to keep the economy under control. The Conservative government of 1970–74, at first opposed to a formal incomes policy, was compelled to change its mind. It had come into office after the wage 'explosion' of 1969–70 and sought at first to limit the rate of inflation by reducing indirect taxes in the budgets of 1971 and 1972 and persuading the CBI to engage in voluntary price restraint. The rate of inflation dropped from 10 per cent in mid-1971 to 6 per cent in mid-1972 but it then accelerated again. The rise in wages in 1972, when the government adopted monetary and fiscal policies that were strongly expansionary, was even higher than it had been in 1970. Protracted negotiations with the trade unions broke down in November and the government then imposed a statutory 90-day wages and prices freeze followed in January 1973 by a limitation of wage increases to £1 per week plus 4 per cent together with rigorous price control. This did not prevent average weekly earnings from continuing to rise, after a preliminary anticipatory surge at the end of 1972, at 13–14 per cent per annum in 1973 – the fastest rise for any year since 1951.[48]

The government then announced on 8 October 1973 a third stage of incomes policy, which was to prove disastrous, that linked increases in pay automatically to the cost of living just as the cost of living was about to take off. International commodity prices were already rising alarmingly and there were strong indications of OPEC's intentions to raise oil prices dramatically. Nevertheless the government thought that there was a fair chance of limiting the rate of inflation to 7 per cent and allowed increases in pay up to that limit with flat rate increases in pay of 40 pence per week for every further increase in prices by 1 per cent.

No attempt was made to amend or renegotiate the arrangement after the fourfold rise in oil prices. It was continued by the Labour government when it took office in March and triggered eleven successive increases in pay between April and November 1974. Great stress is usually laid on this element in the dramatic wage explosion of 1974–75. William Brown points out, however, that threshold agreements were largely confined to the public sector and suggests that 'private sector pay settlements were already surging ahead after the February election'. In his view 'the threshold agreements were in the main used by the public sector to catch up with a private sector pay explosion.'[49] But the evidence points to a substantially faster rise in pay in the public sector than in the private sector in 1974, confirming the importance of the threshold agreements.[50]

By January 1975 weekly wages were up by 29 per cent and retail prices by 20 per cent in comparison with a year before. Wages had become the main factor behind inflation and a rise in real wages had occurred at the very time when there were strong grounds for reducing them. The rise in commodity prices had moved the terms of trade by 25 per cent against the United Kingdom since 1972, imposing a reduction in the national income of over 5 per cent. Yet wage incomes in real terms were over 7 per cent higher at the end of 1974. This was not a sustainable position. It was only possible so long as an enormous current account deficit continued, equal in 1974 to well over £3 billion, or about 4 per cent of GNP, and so long as profits had almost disappeared. It was no coincidence that industry faced a growing liquidity crisis throughout 1974 and that Stock Exchange prices slumped to an extraordinary level, with an earnings yield in excess of 30 per cent.

Profits had been falling since at least the early 1960s. The reasons are not altogether clear but they certainly include government price control and a disposition on the part of business to price on the basis of historic cost rather than replacement cost, leaving an insufficient margin of profit. Profits were also reduced by the practice of charging tax on stock appreciation, which was inevitably boosted by inflation and was reaching formidable proportions by the end of 1974. The price control criteria introduced in 1972 allowed the recovery in price increases of only half any rise in pay, the balance being assumed to be covered by higher productivity. This might be tolerable with wage increases of 10 per cent or less but was far more burdensome when wages were rising at over 30 per cent per annum. Until late in 1974, however, the government turned a blind eye on the downward trend in profits and the even more serious decline in company liquidity, disregarding warnings from the CBI and imposing a 50 per cent increase in Advance Corporation Tax payments in the April Budget.

Yet there was no widespread sense of crisis in 1974 and the measures taken did more to aggravate than to address the problems facing the country. 1974, far more than 1975 or 1976, was the year in which the economy was thrown out of balance. In the first quarter of the year prices in the United Kingdom had risen 7 per cent more since 1970 than the OECD average; a year later the divergence was 14 per cent. This left the United Kingdom level with Japan and Italy but with a price rise twice that in Germany. More important even than the high rate of inflation was the lack of balance within the economy and with the rest of the world. The burden imposed by the shift in the terms of trade had to be reduced and redistributed. There was a

powerful case for lowering consumption in order to sustain investment and lowering wages in order to allow profits to re-emerge.

By the end of 1974 business was in the middle of a liquidity crisis,
the deficit in the balance of payments was formidable, investment
was falling off, the rise in unemployment was accelerating, and so
also was the rise in wages and prices. Yet real wages had been rising
faster than at any time in the past. It has been estimated that in the
first fifteen months of Labour government average earnings in the
public sector rose 12 per cent faster than consumer prices in the
public sector and 4.5 per cent faster in the private sector.[51]

It was abundantly clear in the first half of 1975 that something
would have to be done to check inflation. For the Labour Party that
meant primarily devising an effective incomes policy. For the Conservatives it was coming to mean limitation of monetary growth.
But perhaps the most powerful influence was rising unemployment.
In the two years between the end of 1974 and the end of 1976 unemployment doubled and reached a level of 1.3 million, far above the
peak rate in any earlier postwar depression. Whether because of this
or because of the incomes policy adopted in 1975, the rise in real
wages was reversed and in the next three years there was a progressive reduction to about the level in 1973.

Until November 1974 the government lacked the authority a
majority in the House of Commons would have provided and was
tied by the social contract which it had negotiated with the unions. It
felt unable to renegotiate the threshold arrangements made by the
outgoing government and let a year pass without taking more active
steps to check wage inflation. It was only when prices were rising at
over 30 per cent per annum in the first half of 1975 that an effective
incomes policy began to take shape. The social contract pledged the
unions to accept wage increases in line with cost-of-living increases.
This clearly was not happening. The machinery set up to implement
the social contract approved settlement after settlement that plainly
infringed this condition. Some trade unionists regarded high pay
settlements as a means of inflating the economy. By the middle of
1975 the railwaymen were asking for a 35 per cent increase and had
rejected an offer of 27 per cent. The TUC and the CBI viewed these
developments with growing concern and reached agreement on the
need for a pay limit substantially below current levels. Jack Jones of
the TUC proposed a flat rate increase while others argued for a
simple percentage. In negotiations with the Chancellor, agreement
was reached in July in favour of a flat rate limit of £6 per week,

higher than the £5 Healey wanted and lower than the £7–£8 suggested by Jack Jones.

This formula provided the substance but avoided the form of a
statutory policy, to which the TUC remained strongly opposed. It
proved effective in bringing down the rate of inflation by half. By the
third quarter of 1976 weekly wages were rising at about 14 per cent
per annum and prices had risen by about 13 per cent over the past
year. Wage increases continued to slow down and by the end of 1976
were well under 10 per cent. In the meantime the agreement with the
TUC had been extended for a further year. In his April 1976 Budget
the Chancellor had made large tax allowances conditional on acceptance by the TUC of a 3 per cent limit to increases in pay. What was
ultimately agreed was a maximum increase of £4 per week or 5 per
cent, but with slippage, wages rose faster than this. In 1977 the rise in
wage rates may have been as low as 6.5 per cent but the rise in earnings by 10 per cent casts some doubt on this.

As so often happens, there was a rebound and in 1978–79 the rate
of increase was back up to 18 per cent on the average. But in the
autumn of 1976, before the final slide in the exchange rate, it was
clear that wages were not completely out of control and that,
although the pace was still much too fast, it was at least within limits
of which there was past experience.

CONCLUSION

If the picture of an economy out of control was exaggerated it was
not without some justification. The rate of exchange kept on falling,
the Budget deficit seemed to grow from year to year, prices continued to rise at an unsustainable rate, and unemployment was at a
level never experienced since the war, and still increasing. Mine
workers had brought the Conservative government to defeat in 1974
and the power of wage-earners had since been demonstrated in wage
settlements with a 35 per cent annual rate of increase. The forces of
inflation had appeared in 1975 to be carrying all before them and
although they were in retreat in 1976 there was a danger that they
might revive.

That danger had become associated in the public mind with the
Budget deficit and the increase in public expenditure through boom
and slump with little reconsideration or drawing back as costs and
prices rose. The growth in the PSBR was thought to put in question
the government's power to finance it without large-scale borrowing

from the banks and such borrowing might jeopardise what control over the money supply the authorities retained. From that loss of control, so it was thought, inflation would result.

Control mattered as a means of attaining all the government's objectives. Among these the most important were to maintain a high level of employment and prosperity, reasonable stability in prices and a satisfactory balance in foreign trade. All three suffered from the government's inability to control the economy. The balance of payments might soon be rescued by North Sea oil but in the immediate future the choice was between direct control over imports or more foreign borrowing despite the unwelcome conditions that would be attached to a loan from the only organisation likely to provide one. Inflation had been tackled, not by cutting expenditure and adding to unemployment or by limitation of the money supply, but directly through incomes policy, which worked more effectively in a slump than it ever did in a boom. As a result, the immediate danger of an escalation in wages had passed. Enough had been done, or so the Cabinet thought, to bring public expenditure under control, limit inflation and restore a degree of balance to the economy, to justify resistance to measures that would raise unemployment and do more damage to output and investment.

Ever since Labour took office, unemployment had risen quarter by quarter. By the end of 1976 it was a million higher than ten years previously and affected 5 per cent of the working population; in 1966 it had been 1.5 per cent. If the government hesitated to cut public expenditure once again it was primarily because of the unemployment it expected would follow. It was conscious, too, that the regeneration of British industry, on which it set such store, was out of the question when the cuts inevitably fell with greater severity on capital investment. Mrs Thatcher might tell Robin Day when interviewed on the radio that cuts of £5.5–£6.5 billion were possible without damage to the economy. But when her turn came, she never succeeded in making cuts of that size.

In any event the Labour government could assert control only within the limits of what was politically possible. There was no point in putting forward proposals that would not command the support of the party to whatever extent was required to see them voted through the House of Commons. Nor could it accept conditions from the IMF that would never attract such support. Given the attitudes of financial markets and the strength of feeling on the left of the party, their room for manoeuvre was extremely limited. The

Chancellor excited derision for his invariable optimism. But no one else could have stood up to all the pressures on him and succeeded in the end in securing the acceptance of all concerned: the Prime Minister (belatedly, as part of what he took to be a necessary strategy); the Cabinet (thanks to that strategy); the Party (in spite of dissent); and the IMF (by the narrowest of margins).

CHAPTER 8

Comparisons and Conclusions

We have argued that 1976 was a turning point in ideas about economic management. It was undoubtedly a year of crisis. But was there also a difference in economic policy and performance from other years? Or from other countries? Was there some intelligible reason why the crisis in thinking and events occurred in 1976?

If we confine ourselves first to what was going on within the United Kingdom it is not at all obvious that the situation in 1976 was more critical than at other times in the 1970s. The problems that came to a head in that year extended much further back. The slide in the pound had begun in 1972 and went on throughout the next four years; the balance of payments had been in much heavier deficit in 1974 and 1975; the rise in wages, prices and the money supply had slowed down greatly; thanks to inflation, the national debt, in spite of the large Budget deficit, was falling, both in real terms and as a proportion of GDP. The arguments in progress – over monetary targets, how to deal with inflation, the scope for cuts in public expenditure, the possible use of import limitation – had all been going on for a long time. Apart from the continuing fall in sterling, the outlook in 1976 was in many ways more reassuring than in either of the two preceding years.

It was on these hopeful signs that Denis Healey dwelt when he introduced his Budget on 6 April. The pay policy introduced in 1975 had brought down wage settlements, and inflation had been dropping month by month since September. The rate of inflation had already been cut by half, and with luck would be halved again and end the year 'well below 10 per cent'.[1] The rise in unemployment had slowed down and vacancies were on the increase. The growth of the

215

money supply was being contained: it had been no more than 8 per cent in 1975 whereas the national income at current prices was up by 26 per cent. More than half the borrowing requirement had been financed outside the banking system by sales of public sector debt. Looking ahead, the Chancellor forecast an increase in output of 3.5 per cent – 1 per cent more than the average for the whole postwar period.

To this favourable view of domestic prospects he rashly added a confident assessment of the outlook for the balance of payments. The large deficit on current account in 1975 had already been halved and could be expected to fall further in 1976. The competitive position of the United Kingdom had improved in 1975, the terms of trade were a good deal better and exports were expected to rise at 9 per cent per annum. As if this were not sufficiently reassuring, the Chancellor emphasised that with the exception of the oil facility provided by the IMF, no inroads had been made into the extensive lines of international credit available to the United Kingdom. 'We should thus have no difficulty,' he boldly concluded, 'in meeting our external financing needs this year.' But he was careful to add that 'this depends on our success in fighting inflation and in maintaining confidence in our determination to pay our way in the world.'[2]

In view of what happened later in the year there is a certain irony in the Chancellor's words. Confidence was *not* maintained. But was his assessment of the economic outlook mistaken? Was he too sanguine? Mrs Thatcher, acting as spokesperson for the Opposition, certainly thought so. She fastened on two points central to later events. The PSBR had been underestimated (by nearly £2 billion) in 1975: it was highly likely to have been underestimated again in 1976, she argued, and even if this were not so, a deficit of £12 billion was simply too great. Secondly, the dollar rate of exchange had fallen since the last Budget from 2.37 to 1.87 – nearly a cent per week. That hardly made for confidence.

Yet in many ways things did fall out as the Chancellor had suggested. Gross domestic product is now thought to have increased by 2.6 per cent – below the forecast of 3.5 per cent but about as fast as in any year between 1973 and 1983.[3] The balance of payments continued to improve; North Sea oil began to flow; the volume of exports grew by 9 per cent as forecast. The rise in unemployment slowed down considerably, hourly earnings rose less steeply than in any year in the 1970s, and output per man-hour in manufacturing rose by more than in all the years 1974–79 taken together. The rate of inflation fell quarter by quarter and in the second half of the year was under 10 per cent.[4] Broad money and narrow money were both increasing more slowly than money incomes. Most impressive of all, consumer spending, which had fallen in real terms over each of the two pre-vious years – something almost unprecedented in postwar Britain – hardly rose at all in 1976 when the national income registered an in-crease of 2.6 per cent.[5] These were all helpful adjustments; and so far as they went, they showed that the Chancellor had not altogether misjudged the situation in his Budget.

Even if one turns to the Budget itself and public expenditure, things turned out better than expected. The level of public expendi-ture, which caused so much excitement, was no longer climbing; in volume it had reached its peak, by one measure at least, in 1974–75 and as a proportion of GDP, in 1975–76.[6] By the autumn of 1976, before the IMF appeared, cash limits had taken effect on public ex-penditure more powerfully than was realised. The PSBR had been falling from the beginning of the year and was well below the fore-cast.[7] As for the finance needed to cover the deficit, recourse to the banks over the year as a whole was negligible and sales of gilts to the non-bank public, although a recurring source of anxiety, were higher in 1976 than in any previous year.[8]

The one fresh source of disquiet had nothing to do with United Kingdom policy. It was a renewed rise in international commodity prices from the trough into which they had fallen in 1975. Exports from primary producers fetched prices in dollars that touched bot-tom in the last quarter of 1975 and had risen 22 per cent by the last quarter of 1976, the rise being particularly strong in foodstuffs. The rise in sterling import prices, boosted by the fall in the pound, was 27 per cent over the same period, well ahead of domestic prices. This re-inforcement of domestic inflation helps to account for the rise in re-tail prices of 14 per cent over the year, slightly faster than in the second half of 1975, although some further slowing down had been expected.

Yet in spite of all the improvements in the situation there was a crisis of confidence in sterling that continued for nine months until the IMF gave its approval. It had two aspects that were linked but distinct. One was the British government's need to raise funds in sterling in order to cover its borrowing requirement. The other was its need to raise funds in dollars to cover its external deficit including withdrawals of sterling balances. There were those, as described in Chapter 5, who thought that the borrowing requirement created the exchange requirement. But whatever validity this idea had in relation to a current account deficit in the balance of payments – and it would seem to have had only limited validity – it did not extend to speculative sales of pounds, spot or forward, or to movements of funds out of sterling into what seemed a safer currency. These operated to inflate the PSBR rather than the other way round.

The fall in the exchange rate arose precisely out of such transactions. The notion which seems to have taken firm root that it was difficulties in financing the large PSBR that occasioned the crisis has substance only in so far as the size of the PSBR created mistrust in foreign holders of sterling or reacted on the current account by raising the level of domestic demand, including demand for imports. The government undoubtedly did have problems in financing its borrowing without aggravating inflation. But its difficulties in raising sterling funds were not insuperable provided it was prepared to offer high enough interest rates. It was the difficulty of raising enough in foreign exchange that was the crucial obstacle.[9]

We turn next to ask why other European countries, Italy excepted, should have escaped the exchange crisis that hit Britain. The problems with which Britain was wrestling in the mid-1970s were much the same, in kind if not in degree, in nearly all industrial countries. All had been affected by the world boom of 1973 when international commodity prices shot up at rates not experienced since the Korean War in 1950–51. The first oil shock at the end of 1973 had then multiplied oil prices fourfold and created a major imbalance in international trade and payments. The oil producers moved into balance of payments surplus on an enormous scale while countries importing oil, including nearly all the major industrial countries, ran into corresponding deficits. For example, the rise in Britain's import bill for oil in 1974 was estimated to account for £2.5 billion out of its balance of payments deficit of £3.4 billion in that year.

Even before these events there had been a universal speeding up of inflation. Between the autumn of 1972 and the spring of 1974 staple commodities exported by primary producing countries doubled in price and the price of exports of manufactures from advanced industrial countries rose nearly as fast. What were export prices for one set of countries were import prices for another and the rise in import prices tended to lever up other domestic prices until the rise in the cost of living provoked higher wage demands which, when granted, made prices rise faster still.

There was an initial difference in the response of the United Kingdom to these events. Throughout 1974 Denis Healey had called for the adoption by the industrial countries in OECD of policies to sustain the level of world activity by borrowing to finance emerging deficits. If the rise in the price of oil increased the revenues of the oil producers at a rate well beyond what they could spend abroad, the importing countries should reconcile themselves to the inevitable collective deficit that would result and not seek to escape their share of the deficit by deflating and passing it on to their neighbours. Mr Healey was treated like the fox that lost its tail: his advice was not heeded. 'Most industrial countries other than the United Kingdom,' the National Institute reported in February 1975, adopted 'restrictive monetary and fiscal measures intended to check the rise both in domestic prices and in balance of payments deficits.'[10] These measures were thought to be achieving considerable success 'though at a heavy social cost'. As the National Institute observed in the same issue of its *Economic Review*, 'the world economy seems to be moving rapidly towards the deepest recession since the war.'[11] Unemployment began to rise sharply in 1974 in nearly all the leading industrial countries except the United Kingdom and Italy and in 1975 rose almost everywhere, not excepting the United Kingdom. In consequence, by 1975 inflation was slowing down in virtually all industrial countries, although not in the United Kingdom.

The rapid rise in prices in the United Kingdom in 1974–75, combined with rising unemployment, made other countries feel entitled to look askance at the management of its affairs; while the Chancellor tended to attribute his difficulties to the persistence of other countries in mistaken policies in spite of his efforts to set a good example. After 1974, however, other industrial countries were at least as expansionary as the United Kingdom; and even in 1974, whatever may have been done to sustain activity in the United Kingdom, the falling-off in the growth of GDP from its 1973 peak was well beyond the fall experienced in other European countries. A rise of 7.2 per cent in 1973 was succeeded by a fall of 1.7 per cent (the heaviest fall since 1945) while the typical European experience was a reduction in the previous rate of growth by about 2 per cent. It was slightly less than that in Italy, slightly more in France, and only in Germany was it markedly different, GNP hardly rising in 1974 – by 0.2 per cent – after increasing by 4.7 per cent in 1973.[12] It is true that in 1975 the United Kingdom shows to better advantage with a smaller fall in GDP than the United States, Germany and Italy (but not France). Taking the two years together, however, the swing from expansion in 1973 to contraction in 1975 was greater in Britain than in all the countries mentioned except Italy.

Even before the end of 1974 the rise in unemployment on the Continent was bringing about a change in policies which were reported to be 'increasingly expansionary'.[13] In Germany, for example, where economic policy in 1974 had been 'single-mindedly focused on economic restraint to keep inflation down to a minimum', the government introduced a new economic programme in December to encourage private investment, restore economic growth and reverse the downward trend by the second half of 1975.[14] In the United States, where restrictive monetary and fiscal policies had produced a severe recession, the President had begun in January 1975 to shift the emphasis from fighting inflation to countering recession and was recommending expansionary measures.[15] In France, two-thirds of the government's annual budgeted spending was brought forward to the first half of 1975, Bank Rate was cut and aid was given to the car, engineering and building industries.[16] Other countries faced with much the same problems, adopted much the same remedies.

But there was one marked difference, even at that stage, between the priorities of the Wilson government and those of governments in other industrial countries. Where other countries made control of inflation their primary objective and took expansionary action only after efforts to limit the surge in prices, government policy in Britain in 1974–75 gave clear precedence to maintaining employment and relied on agreement with the trade unions as a means of holding down prices. This proved completely ineffective in the critical period up to the middle of 1975 while the harsher measures elsewhere were somewhat more successful.

One measure of this success is given by a comparison of the increase in wages and prices in different countries over the eighteen months between the first quarter of 1974 and the third quarter of 1975. The results are shown in Table 16. While they should be regarded as at best approximations (especially as the figures are not seasonally adjusted), the table brings out the wide difference between Germany and the United States on the one hand and Italy and the United Kingdom on the other, with France in an intermediate position. Inflation in the United Kingdom, whether of wages or of prices, was faster than in any of the other four countries; and what is more, the fall in output (Table 17) and the rise in unemployment was greater. The picture provided by Tables 16 and 17 is one that financial markets were forming through 1975 and it coloured their apprecia-

Table 16

Percentage increase in wages and prices in five leading countries, 1974–76

	Consumer prices		Hourly earnings in manufacturing		Output per man-hour in manufacturing	
	Q1 1974– Q3 1975	Q3 1975– Q4 1976	Q1 1974– Q3 1975	Q3 1975– Q4 1976	Q1 1974– Q3 1975	Q3 1975– Q4 1976
US	15	7	14	10	4	3
Germany	9	5	17	7	2	8
France	19	12	29	18	−6	13
Italy	29	24	40	30	−3	11
UK	38	18	42	17	−3	5

Source: National Institute, *Economic Review,* 1975–77.

Table 17

Changes in key variables in seven countries, 1973–76
(% increase from 1973 to 1976)

	GNP	Unemploy-ment[1]	Consumer prices	Hourly earnings in manu-facturing	Output per man-hour in manu-facturing
UK	0.3[2]	3.2	66.9	78.9	4.2
US	2.6	2.8	28.1	27.3	9.7
Canada	7.4	1.5	32.1	49.2	6.9
Japan	7.0	0.8	50.6	66.1	11.3
France	6.8[2]	1.4	39.1	60.6	9.8
Germany	2.7	3.1	18.5	26.9	14.4
Italy	5.4[2]	0.2	63.1	87.2	7.2

1. Addition to unemployment as percentage of labour force.
2. GDP.

Source: National Institute, *Economic Review*, various issues.

tion of policies in 1976. Germany and the United States felt entitled in the light of their own success to preach to the United Kingdom and to call for a radical change to what they thought of as more responsible policies.

If we carry the picture forward to the end of 1976 not much

changes. The rise in wages and prices slowed down in the second period but it remained much faster in the United Kingdom than in Germany and the United States and compared favourably only with Italy and (in respect of earnings) with France.

In the three years from 1973 to 1976 (Table 17) hourly earnings in manufacturing in Britain rose nearly three times as fast as in Germany and the United States. In consumer prices the contrast was even greater, especially in relation to Germany where the rise in prices was 19 per cent compared with 67 per cent in Britain. Over the same period productivity, as measured by output per man-hour in manufacturing, had hardly risen in Britain. An improvement of over 14 per cent in Germany, and of 10 per cent in France and the United States, compared with an estimated 4 per cent in three years in the United Kingdom. Output and employment did no better. Having had the biggest boom in 1973, the United Kingdom had the most persistent depression in the next few years. In 1976 GDP was not appreciably higher than in 1973 while in France, Italy, Japan and Canada it had grown by between 5.5 and 7.5 per cent and in Germany and the United States by a little under 3 per cent.[17] Unemployment had risen more steeply than in any of those countries and was continuing to increase when it had been falling for some time in Germany, and more hesitantly in the United States. If it had been the Chancellor's object to preserve jobs at the risk of more inflation, he had been less successful than some countries that made control of inflation their first business.

These contrasts can hardly have been encouraging to holders of sterling or to those contemplating a loan to the United Kingdom. The contrast between the rise in earnings and the rise in productivity tells its own story, particularly when put alongside the corresponding figures for Germany. Germany's deflation may have sent unemployment rocketing but it went with wage behaviour and productivity growth that were conspicuously different in the United Kingdom. It is not altogether surprising that Germany was one of the countries running a consistent surplus in its current balance of payments in each year from 1973 to 1976 (see Table 19). Equally it is not surprising that the United Kingdom was one of the countries running a substantial deficit throughout these four years: and it was this, after all, that made British – and Italian – policy so vulnerable to financial opinion abroad.

What is generally assumed to have moved financial opinion was not the external deficit, which was diminishing, but the Budget defi-

Table 18

*Changes in GDP, prices and public expenditure in
ten industrial countries, 1972–78*

	GDP 1976	GDP deflator, 1976	Total outlays of government as % of GDP		
	1972 = 100	1972 = 100	1972	1976	1978
UK	109.1	178.8	39.3	46.3	43.3
US	108.9	133.3	31.3	33.4	31.6
Canada			36.6	39.1	40.3
Japan	118.2	152.9	22.1	27.7	30.5
France	114.4	146.3	38.3	43.9	44.6
Germany	108.9	125.0	40.8	47.9	47.8
Italy	113.6	183.7	38.6	42.2	46.1
Belgium	114.8	146.0	38.8	44.9	47.8
Netherlands	114.1	143.5	45.6	52.9	54.4
Sweden	110.0	148.2	46.2	51.7	59.2

Source: Cols 1 and 2, *National Accounts of OECD Countries,* Vol. 2, 1950–78
and 1972–82 (OECD, Paris); Cols 3–5, *OECD Economic Outlook,*
No. 47 (June 1990), Reference statistics.

cit which in April 1976 was expected to be larger than ever – at least
in nominal terms. But by 1976 was fiscal policy in Britain so very
different from elsewhere? If we compare the growth in public expenditure in Britain and other countries as in Table 18 the results are
rather surprising.

The increase in public spending in the United Kingdom was, it is
true, rather faster between 1972 and 1976 (in proportion to national
income) than in other European countries, but not by much; there
were some countries, including Sweden and the Netherlands, where
things were the other way round. In those two countries public
spending was higher than elsewhere and grew relatively fast. What is
striking is the divergence between the United States, where there
was practically no increase, and Europe as a whole, where the increase was very rapid. If the comparison is extended to 1978, the
level of public expenditure in the United Kingdom forms a *lower*
proportion of GDP than in any of the six European countries in the
table and had risen appreciably less since 1972. This is not at all the
impression conveyed in many surveys of those years.[18]

If we take OECD's figures of general government financial

Table 19

Budget balance and balance of payments in ten countries, 1974–76
(% of GNP/GDP)

	Financial balance of government			Current account of balance of payments		
	1974	1975	1976	1974	1975	1976
UK	−3.9	−4.6	−5.0	−3.8	−1.4	−0.8
US	−0.3	−4.1	−2.2	0.1	1.1	0.2
Canada	+1.9	−2.5	−1.8	−0.9	−2.7	−2.1
Japan	+0.4	−2.8	−3.7	−1.0	−0.1	0.7
France	+0.1	−2.2	−0.6	−1.4	0.8	−1.0
Germany	−1.3	−5.6	−3.4	2.8	1.0	0.8
Italy	−7.8	−12.9	−9.8	−4.3	−0.3	−1.3
Total of above	−0.9	−4.4	−3.2	−0.9	−2.7	−2.1
Belgium	−2.9	−5.3	−6.0	1.4	0.3	0.6
Netherlands	−0.5	−3.0	−2.7	3.1	2.4	2.8
Sweden	+2.0	+2.8	+4.7	−1.0	−0.5	−2.1

Source: OECD Economic Outlook, June 1990.

balances and concentrate on 1975 and 1976 when the United Kingdom ran its largest Budget deficits, it becomes clear that in those years all the governments in Table 19 except the Swedish were in the red. The British deficits are put at about 5 per cent of GDP in both years. Italy was in much deeper trouble; and of the other countries, Germany, Japan, Belgium and the Netherlands all had deficits at least half as large as the United Kingdom's. In pretty well all industrial countries the government was making an unusual call on the private sector for finance. The United Kingdom government went further than the rest, again excluding Italy, but not so very much further than governments of which a very different view was taken.

To sum up. The United Kingdom in 1976 stood out in several respects. It had suffered a rate of inflation exceeded only by Italy. It had increased public expenditure somewhat faster than in almost all other industrial countries. The borrowing requirement was higher than elsewhere, except possibly Italy. The balance of payments was in deficit on current account for four successive years. The reserves were far below the liquid liabilities that had accumulated in the form of sterling balances. Each of these circumstances was the subject of strident press comment that increasingly fastened on public expenditure and the money supply as the source of Britain's difficulties and looked forward to the dictation of what it took to be appropriate remedies by the IMF.

CONCLUSION

Keynes says somewhere that nine times out of ten when things are going wrong and there is a threat of catastrophe, the crisis is avoided or resolved without the upsets that were feared; but 'we run the risk of the tenth time.' In 1976 there was no disaster; but was this because of the intervention of the IMF?

Since it became clear in 1977 that all and more than the IMF asked for was already in train before it arrived it may appear that the IMF had no more than a walking-on part. The peak in public spending had been passed and the PSBR was heading sharply downwards. By 1978, with the additional cuts on which the IMF insisted, the PSBR had been reduced by the £5 billion that the government's critics demanded. But long before these additional cuts could take effect, the economy was out of danger and on the way to recovery. Enough had been done, even though no one knew it, to meet the IMF's requirements.

Was it true, then, as Denis Healey alleges, that it was all a matter of mistaken forecasts: that if he had been given the 'right' forecasts of the PSBR and the balance of payments, he need never have gone to the IMF?[19] No doubt the forecasts left him no option: if things were as bad as his advisers thought, drastic action and the help of the IMF were both required. Indeed, with hindsight, some writers have suspected that the forecasts were deliberately steeped in gloom in order to procure those decisions, but there is no reason to think this was so. Even if the 'right' forecasts had been presented to ministers, they would still have had to go to the IMF and taken such further measures as the IMF required: financial markets would have been little moved by more hopeful forecasts. What they looked for was the acceptance by the IMF that enough had been done. Nothing less would have restored confidence in sterling.

Without a return of confidence how could the international accounts have been balanced? And without an end to the exchange crisis how could recovery have continued? Consider the position at the end of September 1976, when the decision to call in the IMF was taken. The external deficit was still running at over £1 billion per annum, the spot exchange rate was falling steeply, the forward rate was at a discount of well over 10 per cent against the dollar and the discount was still increasing. In the first nine months of the year the authorities had paid out £3.5 billion in foreign exchange to support the pound and had been enabled to do so only by feeding in £1.9 billion from funds advanced by the IMF and other monetary authorities. These funds had been supplemented by foreign currency borrowing on the part of nationalised industries and local authorities to the tune of £1.35 billion so that over those nine months nearly all the necessary finance had come from foreign borrowing.

If things had been allowed to continue after September as they had in the third quarter, it would have been necessary to find the foreign exchange to cover continuing capital withdrawals in addition to the large deficit on current account. Instead of the net inflow of nearly £200 million that actually occurred, a net outflow of £465 million, as in the third quarter, would have had to be financed. The reserves would have dropped to about $3 billion by the end of the year with no prospect of replenishment from an IMF loan and a current account deficit of $2 billion lying ahead in the first half of 1977. Without the reassurance of IMF approval and without the IMF loan to bolster the reserves, desperate remedies would have been necessary. These remedies would undoubtedly have been protectionist and would have had far-reaching consequences. The repercussions of protection would have affected both domestic policy and international relations. They would have multiplied controls long since abandoned, set a dangerous precedent for other countries, provoked retaliation, and soured relationships with fellow members of the European Community, with allies in NATO and with international institutions like the IMF.

It was fortunate that the crisis occcurred in 1976 and not in 1974 or 1975. By that time the world economy had largely recovered from the oil shock. Production and trade were growing rapidly in 1976 so that the international environment of policy was expansionary. In Britain itself the low point had been passed, so the cuts were from an expanding, not a contracting, volume of production and were compatible with some increase in consumption (although not in 1977) after a period in which consumption had fallen.

The course of policy pursued by the government avoided the extremes urged upon it in an atmosphere bordering at times on hysteria. The rate at which wages and prices rose in 1975 produced a state of alarm, even among the trade unions that were adding to inflation, and created a ready audience for extravagant views. The press in

1975–76 gave vent to doctrines and proposed remedies far removed from sobriety. On one side were proposals for large cuts in expenditure and employment to come into effect at once and without much regard to the consequences. On the other was a vision of Fortress Britain cutting itself off from international trade and investment to whatever extent was necessary to restore external balance. While both views could be put in a form that was logically defensible, they were usually carried to extremes by their respective supporters. The government could at least claim that nothing so dramatic as was urged on it proved to be necessary and that, however mistaken its initial moves in 1974, it had guided the economy through the maelstrom without the disasters that were feared.

A year after agreement on the IMF loan the alarms of 1976 seemed a thing of the past. The balance of payments was in increasing surplus, the rate of exchange had begun its long climb to $2.40 to the £1, and the reserves were five times as large as they had been at the end of 1976. The pound had ceased to be a currency to sell and very much a currency to buy: so much so that the problem of the sterling balances was no longer how to slow down their withdrawal but how to limit their accumulation. The domestic economy, too, seemed under much firmer control. The PSBR, without fresh cuts, continued well below the limit of £8.7 billion set by the IMF; domestic credit expansion had risen by only £1 billion at the end of 1977 compared with the limit of £7.7 billion (for 1977–78) in the Letter of Intent; the rise in earnings was at last in single figures and the rise in prices, after allowing for the effect of higher taxes on tobacco and alcohol, was continuing to slow down. Unemployment, it is true, was still increasing but at the end of 1977 a turning point was reached and a gradual fall began.

If these developments met with less than universal relief and enthusiasm in Britain, they must have brought comfort to those allies abroad who had feared a very different outcome and had rallied to Britain's support. Neither the United States nor Germany may have done all that the Prime Minister would have liked but both provided welcome help when it was most needed. Both attached conditions to their assistance and United States officials in particular included some notable hard-liners who had strong views on what the conditions should be. But without the intervention of their governments and central banks the necessary finance would not have been provided.

There were those in America, Germany and elsewhere who hoped that a changed Britain would emerge, phoenix-like, from the crisis, free from past illusions and able to hold to a steady line of policy. They wanted to see, not just the measures that would put an end to the crisis but a change of heart, a forswearing of what they regarded as economic heresies such as deficit financing and over-expansion of the money supply. They wanted, and ultimately got, Thatcherism. But there was little change of heart in the Labour Party. The Prime Minister might denounce public spending as a way of coping with depression, but he was prepared to back a PSBR of not less than £9 billion. The Chancellor had every intention of restoring the cuts when it seemed safe to do so and the PSBR was back above £9 billion by 1978–79, Labour's last year in power. The rank and file demonstrated all too clearly in the winter of discontent that they had undergone no conversion. Apart from the continued issue of monetary targets (which were rarely hit), economic policy in the last years of the Labour government differed little from what it had been before the arrival of the IMF.

APPENDIX

The Letter of Intent

From the Chancellor of the Exchequer

Treasury Chambers, Parliament Street, SW1P 3AG

15th December, 1976

The Government of the United Kingdom hereby requests of the International Monetary Fund a stand-by arrangement under which for a period of two years the Government of the United Kingdom will have the right to purchase from the Fund currencies of other members in exchange for sterling up to an amount equivalent to SDR 3,360 million. Before making purchases under the stand-by arrangement, the Government will consult with the Managing Director on the particular currencies to be purchased from the Fund.

2. The purpose of this request is to support the policies that have been adopted by the Government of the United Kingdom to strengthen the balance of payments and create the conditions in which it will be possible to get both unemployment and domestic inflation down from their present unacceptable levels and keep them down. The stand-by arrangement will also help to repay external debt now falling due and assist in maintaining orderly conditions in the exchange market for sterling. The Government's objectives and policies, which I shall summarize below, have been set out in detail in recent policy pronouncements, including particularly the Prime Minister's speech to the House of Commons on 11 October 1976, my speeches to the House on 11 October and 30 November and my statement in the House this afternoon.

3. Since the summer of 1975, the Government, with the support of both sides of industry, has pursued a medium-term strategy whose objectives are

to reduce the rate of inflation and to achieve a sustainable growth in output, employment and living standards based on a strong expansion in net exports and productive investment. In order to secure this strategy, the White Paper on public expenditure published in February 1976 (Cmnd. 6393) indicated the Government's intention in the years ahead to reduce the share of resources taken by public expenditure. It is also part of this strategy to reduce the public sector borrowing requirement so as to establish monetary conditions which will help the growth of output and the control of inflation. The Government sees this strategy as the basis for a three-year programme which will firmly establish the recovery of the nation's economy and will also allow the United Kingdom to make its proper contribution to the stability and prosperity of the world.

4.   The two pillars on which this strategy is based are the social contract with the trades union movement, which has already allowed us to achieve a substantial reduction in the rate of price and wage inflation and has brought about a dramatic improvement in industrial relations; and the industrial strategy, through which the Government, the trade unions and the employers are seeking to improve the performance of our manufacturing industry and, in particular, its productivity and its ability to compete successfully in world markets. It is our firm intention to continue the policy of securing a progressive deceleration of inflation through voluntary agreement between the Government and the Trades Union Congress. Under the first stage of this policy, the increase in average earnings was reduced to 13.9 per cent in the year ending July 1976, from 27.6 per cent in the corresponding period a year earlier. Under the second stage, the T.U.C. and Government are applying the present pay agreement strictly; average earnings resulting from this second stage policy in the period July 1976 to July 1977 will rise by something like half of the amount of increase in the preceding 12 months. Largely because of this restraint in earnings the rate of price increase has fallen sharply from a rate of 25.9 per cent in the 12 months to October 1975 to one of 14.7 per cent in the 12 months to October 1976. In recent months this progress has been interrupted because of the sharp rise in commodity prices, the effects of the drought and the depreciation of the exchange rate of sterling. Nevertheless the Government is determined to ensure that the rate of inflation continues to fall. Accordingly, it will begin early next year to consider, in consultation with the T.U.C. and the C.B.I., how this objective can best be pursued in the period beyond July 1977. I would aim at reaching agreement through these consultations in the early spring of next year, in time for the Budget. This will ensure that the gains achieved by the sacrifices already made are further improved and that there is continued progress in bringing the rate of inflation in the United Kingdom down to that obtaining in the other main industrial countries.

5.   Work to develop an industrial strategy can produce major results only in the medium-term, but significant progress has been made in the last twelve months. The current phase of the work is directed to increasing mar-

ket shares at home and abroad, through improvements in industrial productivity and non-price competitiveness. It is the Government's policy to create the conditions in which a strong British manufacturing industry can contribute to the improvement of our balance of trade and payments.

6.   I have repeatedly stressed that the Government aims to strengthen the balance of payments progressively over the coming years as one essential condition for sustained growth and a high level of employment. On the basis of our present projections for the growth of world trade and prices, the Government expects that the deficit on current account will fall from over £2 billion in 1976/77 to about £1 billion in 1977/78, and then move into a surplus of some £2–3 billion in 1978/79. In the coming years the current account will increasingly benefit from production of North Sea oil and gas. This prospect together with continued progress in improving the non–oil component of our external accounts will allow us to reduce the large outstanding amount of foreign debt that has been accumulated and at the same time to reconstitute our foreign exchange reserves. However, I must emphasize that an improvement of this magnitude must depend on a satisfactory rate of expansion in world trade. It is not possible for deficit countries to improve their position unless countries with a strong balance of payments ensure a satisfactory rate of growth in their economies and are prepared to accept a deterioration in their own external position.

7.   The Government is determined to carry through a stabilisation programme which will bring the economy into balance and which, if it is not to produce unacceptable social tensions and levels of unemployment, will need to extend over two to three years. The changes required by this programme must proceed at a pace which will not overstrain the consensus on which our policies for regenerating industry and reducing inflation must depend. The Government is deeply conscious that the present state of the economy has brought a waste of human and material resources. The Government's objective is to break decisively away from the constricting pattern of present circumstances and post–war disappointments. It will therefore keep a close watch on the development of the economy, so that if any further action is needed, it can be taken in good time to ensure that conditions are favourable for the necessary shift of resources into exports and productive investment. For this purpose, an essential element of the Government's strategy will be a continuing and substantial reduction over the next few years in the share of resources required for the public sector. It is also essential to reduce the public sector borrowing requirement (PSBR) in order to create monetary conditions which will encourage investment and support sustained growth and the control of inflation. In the following paragraphs of this letter I will describe the policies which the Government will therefore follow over the next two years: the policies for the second year – the financial year 1978/79 – will be reviewed before the end of 1977, in the light of economic developments and prospects.

8.   Our most recent forecast shows the PSBR in 1976/77 to be £11.2 billion.

This is less than the figure of £12 billion forecast when I requested a stand-by arrangement in the first credit tranche in December 1975. This improvement in the expected outcome reflects higher revenues because of the higher rate of inflation referred to in paragraph 4 above and the improved financial position of the public corporations; and it has also been assisted by the progress that has recently been made in establishing firm control over large areas of public expenditures by the use of cash limits and our refusal to sanction expenditure beyond the total set in last February's White Paper for programmes and the contingency reserve.

9. In the White Paper of February this year (Cmnd. 6393) the Government introduced policies to move resources into the balance of payments and investment by reducing public expenditure in both 1977/78 and 1978/79. In July 1976, it made further reductions in public expenditure programmes for the year 1977/78, of the order of £1 billion at 1976 Survey prices. It also announced a surcharge on employers' national insurance contributions, to become effective on 6 April, 1977, which will yield some £1 billion in additional revenue in 1977/78.

10. Since these measures were announced, there have been periods of instability in the exchange market and pressures on monetary aggregates, which have led to a steep increase in interest rates; these, if sustained, would damage our economic performance in several areas. I am therefore convinced that a further reduction in public expenditure and in the public sector borrowing requirement is unavoidable.

11. To remove this instability, therefore, the Government has decided to reduce public expenditure programmes in 1977/78 by a further £1 billion and in 1978/79 by £1½ billion, at 1976 Survey prices in both cases. Details are set out in my statement to the House of Commons today. At the same time I wish to give the maximum possible help to industry and to avoid unnecessary unemployment. I therefore intend to increase expenditure on incentives for industrial investment and expansion and on measures to reduce unemployment in each of the two years 1977/78 and 1978/79 by £200 million. This expenditure will be financed by an increase of 10 per cent in the duties on alcohol and tobacco.

12. As a result of these measures and of a sale during 1977/78 of British Petroleum shares calculated to yield £500 million, the aim is to hold the PSBR to £8.7 billion in that year. As a proportion of GDP at market prices the PSBR will, therefore, fall from about 9 per cent in 1976/77 to about 6 per cent in 1977/78. If, at the time I plan my Budget for 1977/78, I judge that without increasing the PSBR above £8.7 billion there is scope for tax reliefs and if, as I hope, a satisfactory agreement has been reached with the TUC and the CBI on pay arrangements for the period after July 1977, then I would plan to use the available margin to reduce the present burden of direct taxation. My own belief is that present levels of direct taxation have

proved discouraging to effort and efficiency, and if they were to continue unchanged they could threaten the improvement in our economic perform-ance which is an essential objective of the Government's strategy.

13.   The profile of public expenditure after these reductions and those men-tioned earlier in this letter can therefore be stated as follows. The total of public expenditure programmes for the financial year 1976/77 (excluding debt interest and capital finance for nationalised industries) is now expected to be about 1 per cent more in volume than in 1975/76, when it was approxi-mately £50½ billion at 1976 Survey prices. This latest 1976/77 estimate is within the corresponding provision for these programmes and the con-tingency reserve in the last public expenditure White Paper (Cmnd. 6393). The level in 1977/78, after the measures announced in July and the further reductions now decided, is planned to fall to about 1 per cent below that of 1975/76 at 1976 Survey prices without taking account of the proceeds of the planned sale of British Petroleum shares. The planned level for 1978/79 will also be about 1 per cent below that for 1975/76. That part of total ex-penditure which is due to provision for social security benefits for the un-employed is however subject to a margin of fluctuation according to the actual level of unemployment. The revised expenditure programmes in-corporating the changes which I have described will be published in the next public expenditure White Paper. The implication of the figures which I have given is that the published total for programmes plus the contingency re-serve, but excluding on the one hand receipts from the sale of the British Petroleum shares and on the other hand debt interest and capital finance for the nationalised industries, will be around £50 billion or somewhat less in 1977/78 and around £50 billion again in 1978/79, at 1976 Survey prices in both cases. Capital finance for the nationalised industries mobilised by the Government is estimated to be broadly stable over this period.

14.   I also intend to take further fiscal action totalling £0.5 billion at 1976 prices affecting 1978/79 in order to bring the PSBR for that year down to £8.6 billion in nominal terms; this would represent a fall in the level of the PSBR to some 5¼ per cent of GDP at market prices in that year.

15.   The Government has determined these objectives for the PSBR on the basis of a forecast that the gross domestic product will show an increase of about 2 per cent in 1977/78 compared with 1976/77, followed by a some-what larger increase of 2½–3 per cent between 1977/78 and 1978/79.

16.   In carrying out the annual survey of public expenditure programmes in 1977 and in preparing my 1978 Budget, I shall continue to be guided by the need, which is an essential element in our strategy, to shift resources into the export and investment sector and I shall, therefore, take full account of the prospective growth of output and ensure that nothing stands in the way of this shift of resources. In particular, if the forecast rate of growth from the beginning of 1978 to the end of 1979 is in excess of 3.5 per cent per

annum, I shall – in order to allow for it – make an additional fiscal adjustment in 1978/79 of between £500 million and £1,000 million at 1976 prices.
The exact figure would depend on the buoyancy of aggregate demand.

17.   A reduction in the PSBR will go a long way to improve our ability to
control the rate of growth of the monetary aggregates, and will help to reduce the level of interest rates which might otherwise be an impediment to
increased industrial investment. I have repeatedly stressed that our policies
should not be undermined by an excessive expansion of credit. In the first
half of 1976/77, the growth of bank lending rose much more rapidly than
expected, and this contributed to pressures on the pound. To counter these
developments, a series of measures has been taken. In September and
October 1976, the Bank of England increased their minimum lending rate
substantially and called for special deposits from the banking system
amounting in all to 3 per cent of eligible liabilities. In November 1976, the
Bank of England reintroduced the system of supplementary special deposits
which should ensure that the growth of credit and the money aggregates is
brought under control quickly. The Government is determined that bank
credit expansion will not undermine the stability of the exchange market.

18.   I accordingly intend that domestic credit expansion should be kept to
£9 billion in the 12 months ending 20 April 1977 and to £7.7 billion in the 12
months ending 19 April 1978. I intend however to review the latter figure
early in the financial year and to take account of the prospective financial requirements of industry for investment and expansion. It is the Government's intention that the course during each year of Domestic Credit Expansion (DCE), and of the Public Sector Borrowing Requirement within it,
should be consistent with the intended results for the year as a whole and to
take action as appropriate to this end.

19.   In the year ending 18 April, 1979 I expect the expansion of domestic
credit to be further reduced to £6 billion. This, however, will have to be reviewed late in 1977 in the light of the prospects for 1978/79. In that review
an appropriate downward adjustment will be made in the intended rate of
domestic credit expansion for any reduction in the public sector borrowing
requirement for 1978/79 that may result from the review described in paragraph 16.

20.   I intend to fund the major part of the PSBR outside the banking
system, so that there can be room within these levels of domestic credit expansion for bank credit to facilitate the shift of resources into exports and
productive investment. I envisage that the measures which I have now
taken, especially those to reduce the PSBR, will make it possible to reduce
interest rates progressively from their present exceptional levels, while
maintaining effective control of the monetary aggregates.

21.   For at least the immediate future, the supplementary special deposits

scheme, involving guidelines for the growth of banks' interest-bearing liabilities, will be a key instrument for controlling the growth of bank credit to
the private sector. It may also cause some shift of holdings of short-term
public sector debt away from the banking system, distorting the DCE and
money supply statistics, without affecting the underlying state of liquidity
in the economy: if this happens I intend to keep DCE correspondingly
lower than the targets set out above.

22.   While the exact implications of the targets for DCE for the growth of
the money supply, and in particular for sterling M3, will depend on the
speed of progress in achieving our balance of payments objectives, I am
satisfied that the resultant course of sterling M3 will be consistent with a reduction in inflation.

23.   During the past year the problems of financing our external and internal deficits have seriously hampered progress in achieving our goals. The
exchange market, in particular, has been a conspicuous cause of uncertainty,
thereby undoubtedly delaying the recovery of the economy. The measures
now taken by the Government give assurance that private business decisions can be taken against the background of a clearly defined policy.
Intervention will be designed to minimise disruptive short-term fluctuations in the rate and to maintain stability in the exchange markets con-
sistently with the continued maintenance of the competitive position of UK
manufactures both at home and overseas. It is my belief that this, in conjunction with the continued restraint of domestic demand, a steady improvement in non-price competitiveness and progress in aligning our cost
and price inflation to those of our major partners, will alter the long-stand-
ing trend for the UK share of world markets to diminish, and limit more
effectively the continuing penetration of the domestic market by imported
manufactures, thereby promoting industrial growth in the UK. It should
also help to secure us a much-needed improvement in our reserves position.
The United Kingdom authorities stress their support of the Executive
Board Decision of 23 January 1974, on Consultations on Members' Policies
in Present Circumstances, and reiterate their intention to collaborate with
the Fund in accordance with the provisions of Article IV, Section 4(a).

24.   The Government remains firmly opposed to generalised restrictions
on trade and does not intend to introduce restrictions for balance of payments purposes. It continues to believe, however, that in current economic
circumstances there may be cases where particular industries which are via-
ble in the long-term are suffering serious injury as a result of increased imports. The Government has introduced certain temporary selective
measures in a number of such cases and has stated that it is prepared to consider the further use of such measures where they may be justified in similar
cases which may arise. It will be the Government's policy to reduce such
protective measures as soon as circumstances permit. During the period of
the stand-by arrangement, the Government does not intend to introduce

any multiple currency practices or impose new or intensify existing restrictions on payments and transfers for current international transactions.

25.   The Government believes that the policies set out in this letter are adequate to achieve the objectives of its programme, but will take any further measures that may become appropriate for this purpose. The United Kingdom Government will consult the Fund in accordance with the policies of the Fund on such consultation on the adoption of any measure that may be appropriate. In any case, the United Kingdom authorities will reach understandings with the Fund before 16 January, 1978 on their policy intentions for the remaining period of the stand-by arrangement.

(DENIS HEALEY)

NOTES

Introduction: 'Goodbye, Great Britain'

1   Alan Budd, in Frances Cairncross (ed.), *Changing Perceptions of Economic Policy* (London: Methuen, 1981), p. 56.
2   There are many different measures of the stock of money. The most common measures in use in the 1970s were M1 ('narrow money') and M3 ('broad money'). Of these M1 included notes and coin held by the public, banks' till money and balances with the Bank of England and (much the largest item) demand deposits held by the private sector with UK banks. M3 included notes and coin in circulation plus all sterling bank deposits (including time deposits and certificates of deposit) held by UK residents in both public and private sectors plus private sector deposits held by UK residents in other currencies. £M3, which did not come into use until the mid-1970s, excluded the last of these items. The use of M3 and £M3 was discontinued in the course of the 1980s and other measures introduced.
3   *The Economist*, 19 April 1975, p. 90.
4   *Ibid.*, p. 80.
5   The United States in May 1975 intended to cut taxes by $23 billion and was running a Budget deficit estimated at $80 billion a year (*The Economist*, 3 May 1975, p. 33).
6   *The Economist*, 19 April 1975, p. 90.
7   *The Banker*, March 1975, p. 241. The OECD (Organisation for European Co-operation and Development) countries are Britain, France, Germany, Italy, Belgium, the Netherlands, Spain, Luxembourg, Austria, Canada, Denmark, Greece, Iceland, Norway, Ireland, Portugal, Sweden, Switzerland, Turkey, the US, Australia, Japan, New Zealand and Finland.
8   *The Times*, 1 October 1976, p. 4.

Chapter 1: What's Past is Prologue

1   William Keegan and R. Pennant-Rea, *Who Runs the Economy?* (London: Maurice Temple Smith, 1979), p. 166; for quotation see Karen Bernstein, 'The International Monetary Fund and Deficit Countries: the Case of Britain, 1974–77' (Stanford University Ph.D. thesis, 1983), p. 118.
2   Quoted in Stephen Fay and Hugo Young, 'The Day the £ Nearly Died', *The Sunday Times*, 14 May 1978. A substantial minority in the Cabinet argued strongly for import controls, and the Chancellor of the Exchequer, Denis Healey, certainly toyed with the idea. See Chapter 4.
3   Analogies were drawn between Britain and the simultaneous financial crisis in New York City. Fay and Young, 'The Day the £ Nearly Died', 14 May 1978, p. 34.
4   Susan Strange, *Sterling and British Policy: A Political Study of an International Currency in Decline* (London: Oxford University Press, 1971), pp. 5–48.

5 Kathleen Burk, *Britain, America and the Sinews of War 1914–1918* (London: Allen & Unwin, 1985), ch. 9, and K. Burk, 'Money and Power: the Shift from Great Britain to the United States', in Y. Cassis (ed.), *Finance and Financiers in European History, 1880–1960* (Cambridge: Cambridge University Press, 1992), pp. 359–69.

6 Both the Swiss and the Germans took the position of Britain in this respect as an awful warning and fought against allowing their currencies to become reserve currencies. Germany, for example, does not sell the equivalent of gilts or Treasuries. Switzerland even goes on the attack: in 1966, for example, J.P. Morgan & Co. of the US and Morgan Grenfell & Co. of London collaborated on issuing the first Eurobonds denominated in Swiss francs (on behalf of the City of Copenhagen); among other retaliatory moves, Switzerland reportedly told Washington that if there were any more such flotations, Switzerland would convert an equivalent amount of her dollar reserves into gold. See Kathleen Burk, *Morgan Grenfell 1838–1988: the Biography of a Merchant Bank* (Oxford: Oxford University Press, 1989), pp. 231–2.

7 Robert O. Keohane and Joseph S. Nye, *Power and Interdependence*, 2nd edn (Glenview, Ill.: Scott, Foresman, 1989), pp. 125–6.

8 Sidney Dell, 'On Being Grandmotherly: the Evolution of IMF Conditionality' (*Princeton Essays in International Finance*, No. 144, October 1981), pp. 1–10.

9 Joseph Gold, *The Stand-by Arrangements of the International Monetary Fund* (Washington: IMF, 1970), pp. 7–15.

10 Dell, 'On Being Grandmotherly', p. 10.

11 Bernstein, 'The IMF and Deficit Countries', pp. 50–5.

12 Robert Solomon, *The International Monetary System 1945–1981* (New York: Harper & Row, 1982), p. 43.

13 Interview with Herr Dr Wolfgang Rieke of the Bundesbank, 1 December 1989. Susan Strange, *International Monetary Relations* (London: Oxford University Press, 1976), pp. 112–16. The Group of Ten includes the US, the UK, France, Germany, Italy, Belgium, the Netherlands, Canada, Japan and Sweden.

14 For details see Alec Cairncross and Barry Eichengreen, *Sterling in Decline: The Devaluations of 1931, 1949 and 1967* (Oxford: Basil Blackwell, 1983), ch. 5; Kathleen Burk et al., 'The 1967 Devaluation', *Contemporary Record*, Vol. 1, no. 4 (1988), 44–53; James Callaghan, *Time and Chance* (London: Collins, 1987), pp. 209–25; John Brooks, 'In Defence of Sterling: The Bankers, the Pound, and the Dollar', in *Business Adventures* (Harmondsworth: Penguin Books, 1971), pp. 294–370.

15 Interview with Scott Pardee, 27 July 1989. Mr Pardee ran the foreign exchange desk at the Federal Reserve Bank of New York in 1976.

16 Margaret Garritsen de Vries, *The International Monetary Fund 1966–1971: The System Under Stress, Vol. I* (Washington: IMF, 1976), pp. 343–7. Although many IMF stand-by arrangements had been approved for developing countries, this stand-by for the UK was the first for a large industrial member (*ibid.*, p. 341). Dell, 'On Being Grandmotherly', pp. 12–13.

17 Quotation from interview with Sir Alan Whittome, 25 July 1989.

18 746 H.C. Deb., col. 1322, 9 May 1967, quoted in Strange, *International Monetary Relations*, p. 155.

19 Interview with Sir William Ryrie, 28 July 1989.

20 *The Times*, 20 May 1968, quoted in Strange, *International Monetary Relations*, p. 159.

21 Strange, *International Monetary Relations*, p. 161. Harold Lever, then Financial Secretary to the Treasury, claimed that the Bank and Treasury were 'bitterly opposed'. Interview with Lord Lever, 4 May 1989.

22 Bank for International Settlements, *Thirty-Ninth Annual Report* (Basle: BIS, June 1969), p. 24.

23 *Who Runs the Economy?*, p. 157.

24 'The floating pound was costly for the United Kingdom in respect of both the exchange rate guarantee associated with the Basle Group Arrangement of 1968 and the unilateral guarantee which superseded it in September 1973. The former called for payments totalling £59 million; the latter had cost £80 million before it was in turn superseded in March 1974 by yet another scheme.' F.T. Blackaby (ed.), *British Economic Policy 1960–74* (Cambridge: Cambridge University

Press for NIESR, 1978), p. 352.
25 According to Keegan and Pennant-Rea (*Who Runs the Economy?*, p. 161), 'Market sources at the time insist that the sale was by Nigeria . . .'. However, Denis Healey, the Chancellor, insisted in Cabinet that 'it wasn't true that Nigeria was selling sterling', although he failed to say who was. Barbara Castle, *The Castle Diaries 1974–76* (London: Weidenfeld & Nicolson, 1980), p. 683 (entry for 11 March 1976).
26 Interview with Sir William Ryrie, 28 July 1989.
27 Remarks at the Conference on Economic Policy 1974–79, Oxford, 1 December 1989.
28 Tony Benn, *Against the Tide: Diaries 1973–76* (London: Hutchinson, 1989), pp. 96 and 278.
29 Interview with Andrew Graham, 22 June 1990.
30 Keegan and Pennant-Rea, *Who Runs the Economy?*, p. 31.
31 Kathleen Burk *et al.*, 'Symposium: the 1976 IMF Crisis', *Contemporary Record*, Vol. 3, no. 2 (November 1989), p. 41.
32 Castle, *The Castle Diaries, 1974–76*, p. 181.
33 Leo Pliatzky, *Getting and Spending* (Oxford: Basil Blackwell, 1982), p. 213.
34 881 H.C. Deb., col. 279, 12 November 1974.
35 Margaret Garritsen de Vries, *The International Monetary Fund 1972–78: Cooperation on Trial, Volume I: Narrative and Analysis* (Washington: International Monetary Fund, 1985), p. 464.
36 Information from Sir Douglas Henley and Harold Copeman; *Public Expenditure to 1979–80* (Cmnd 6393), February 1976, paras 14 and 15. The cash limit system excluded social security payments in cash and various other expenditures not under short-term control by the government.
37 See Chapter 7, Tables 9 and 10 (pp. 189 and 195). Responsibility for ensuring that cash limits stuck fell to Sir Leo Pliatzky, the Treasury's Second Permanent Secretary, Public Expenditure. See his *Getting and Spending*, pp. 138–75.
38 According to Castle, in Cabinet on 12 June 1975, 'Denis burst out with all his suppressed anxieties about the state of sterling. "This morning we have had the most severe attack on sterling we have ever had . . . It has cost us 500 million

dollars to hold the rate even here. We have got to stop the slide. I have been talking to the central bankers in Paris and the real reason for this run is the widespread feeling that we lack the will to deal with inflation" (*Castle Diaries*, p. 417).
39 Jack Jones, *Union Man: The Autobiography of Jack Jones* (London: Collins, 1986), pp. 296–8.
40 The countries providing funds included Iran, Kuwait, Nigeria, Oman, Saudi Arabia and Venezuela (all OPEC members), plus Austria, Belgium, Germany, the Netherlands, Norway, Sweden, Switzerland, and the Central Bank of Trinidad and Tobago. Garritsen de Vries, *The International Monetary Fund 1972–78, Volume I*, p. 345.
41 *Ibid.*, pp. 343–9.
42 *Ibid.*, pp. 465–6.
43 Benn, *Against the Tide*, pp. 528–33.

Chapter 2: The Gathering Storm: March–September 1976

1 As Sir Douglas Wass was later to say, 'this increasing internationalisation of economic and financial activity . . . is . . . the single most important structural change in the world economy in the second half of the twentieth century. Its implications for the independence of national economic management are still not fully grasped.' 'The Changing Problems of Economic Management', lecture given to the Johnian Society, Cambridge, 15 February 1978, para. 9. See Chapter 6.
2 'U.S. Foreign Economic Policy Issues: The United Kingdom, France, and West Germany', A Staff Report Prepared for the Use of the Subcommittee on Foreign Economic Policy of the Committee on Foreign Relations, United States Senate, 95th Congress, 1st Session (March 1977), p. 3.
3 Stephen Fay and Hugo Young, 'The Day the £ Nearly Died', *The Sunday Times*, Part I, 14 May 1978, p. 34.
4 *Ibid.*
5 William Keegan and R. Pennant-Rea, *Who Runs the Economy?* (London: Maurice Temple Smith, 1979), p. 161.
6 Pliatzky, *Getting and Spending* (Oxford: Basil Blackwell, 1982), p. 147.
7 *Ibid.*, p. 148.
8 Joel Barnett, *Inside the Treasury* (London: André Deutsch, 1982) and Bernard

Donoughue, *Prime Minister: The Conduct of Policy under Harold Wilson and James Callaghan* (London: Jonathan Cape, 1987) have nothing substantial to add, Donoughue contenting himself with attributing the policy to the Treasury and blaming the Bank for mishandling the technical aspects (p. 85).

9   Denis Healey, *The Time of My Life* (London: Michael Joseph, 1989), p. 426.

10 The journalist Malcolm Crawford, in his review of Healey's book, wrote that 'Later, he blames the Bank of England for allowing the pound to fall below \$2 on March 4, 1976. But it did not fall by mistake: it was pushed by Healey's policy of competitive depreciation to assist industrial recovery. I lunched that day with a senior Treasury official, who talked openly about the policy and its supporters and opponents.' *Business* (December 1989), p. 173.

11 Healey, *Time of My Life*, p. 390.

12 Edmund Dell, *A Hard Pounding: Politics and Economic Crisis, 1974–76* (Oxford: Oxford University Press, 1991), p. 68.

13 *Ibid.*, pp. 40–1.

14 *Ibid.*, pp. 179–80.

15 Interview with Sir William Ryrie, 28 July 1989.

16 Dell, *A Hard Pounding*, p. 163.

17 *Ibid.*, p. 195.

18 Interview with Sir Derek Mitchell, 3 September 1991. Sir Derek also recalled that the Treasury had produced a memorandum in March 1975 on possible step devaluations of 10 per cent, 15 per cent and 20 per cent.

19 Hopkin to Burk, 15 August 1991.

20 Interview with Sir Kit McMahon, 3 September 1991.

21 Quoted in Burk *et al.*, 'Symposium: the 1976 IMF Crisis', *Contemporary Record*, Vol. 3, no. 2 (November 1989), p. 42.

22 Dell, *A Hard Pounding*, pp. 208–9.

23 Hopkin to Burk, 15 August 1991.

24 If it doesn't, *then* there's something to worry about.

25 Comments by Wass, Oxford, 1 December 1989.

26 Hopkin to Burk, 15 August 1991. For the importance of capital flows see Chapter 6, pp. 174–6.

27 *The Times*, 4 March 1976, p. 21. In this context a hundred points equal one cent.

28 13 March 1976, p. 73.

29 *The Times*, 5 March 1976, p. 19.

30 *Ibid.*, 6 March 1976, p. 1.

31 *The Economist*, 13 March 1976, p. 9.

32 Bank of England, *Quarterly Bulletin*, June 1976, pp. 171–2.

33 *The Times*, 9 March 1976.

34 Barnett, *Inside the Treasury*, p. 87; Tony Benn, *Against the Tide: Diaries 1973–76* (London: Hutchinson, 1989), p. 529; and James Callaghan, *Time and Chance* (London: Collins, 1987), pp. 390–1.

35 Donoughue in fact says that Wilson told him in March 1974 to arrange for two years' leave from the London School of Economics because he would retire in the spring of 1976 when he became sixty. *Prime Minister*, p. 86.

36 *Ibid.* Callaghan, *Time and Chance*, pp. 386–7, 391.

37 Callaghan, *Time and Chance*, p. 414. 1 January 1976 is clearly a rounding, quarterly date, since no significant support was required until 4 March.

38 *Ibid.*

39 Keegan and Pennant-Rea, *Who Runs the Economy?*, p. 162.

40 *Ibid.* Dell also supports this: *A Hard Pounding*, p. 206.

41 Callaghan, *Time and Chance*, p. 418.

42 Phillip Whitehead, *The Writing on the Wall* (London: Michael Joseph, 1985), p. 184.

43 Callaghan, *Time and Chance*, pp. 415–17; Donoughue, *Prime Minister*, p. 88.

44 Garritsen de Vries, *The International Monetary Fund 1972–1978*, Vol. I, p. 466.

45 *Who Runs the Economy?*, p. 163.

46 Fay and Young, 'The Day the £ Nearly Died', 14 May 1978, pp. 33–4.

47 *Ibid.*, p. 34.

48 Interview with Scott Pardee, 26 July 1989.

49 Scowcroft to Greenspan and to Lynn, 24 February 1976, Box 57, File CO160 – 1/1/76–2/29/76, White House Central Files, Gerald Ford Papers, Ford Presidential Library, Ann Arbor, Michigan. Emphasis in the original.

50 Quoted in Fay and Young, 'The Day the £ Nearly Died', 14 May 1978, p. 34.

51 Interview with Herr Dr Karl-Otto Pöhl, 15 December 1989.

52 Fay and Young, 'The Day the £ Nearly Died', 14 May 1978, p. 34. Interview with Sir Derek Mitchell, 3 September 1991.

53 Interview with Lord Lever, 4 May 1989.

54 *Ibid.*, also printed in *Contemporary Record*,

Vol. 3, no. 2 (November 1989), p. 45.

55 Healey, *Time of My Life*, p. 427.

56 'The Day the £ Nearly Died', 14 May 1978, p. 33.

57 Interview with Sir Kit McMahon, 3 September 1991. Box 113, File UK Loan from Group of 10, June 1976, Arthur Burns Papers, Ford Presidential Library, Ann Arbor, Michigan.

58 Interview with Scott Pardee, 26 July 1989.

59 'The Day the £ Nearly Died' 14 May 1978, p. 33.

60 Interview with Stephen Axilrod, 27 July 1989. The Federal Open Market Committee (FOMC) is made up of the seven members of the Federal Reserve Board, the president of the Federal Reserve Bank of New York, who has a permanent seat on the FOMC, and four other members drawn by rotation from the remaining eleven Federal Reserve bank presidents. Donald F. Kettl, *Leadership at the Fed* (New Haven: Yale University Press, 1986), p. 5. See also William Greider, *Secrets of the Temple: How the Federal Reserve Runs the Country* (New York: Simon & Schuster, 1987, Touchstone pb, 1989).

61 Interview with Stephen Axilrod, 27 July 1989.

62 Nor had Ford been elected Vice-President: Republican Congressman from Michigan and Minority Leader of the House of Representatives, Ford had been chosen by President Nixon to succeed Vice-President Spiro Agnew, who was forced to resign in December 1973 because of allegations of bribery.

63 Kenneth W. Thompson (ed.), *The Ford Presidency: Twenty-two Intimate Perspectives of Gerald R. Ford* (Lanhan: University Press of America, 1988).

64 Fay and Young, 'The Day the £ Nearly Died', 14 May 1978, p. 35

65 Interview with Scott Pardee, 26 July 1989.

66 Box 113, File UK Loan from Group of 10, June 1976, Burns Papers.

67 'Passage the Chancellor proposes to include in his speech today. It is wrong to suggest that there is any reluctance on the part of the United States authorities to provide $2 billion as part of an international operation. On the contrary, U.S. was helpful in putting the package together. Distribution of the amount between the Treasury and the Federal Reserve is an internal matter, but in this connection it is relevant to recall that in a number of previous support operations the U.S. contribution has been divided between the Federal Reserve System and an agency of the Government.' *Ibid.*, Burns Papers.

68 'The Day the £ Nearly Died', 14 May 1978, p. 33.

69 Interview with Sir Kit McMahon, 3 September 1991.

70 H.C. Deb. 912, col. 915, 7 June 1976.

71 Interview with Scott Pardee, 26 July 1989.

72 Box 113, File UK Loan from Group of 10, June 1976, Burns Papers. This concern about liquidity is very odd, given the change in M3.

73 *Ibid.*: notes by Scott Pardee on cable from Bank of England, 6 June 1976.

74 Garritsen de Vries, *International Monetary Fund 1972–1978. Vol. I*, p. 25; interview with Scott Pardee, 26 July 1989; Reuter announcement, 7 June 1976, in Box 113, File UK Loan from Group of 10, June 1976, Burns Papers.

75 'The Day the £ Nearly Died', 14 May 1978, p. 35.

76 Healey, *Time of My Life*, p. 427.

77 Dell, *A Hard Pounding*, pp. 225, and 223 for quote.

78 *Ibid.*, p. 222.

79 From the private political diaries and papers of Tony Benn, 2 July 1976, in the Benn Archives, London (hereafter Manuscript Diary).

80 *Ibid.*

81 Benn, *Against the Tide*, pp. 588–9.

82 Donoughue has noted that during Callaghan's first month as prime minister, the whole of the year's contingency reserve had been allocated to various spending programmes. *Prime Minister*, p. 88.

83 According to Leo Pliatzky, 'the factors which had influenced the Treasury to go for public expenditure cuts were first that the Governor of the Bank of England had been in two or three times in June and demanded £3 billion's worth of cuts immediately, and second, that the Treasury was deeply wounded by the general charge that public expenditure was out of control.' Benn, *Against the Tide*, entry for 9 July 1976, p. 593.

84 *Ibid.*, p. 591.

85 *Inside the Treasury*, p. 89.

86 Benn, Manuscript Diary, entry for 6 July 1976.

87 Ibid.

88 Barnett, Inside the Treasury, p. 90.

89 Ibid., pp. 91–3. Although he says the Cabinet took place on 13 July, Benn's Manuscript Diary gives the date as 15 July.

90 Interview with Sir Derek Mitchell, 3 September 1991.

91 Barnett, Inside the Treasury, pp. 93–5.

92 'The Day the £ Nearly Died', 14 May 1978, p. 35.

93 Benn, Manuscript Diary, 2 August 1976.

94 Garritsen de Vries, International Monetary Fund 1972–1978. Vol. I, p. 467.

95 Interview with Sir Derek Mitchell, 3 September 1991.

96 Public sector debt is made up of central government debt, such as Treasury bills, gilt-edged stock, National Savings and tax instruments, and local authority debt.

97 The dollar value of all the balances (not just those held by OPEC countries) declined from $14.8 billion at the end of December 1975 to $10.3 billion at the end of September 1976. David H. Howard, 'Sterling Balances', 22 November 1976, Box 113, File UK General November 1976–1977, Burns Papers.

98 Bank of England, Quarterly Bulletin (December 1976), p. 428.

99 Interview with Jeremy Wormell, who in 1976 was Head of Research, Pember & Boyle (gilt brokers). Gold's book was published by the IMF in Washington, 1970. Other evidence supports this, and indeed, extends it beyond the gilts sector. The Staff Report for the Committee on Foreign Relations noted that 'during this period [roughly March to October 1976], it was ... becoming difficult for Britain to resort to the commercial banking sector for new credits ... [T]he international banks have become increasingly reluctant to provide additional new credits.'

100 Interview with Scott Pardee, 26 July 1989.

101 There were technical reasons for this, including an Irish bank strike and the continuing rise in international commodity prices.

102 Interview with Jeremy Wormell, 12 September 1991.

103 Bank of England, Quarterly Bulletin (October 1976), p. 429.

104 Keegan and Pennant-Rea, Who Runs the Economy?, p. 165.

105 Time and Chance, p. 422.

106 Figures from Federal Reserve Board papers show intervention supplies of dollars provided to the market to the extent of $675 million in September, $372 million in October and $112 million in the first three weeks of November. 'Economic and Financial Indicators', 22 November 1976, Box 113, File UK General November 1976–1977, Burns Papers.

107 Dell, A Hard Pounding, p. 235; Keegan and Pennant-Rea, Who Runs the Economy?, p. 165; Fay and Young, 'The Day the £ Nearly Died', 14 May 1978, p. 35; interview with Jeremy Wormell, 12 September 1991.

108 Fay and Young, 'The Day the £ Nearly Died', 14 May 1978, p. 35. Treasury forecast from Callaghan, Time and Chance, p. 424.

109 It had been $1.77 for a period already.

110 Burk et al., 'The 1976 IMF Crisis', p. 44.

111 Benn, Manuscript Diary; Dell, A Hard Pounding, p. 236; Callaghan, Time and Chance, p. 428; Fay and Young, 'The Day the £ Nearly Died', 14 May 1978, p. 35.

112 Callaghan, Time and Chance, pp. 427–8.

113 Ibid., pp. 425–6.

114 Benn, Manuscript Diary, entry for 28 September 1976; Callaghan, Time and Chance, p. 429.

115 Keegan and Pennant-Rea, Who Runs the Economy?, p. 166.

116 Garritsen de Vries, International Monetary Fund 1972–78. Vol. I, p. 468.

117 Interviews with Sir William Ryrie, 28 July 1989, and Sir Kit McMahon, 3 September 1991.

118 Benn, Against the Tide, p. 616.

Chapter 3: The Crisis Breaks: October–December 1976

1 Joel Barnett, Inside the Treasury (London: André Deutsch, 1982), p. 98.

2 Ibid., p. 100.

3 James Callaghan, Time and Chance (London: Collins, 1987), p. 430.

4 Economic Trends Annual Supplement 1991 (London: HMSO, 1991), various tables.

5 Denis Healey, quoted in Institutional Investor (June 1987), 68, cited in Edmund Dell, A Hard Pounding: Politics and Eco-

nomic Crisis 1974–76 (Oxford: Oxford University Press, 1991), p. 238. In fact, by October 1977 it was 5 per cent.

6   Denis Healey, *The Time of My Life* (London: Michael Joseph, 1989), p. 431. Dell had left the Treasury and joined the Cabinet on 8 April 1976 as Secretary of State for Trade.

7   From the private political diaries and papers of Tony Benn, in the Benn Archives, London (hereafter Manuscript Diary), entry for 7 October 1976.

8   Healey, *Time of My Life*, p. 431; Phillip Whitehead, *The Writing on the Wall* (London: Michael Joseph, 1985), pp. 190–1; Dell, *A Hard Pounding*, p. 238. Dell notes (*ibid.*) that the increase in interest rates was acompanied by a further call for special deposits, this time for £700 million. The two measures together produced a sharp slowdown in monetary growth in 1976–77 – £M3 grew by just 7 per cent. The sale of gilts in the fourth quarter of 1976 totalled £2,338 million.

9   Stephen Fay and Hugo Young, 'The Day the £ Nearly Died', *The Sunday Times*, 21 May 1978, p. 33.

10 Fay and Young (*ibid.*) claim that Callaghan now decided that with Crosland as his ally, 'he would run the economy'. William Keegan and R. Pennant-Rea state that Callaghan 'seized control of economic strategy' *vis-à-vis* the US and the IMF. *Who Runs the Economy?* (London: Maurice Temple Smith, 1979), p. 167.

11 Callaghan, *Time and Chance*, pp. 429–30.

12 This is a direct quote from the US Constitution.

13 White House Central Files, Box 57, File CO160. 10/1/76–11/30/76, Ford Papers.

14 Callaghan printed the final two-thirds of the letter in *Time and Chance*, p. 429.

15 White House Central Files, Box 57, File CO160. 10/1/76–11/30/76, Ford Papers.

16 *Time and Chance*, p. 430.

17 Fay and Young, 'The Day the £ Nearly Died', 21 May 1978, p. 33.

18 *Ibid.*

19 Callaghan, *Time and Chance*, p. 431.

20 *Ibid.*

21 *Ibid.*, p. 432.

22 *Ibid.*

23 Interview with Dr Karl-Otto Pöhl, 15 December 1989. Schmidt and Pöhl were once very close, and indeed, Schmidt had appointed Pöhl as President of the Bun-

desbank. However, the clash between the German government and the Bundesbank in 1981 over growth versus control of inflation was instrumental in Schmidt's resignation, for which he apparently blamed Pöhl and the Bundesbank. Pöhl's comments now are thus perhaps more dismissive than they might have been in the 1970s.

24 Ellen Kennedy, *The Bundesbank: Germany's Central Bank in the International Monetary System* (London: Pinter Publishers/Royal Institute of International Affairs, 1991), chs 2 and 3.

25 Benn, Manuscript Diary. Callaghan himself had told Benn on 7 October that 'Helmut Schmidt and I are going to have a long, comprehensive financial talk with nobody present from the Foreign Office, nobody from the Treasury, they'll wreck it. But Helmut Schmidt has got $32 billion dollars in reserves. They could fund the entire sterling balances. He's from Hamburg and they all like the English.' Tony Benn, *Against the Tide: Diaries 1973–76* (London: Hutchinson, 1989), p. 624.

26 Benn, Manuscript Diary.

27 *Time and Chance*, pp. 431–2.

28 Interview with Dr Karl-Otto Pöhl, 15 December 1989.

29 Fay and Young, 'The Day the £ Nearly Died', 21 May 1978, p. 33.

30 Pöhl has commented that Germany has two men at the IMF, the Executive Director and his alternate, and one is from the government and one from the Bundesbank, but they alternate. 'They are under instruction from the government, but the government gives instructions only with the agreement from the Bundesbank. There's a contract between the government and the Bundesbank, but in practice there's always conflict. . . . Normally the government usually decides, and we are more the number 2 in that. So Schmidt could have been exerting influence there. If the Finance Ministry says yes, he [IMF representative] has to do it.' Interview with Dr Karl-Otto Pöhl, 15 December 1989.

31 Margaret Garritsen de Vries, *The International Monetary Fund 1972–1978. Cooperation on Trial, Volume I: Narrative and Analysis* (Washington: International Monetary Fund, 1985), p. 470; Dell, *A Hard Pounding*, p. 239.

32 Whitehead, *The Writing on the Wall*, p. 191.
33 Interview with Sir Alan Whittome, 25 July 1989.
34 'The Day the £ Nearly Died', 21 May 1978, p. 33.
35 But not the Foreign Office?
36 Benn, Manuscript Diary, entry for 28 October 1976.
37 Karen Bernstein, 'The International Monetary Fund and Deficit Countries: the Case of Britain, 1974–77' (Stanford University Ph.D. thesis, 1983), pp. 118–21.
38 *Inside the Treasury*, p. 103.
39 Garritsen de Vries, *The International Monetary Fund 1972–1978. Vol. I*, p. 471.
40 *Ibid.*, p. 470. Bernstein, too, emphasises the importance of this set of negotiations to the IMF itself. 'The IMF and Deficit Countries', pp. 488, 518–21
41 'The Day the £ Nearly Died', 21 May 1978, p. 34.
42 Benn, Manuscript Diary, entry for 3 November 1976.
43 Interview with Sir Derek Mitchell, 3 September 1991.
44 Interview with Sir William Ryrie, 28 July 1989.
45 Interview with Sir Derek Mitchell, 3 September 1991.
46 Fay and Young, 'The Day the £ Nearly Died', 21 May 1978, p. 34. They assumed that the writer was Peter Jay, the Economic Editor and Callaghan's son-in-law. Barnett confirms the PSBR estimate of £11.2 billion, which was later scaled down to £10.5 billion. *Inside the Treasury*, p. 102.
47 Dell, *A Hard Pounding*, p. 252.
48 Benn, Manuscript Diary, 3 November 1976.
49 According to Benn, Nicholas Kaldor told him that 'Sir Douglas Wass . . . and Leo Pliatzky were both very sympathetic to us'. Benn, *Against the Tide*, p. 652. This should be taken as unproven gossip.
50 Dell, *A Hard Pounding*, pp. 249–50. Others noted another type of split, a generation gap: 'the younger economists tend to be monetarist and the older ones Keynesians so that there are disagreements about policy within both organisations [the Treasury and the Bank of England].' Alec Cairncross (Diary entry for 25 November 1976).
51 According to Bernard Donoughue, the head of the Prime Minister's Policy Unit, 'in the middle of this crisis I was privately summoned to the United States Embassy for a secret meeting with a very senior official there who said "You should be aware of something, which is that parts of the Treasury are in very deep cahoots with parts of the US Treasury and with certain others in Germany who are of very right-wing inclination and they are absolutely committed to getting the IMF here and if it brings about the break-up of this government, they will be very, very happy." He actually showed me a copy of a secret communication between London and Washington which seemed to confirm this view . . . Treasury individuals were in direct communication with some people in Washington about these developments and the desirability of getting the IMF in and being able to change the basic drift of this government's policy.' Kathleen Burk *et al.*, 'Symposium: the 1976 IMF Crisis', *Contemporary Record*, Vol. 3, no. 2 (November 1989), 43.
52 Fay and Young, 'The Day the £ Nearly Died', 21 May 1978, p. 33.
53 Benn, *Against the Tide*, p. 652.
54 Fay and Young, 'The Day the £ Nearly Died', 21 May 1978, p. 33.
55 Interviews with Sir Derek Mitchell, 12 February 1991 and 3 September 1991.
56 Interview with Dr Karl-Otto Pöhl, 15 December 1989. According to Pöhl, Mitchell 'was knighted and fired', but this was not true. First of all, he had already received a knighthood in 1974. Secondly, he had been offered the posts of Permanent Secretary to Trade and to the Overseas Development Administration, but declined them both. Some years earlier he had decided that he would retire from the Civil Service at the age of fifty-five, and he did, joining the merchant bank, Guinness Mahon. Interview with Sir Derek Mitchell, 3 September 1991.
57 One difficulty with tracing the pattern of events is that many of those participants who have given accounts have treated matters with little reference to dates. It is clear that forecasts changed, perceptions changed, opinions changed and coalitions changed, but when, and therefore why, is more difficult to pin down.
58 According to Bernstein, this was the least

contentious part of the Agreement. 'The IMF and Deficit Countries', p. 509.

59 Garritsen de Vries, *The International Monetary Fund 1972–1978. Vol. I*, p. 471.

60 *Inside the Treasury*, p. 103. Fay and Young write that when the IMF team got hold of the PSBR, 'they, too, reckoned it was too high, and scaled it down from £11.2 billion to £10.5 billion.' 'The Day the £ Nearly Died', 21 May 1978, p. 34.

61 Bernstein, 'The IMF and Deficit Countries', pp. 499–500.

62 Fay and Young, 'The Day the £ Nearly Died', 21 May 1978, p. 34. Bernstein, 'The IMF and Deficit Countries', p. 508. Interview with Alan Whittome, 25 July 1989.

63 'The Day the £ Nearly Died', 21 May 1978, p. 34.

64 He told his friend Pöhl later that his telephones were bugged.

65 'The Day the £ Nearly Died', 21 May 1978, p. 34. Interview with Alan Whittome, 25 July 1989.

66 Barnett, *Inside the Treasury*, pp. 100–3.

67 *Ibid.*, p. 102.

68 *Time and Chance*, p. 386.

69 Healey, *Time of My Life*, p. 389; and others.

70 *Ibid.*, p. 389.

71 Interview with Lord Lever, 4 May 1989.

72 According to Donoughue, the need to include ministers in discussions about monetary matters led to the formation of a small 'mixed' committee of ministers and officials, in which the normal rights of ministerial attendance did not apply. The Prime Minister chaired, and regular attenders included the Chancellor, the Permanent Secretary and the Second Permanent Secretary, Overseas Finance, from the Treasury, the Governor of the Bank of England, Harold Lever, the Secretary to the Cabinet, the Principal Private Secretary to the Prime Minister, and the Head of the Policy Unit. Occasionally the President of the Board of Trade or other officials might attend if relevant. He says that this 'Seminar' met regularly in 1977–79. *Prime Minister: The Conduct of Policy under Harold Wilson and James Callaghan* (London: Jonathan Cape, 1987), pp. 101–2. According to Healey, the 'Seminar' was set up in 1977. *Time of My Life*, p. 450.

73 Fay and Young, 'The Day the £ Nearly Died', 21 May 1978, p. 34. It is unclear if

Callaghan's letter or a telephone message, or both, arrived on 9 November; the briefing paper for the Ford/Lever meeting on 16 November refers only to 'Prime Minister Callaghan's message of November 9'. Brent Scowcroft, Briefing Paper, 12 November 1976, White House Central Files, Box CO160, File PR7-1, 1 October–30 November 1976, Ford Papers.

74 Fay and Young, 'The Day the £ Nearly Died', 21 May 1978, p. 34.

75 *Ibid.*

76 *Ibid.*

77 According to Yeo, the meeting between Simon and Lever was 'like bidding between two bridge players who knew each other's hand'. *Ibid.*

78 Interview with Lord Lever, 4 May 1989, and with Sir William Ryrie, 28 July 1989.

79 Interview with Lord Lever, 4 May 1989.

80 Interview with Sir William Ryrie, 28 July 1989.

81 Fay and Young, 'The Day the £ Nearly Died', 21 May 1978, p. 34.

82 Ryrie, however, remembered the meeting as ending on a 'nebulous note, with Kissinger sort of vaguely acknowledging some of the political concerns'. Interview with Sir William Ryrie, 28 July 1989.

83 *Ibid.*

84 Interview with Lord Lever, 4 May 1989.

85 12 November 1976, File CO160, White House Central Files, Ford Papers.

86 'The Day the £ Nearly Died', 21 May 1978, p. 34.

87 Callaghan to Ford, 3-page letter, 12 November 1976, File CO160, White House Central Files, Ford Papers. The paper is cited here as listed in the catalogue, but the author was unable to convince the National Archives to declassify it.

88 Interview with Lord Lever, 4 May 1989.

89 'The Day the £ Nearly Died', 21 May 1978, p. 34.

90 Interview with Lord Lever, 4 May 1989.

91 Fay and Young, 'The Day the £ Nearly Died', 21 May 1978, p. 34.

92 *Ibid.*

93 *Ibid.*

94 Interview with Sir William Ryrie, 28 July 1989; Dell, *A Hard Pounding*, p. 256.

95 Interview with Fred Bergsten, 24 July 1989. Ryrie's assessment of Bergsten's response was less that he was taking Yeo's position than that he was not going to

take responsibility for something before he himself had the responsibility. Interview with Sir William Ryrie, 28 July 1989. Keegan and Pennant-Rea confirm that Carter and Michael Blumenthal, the future Treasury Secretary, agreed with the Ford approach. *Who Runs the Economy?*, p. 167. Fay and Young point out that Simon had alerted Carter to his fears about what Lever was up to. 'The Day the £ Nearly Died', 21 May 1978, p. 34.

96 Interview with Lord Lever, 4 May 1989.
97 Callaghan, *Time and Chance*, p. 433.
98 *Ibid.*, p. 437. Fay and Young, 'The Day the £ Nearly Died', 21 May 1978, p. 35, for the quotation.
99 It is not clear who initiated this meeting, the Prime Minister, the Chancellor, the CBI or the IMF mission. Methven and MacDougall met with the Chancellor on 9 November, and 'he wanted to know what we were going to say to Whittome and Finch.' MacDougall in Burk *et al.*, 'Symposium: 1976 IMF Crisis', p. 45.
100 Bernstein, 'The IMF and Deficit Countries', p. 513.
101 *Ibid.*, p. 44.
102 Leo Pliatzky, *Getting and Spending* (Oxford: Basil Blackwell, 1982), p. 153.
103 *Ibid.*, p. 155.
104 Benn, Manuscript Diary, entry for 17 November 1976.
105 Benn, *Against the Tide*, p. 647.
106 Callaghan, *Time and Chance*, p. 434.
107 Dell, *A Hard Pounding*, pp. 257–8.
108 *Ibid.*, p. 258.
109 Susan Crosland, *Tony Crosland* (London: Jonathan Cape, 1982), p. 376.
110 'The Day the £ Nearly Died', 21 May 1978, p. 35. Ruth Winstone, Editor of Benn's published diaries, notes that Benn mentions in his notes that Benn, Kaldor and Shore met in the late afternoon. Winstone to Burk, 8 April 1991.
111 Benn, Manuscript Diary, entry for 23 November 1976.
112 *Ibid.*
113 In fact, the National Institute of Economic and Social Research's forecast was for a PSBR £2.5 billion lower than the Treasury had forecast. According to Fay and Young, Crosland had heard about it, and the Treasury knew, but it wasn't scheduled for publication until 26 November. Crosland 'primed his Permanent Secretary at the Foreign Office, Sir

Michael Palliser, to mention it at the next meeting of "the generals," as the weekly gathering of all Whitehall permanent secretaries is known. Somewhat shamefacedly, Douglas Wass produced a copy from his inside pocket.' 'The Day the £ Nearly Died', 21 May 1978, p. 35.
114 This is debatable: Whittome has said that the Fund would probably have accepted short-term import controls. Dell, however, thinks Whittome is mistaken: 'it would have caused a major international row.' Dell to the author, 26 July 1991.
115 Crosland, *Tony Crosland*, pp. 377–8.
116 Manuscript Diary, entry for 23 November 1976.
117 *Ibid.*
118 Dell, *A Hard Pounding*, p. 262.
119 Callaghan, *Time and Chance*, p. 437.
120 Interview with Dr Karl-Otto Pöhl, 15 December 1989.
121 Benn, *Against the Tide*, p. 658.
122 'The Day the £ Nearly Died', 21 May 1978, p. 35.
123 Crosland, *Tony Crosland*, p. 379.
124 *Ibid.* Fay and Young, 'The Day the £ Nearly Died', 21 May 1978, p. 35, for the quotation.
125 Benn, *Against the Tide*, pp. 655–8.
126 Callaghan, *Time and Chance*, p. 422. Benn, Manuscript Diary, entry for 13 October 1976.
127 Benn, *Against the Tide*, p. 657.
128 Crosland, *Tony Crosland*, p. 379. Benn, Manuscript Diary, entries for 1 and 2 December 1976. Dell, *A Hard Pounding*, p. 266, for the first quotation. Interview with Sir Derek Mitchell, 12 February 1991. Interview with Alan Whittome, 25 July 1989, for the second quotation.
129 'The Day the £ Nearly Died', 21 May 1978, p. 35, for first quotation. Interview with Alan Whittome, 25 July 1989, for second.
130 *Ibid.* (Interview).
131 Interview with Dr Karl-Otto Pöhl, 15 December 1989.
132 'The Day the £ Nearly Died', 21 May 1978, p. 35.
133 *Ibid.*
134 Whitehead, *The Writing on the Wall*, p. 197.
135 Fay and Young, 'The Day the £ Nearly Died', 21 May 1978, p. 35.
136 Interview with Dr Karl-Otto Pöhl, 15 December 1989.
137 *Ibid.* Dr Otmar Emminger, the Deputy

Governor of the Bundesbank, accompanied Pöhl to Washington, but he apparently played no role; he had not attended the meeting with Burns.

138 Fay and Young, 'The Day the £ Nearly Died', 28 May 1978, p. 33. Callaghan, *Time and Chance*, p. 438.

139 *Time and Chance*, pp. 436–8.

140 Crosland, *Tony Crosland*, pp. 380–1.

141 Whitehead, *The Writing on the Wall*, pp. 197–8, for the quotation. Garritsen de Vries, *The International Monetary Fund 1972–1978. Vol. I*, pp. 471–2. Interview with Alan Whittome, 25 July 1989.

142 Interview with Sir William Ryrie, 28 July 1989.

143 Benn, *Against the Tide*, p. 672.

144 Garritsen de Vries, *The International Monetary Fund 1972–1978. Vol. I*, p. 472.

145 Interview with Alan Whittome, 25 July 1989.

146 'The Day the £ Nearly Died', 28 May 1978, p. 33.

147 Benn, *Against the Tide*, p. 672.

148 Healey, *Time of My Life*, p. 431.

149 Donoughue, *Prime Minister*, p. 97.

150 *Ibid.*, pp. 97–8.

151 Benn, *Against the Tide*, p. 661.

152 *Ibid.*, p. 662.

153 *Ibid.*, pp. 662–5.

154 'The Day the £ Nearly Died', 28 May 1978, p. 33.

155 Benn, *Against the Tide*, p. 666.

156 *Ibid.*, pp. 665–6.

157 'The Day the £ Nearly Died', 28 May 1978, p. 33.

158 Benn, *Against the Tide*, pp. 665–7.

159 *Ibid.*, p. 667.

160 'The Day the £ Nearly Died', 28 May 1978, p. 33.

161 Crosland, *Tony Crosland*, p. 380.

162 Benn, Manuscript Diary, entry for 1 December 1976.

163 *Tony Crosland*, p. 380.

164 Benn, Manuscript Diary, entry for 1 December 1976.

165 Fay and Young, 'The Day the £ Nearly Died', 28 May 1978, p. 33.

166 *Ibid.*

167 Callaghan, *Time and Chance*, pp. 438–9.

168 Fay and Young, 'The Day the £ Nearly Died', 28 May 1978, p. 34.

169 Callaghan, *Time and Chance*, p. 439.

170 *Ibid.* Dell, *A Hard Pounding*, p. 240. Benn, *Against the Tide*, p. 670.

171 Benn, *Against the Tide*, p. 673. Crosland, *Tony Crosland*, pp. 381–2. Dell, *A Hard Pounding*, p. 270.

172 Benn, *Against the Tide*, pp. 678–9.

173 Healey, *The Time of My Life*, p. 432.

174 Callaghan, *Time and Chance*, pp. 440–1.

175 *Ibid.*, p. 441.

176 Bernstein, 'The IMF and Deficit Countries', pp. 524–5. She added that this was confirmed in a letter to her from a UK Treasury official in 1982. On the other hand, another anonymous participant has commented that from beginning to end the negotiations were about cuts in each of the two years 1977–78 and 1978–79.

177 Benn, Manuscript Diary, entry for 6 December 1976, for the quotation. Barnett, *Inside the Treasury*, p. 105.

178 Benn, Manuscript Diary, entry for 6 December 1976.

179 *Ibid.*, 7 December 1976.

180 *Inside the Treasury*, p. 106. Benn, Manuscript Diary, 7 December 1976, agrees and gives much additional detail on this Cabinet meeting and on most others.

181 Benn, Manuscript Diary, entry for 7 December 1976. Pliatzky, *Getting and Spending*, p. 157. Barnett, *Inside the Treasury*, p. 106–8.

182 Callaghan, *Time and Chance*, p. 442. Benn, Manuscript Diary, entry for 7 December 1976.

183 Manuscript Diary, entry for 7 December 1976.

184 Callaghan, *Time and Chance*, pp. 442–3.

185 Garritsen de Vries, *The International Monetary Fund 1972–1978. Vol. I*, p. 472. Benn, Manuscript Diary, entry for 14 December 1976. Benn, *Against the Tide*, p. 687.

186 Dell, *A Hard Pounding*, pp. 272–4. Letter of Intent, 15 December 1976. The final letter varies slightly from the draft in its wording, e.g. in the two selections quoted by Dell. Donoughue, *Prime Minister*, pp. 99–100.

187 Dell, *A Hard Pounding*, p. 274. Benn, *Against the Tide*, p. 687. Barnett, *Inside the Treasury*, p. 109.

188 Whitehead, *The Writing on the Wall*, p. 200.

189 Arrangements had had to be made to allow Healey to announce the UK measures to Parliament before the Executive Board of the IMF had met to approve them, but the executive directors had been told informally of the main lines of the agreement. Garritsen de

Vries, *The International Monetary Fund 1972–1978. Vol. I*, pp. 472–3.

190 This was re-emphasised later in his address, when he said that 'The stand-by arrangements this time cover a two-year period, so that we can make the necessary adjustment without imposing unacceptable strains on the social contract and the industrial strategy.' H.C. Deb. 922, col. 1535, 15 December 1976.

191 *Ibid.*, cols 1525–37.

192 Dell, *A Hard Pounding*, p. 275. Barnett, *Inside the Treasury*, p. 110. Healey, *The Time of My Life*, p. 432.

193 'The TUC understands the circumstances which have forced the Government to take the measures adopted, and recognizes that the Government has managed to limit the deflationary impact of the conditions laid down by the IMF. It has to be accepted that there was no real alternative to seeking financial support from abroad if the pound was to be protected against continuing downward pressure, the consequence of which would have been even more difficulties on the balance of payments and even more unemployment.' General Council statement, 16 December 1976, in *TUC Report*, 1977, p. 219, quoted in Bernstein, 'The IMF and Deficit Countries', p. 597.

194 Callaghan, *Time and Chance*, p. 443. Benn, Manuscript Diary, entry for 16 December 1976. Simon quoted in Dell, *A Hard Pounding*, pp. 274–5.

195 Benn, Manuscript Diary, 16 December 1976.

196 Barnett, *Inside the Treasury*, p. 110.

Chapter 4: Getting Rid of the Sterling Balances

1 James Callaghan, *Time and Chance* (London: Collins, 1987), pp. 431–2. Damage in this area was caused by an article by Samuel Brittan in October. Apparently Brittan spoke to people in Basle, and then wrote that the Bank and the Treasury were being disloyal to the government by not taking up an offer to help with the balances. According to McMahon, Brittan did not check with the Bank, where he would have learned that they did not take up the offer because they knew that the US would not have agreed to it – and the Bank was afraid that even raising the issue would sour the

IMF negotiations. Interview with Sir Kit McMahon, 3 September 1991.

2 Interview with Sir Derek Mitchell, 3 September 1991.

3 Interview with Dr Wolfgang Rieke, 15 December 1989.

4 *Ibid.* Rieke drew a distinction between not encouraging the accumulation of future balances and positively discouraging it.

5 F.T. Blackaby (ed.), *British Economic Policy 1960–74* (Cambridge: Cambridge University Press for NIESR, 1978), pp. 351–2.

6 Bank of England, *Sterling Balances*, 5 November 1976.

7 *Ibid.*

8 David H. Howard, 'Sterling Balances', 22 November 1976, File UK: Sterling Balances Problem 11/76–1/77 (1), Box 113, Arthur Burns Papers, Ford Presidential Library, Ann Arbor, Michigan.

9 E.M. Truman, 'An Analysis of Two Approaches to the "Sterling Balance Problem"', 23 November 1976, File UK: Sterling Balances Problem 11/76–1/77 (1), Box 113, Burns Papers.

10 Stephen Fay and Hugo Young, 'The Day the £ Nearly Died', *The Sunday Times*, 28 May 1978, p. 34.

11 Interview with Sir Kit McMahon, 3 September 1991.

12 'Comparison of Plans for Dealing with Sterling Balances', 11 December 1976, File UK: Sterling Balances Problem 11/76–1/77 (2) and Paul A. Volcker, 'Possible Approach toward Sterling Balance Problem', 9 December 1976, File UK: Sterling Balance Problem 11/76–1/77 (1), both Box 113, Burns Papers.

13 'Comparison of Plans for Dealing with Sterling Balances', 11 December 1976, File UK: Sterling Balances Problem 11/76–1/77 (2), Box 113, Burns Papers; US Treasury, 'Outline of a Proposed Comprehensive Multilateral Approach to Resolution of the Sterling Balances'.

14 Fay and Young, 'The Day the £ Nearly Died', 28 May 1978, p. 34.

15 Interview with Sir Derek Mitchell, 5 September 1991.

16 Fay and Young, 'The Day the £ Nearly Died', 28 May 1978, p. 34.

17 *Ibid.*

18 *Ibid.*

19 Pöhl apparently visited Witteveen on 14 December, and it is likely that he and

Emminger saw Burns on that visit. Interview with Sir Derek Mitchell, 3 September 1991.

20 *Ibid.*

21 Interview with Sir Kit McMahon, 3 September 1991.

22 The G10 countries would provide SDR 2,560 million and Switzerland SDR 300 million.

23 The GAB calls for consultation using 'the facilities of the international organizations to which they belong', prior to any call by the IMF on the supplementary resources available under the GAB. Letter from M. Wilfred Baumgartner, Minister of Finance, France, to Mr Douglas Dillon, Secretary of the Treasury, USA, 15 December 1961.

24 Interview with Dr Wolfgang Rieke, 15 December 1989.

25 *Ibid.*

26 *Ibid.*

27 Interview with Sir Derek Mitchell, 3 September 1991.

28 Interview with Dr Wolfgang Rieke, 15 December 1989.

29 Margaret Garritsen de Vries, *The International Monetary Fund 1972–1978. Volume I.* (Washington, IMF, 1985) pp. 474–5.

30 The amounts: Belgium $150m; Canada $100m; Germany $600m; Japan $450m; Netherlands $150m; Sweden $50m; Switzerland $300m; US $1,000m; other countries $80 m; BIS $120m. 'Agreement of Participating Central Banks on Main Components of Sterling Balance Facility', 10 January 1977, File UK: Sterling Balances Problem 11/76–1/77 (2), Box 113, Burns Papers. Unless it is hidden under 'other countries', the OPEC countries made no contribution, contrary to the hopes of Volcker and the Fed staff.

31 *Ibid.*, and Garritsen de Vries, *The International Monetary Fund 1972–1978. Vol. I,* pp. 475–6.

32 1923 H.C. Deb., col. 1260, 11 January 1977. To assuage Yeo's fears that Britain might encourage the building up of the private balances as a way of getting access to non-IMF conditional funds, Healey stated that the UK 'would not wish large new inflows into private holdings to be a means of financing' the UK balance of payments deficit on current account (col. 1261). He also noted that France and Italy were not part of the agreement (col. 1266).

33 The terms were 7–8 per cent over LIBOR (London interbank official rate) for the first two years and 1 per cent over LIBOR for the subsequent five years. The Chancellor's comments were made in his 29 March 1977 Budget speech. 929 H.C. Deb., col. 261, quoted in Karen Bernstein 'The International Monetary Fund and Deficit Countries: the Case of Britain, 1974–77' (Stanford University Ph.D. thesis, 1983), p. 605.

34 Garritsen de Vries, *The International Monetary Fund 1972–1978. Vol. I,* p. 476. Richardson to Burns, 21 January 1977, File UK Sterling Balances Problem 11/76–1/77 (2), Box 113, Burns Papers.

35 Joel Barnett, *Inside the Treasury* (London: André Deutsch, 1982), pp. 110, 115–16.

36 William Keegan and R. Pennant-Rea, *Who Runs the Economy?* (London: Maurice Temple Smith, 1979), p. 169. They went on to note that there was hardly any fuss in Parliament in the autumn of 1977 when Healey chose to retain Fund surveillance over British policy. Indeed, 'by the autumn of 1977 the ebullient Healey was almost boasting of the way in which Britain had gone to the Fund; and in his new capacity as chairman of the IMF's key policy committee of ministers he was even preaching the virtues of IMF "conditionality".' *Ibid.*

37 Garritsen de Vries, *The International Monetary Fund 1972–1978. Vol. I,* pp. 475–7.

38 David H. Howard, 'Some Recent Developments in the United Kingdom', File International Monetary Meetings: Briefing Book, 22 September 1977 (2), Box 72, Burns Papers.

39 Anonymous Bank of England official, quoted in Bernstein, 'The IMF and Deficit Countries', p. 587.

40 Interview with Sir Kit McMahon, 3 September 1991.

41 Callaghan, *Time and Chance*, p. 446.

42 Garritsen de Vries, *The International Monetary Fund 1972–1978, Vol. I,* p. 478.

Chapter 5: The Movement of Opinion

1 Sir William Armstrong, 'Some Practical Problems in Demand Management', Stamp Memorial Lecture, 1968 (London: Athlone Press, 1969); Sir Douglas Wass, lecture to the Johnian Society, Cam-

bridge, 15 February 1978 on 'The Changing Problems of Economic Management'; Sir Peter Middleton, 'Economic Policy Formulation in the Treasury in the Post-War Period', NIESR Jubilee Lecture, 28 November 1988 (National Institute, *Economic Review*, 1989).

2   Wass, 'Changing Problems', p. 2.

3   N.J. Kavanagh and A.A. Walters, 'The Demand for Money in the United Kingdom, 1877–1961', *Bulletin of the Oxford University Institute of Economics and Statistics* (1966), pp. 93–166. For a previous, but neglected, attempt see R.P. Higonnet, 'Bank Deposits in the United Kingdom 1870–1914', *Quarterly Journal of Economics* (August 1957), pp. 329–58.

4   F. Blackaby, 'British Economic Policy, 1960–74: a General Appraisal', National Institute of Economic and Social Research, *Economic Review* (May 1977), p. 43.

5   M. Friedman, 'The Role of Monetary Policy', *American Economic Review* (March 1968) pp. 1–17. See also the articles by Friedman, Wincott and Tooby, in 'The Money Supply Debate', *The Banker* (December 1968) pp. 1096–1115.

6   A.A. Walters, *Britain's Economic Renaissance: Margaret Thatcher's Reforms 1979–84* (New York and Oxford: Oxford University Press, 1986), p. 116.

7   This distinction goes well back in the development of monetary theory. It was made with particular emphasis in Lauchlin Currie's *The Supply and Control of Money in the United States* (Cambridge, Mass: Harvard University Press, 1934).

8   Harold Wincott, 'L'Impasse in Britain', in 'The Money Supply Debate', *The Banker* (December 1968), pp. 1101–1106.

9   S. Brittan, in *The Financial Times*, 9 March 1972.

10 T. Congdon, 'The Futility of Deficit Financing as a Cure for Recession', *The Times*, 23 October 1975.

11 Walters, *Britain's Economic Renaissance*, pp. 27–32.

12 Below, pp. 193–7 and 207–8.

13 *The Times*, 20 October 1976. A reply by Lord Kaldor appeared on 26 October, a rejoinder by Ball and Burns on 28 October, and a further letter from Lord Kaldor on 3 November. The Letters to the Editor columns of *The Times* contain more letters from economists at this period than perhaps at any other time.

14 Robert Bacon and Walter Eltis, *Britain's Economic Problem: Too Few Producers* (London: Macmillan, 1976).

15 *Ibid.*, p. 93.

16 *Ibid.*, pp. 84–5.

17 *Ibid.*, p. 15.

18 The 'New Cambridge' thesis was examined by the Expenditure Committee in 1974 (*Public Expenditure, Inflation and the Balance of Payments*, H.C. 328) which heard extensive evidence from economists including Godley, Worswick, Laidler, Lord Kahn, Posner, and Dow.

19 *The Financing of Public Expenditure*, First Report of the Expenditure Committee, Session 1975–76, Vol. I, *Report*, H.C. 69 I, 11 December 1975. Sedgemore's draft was rejected by the Expenditure Committee. But the same arguments were advanced in Cabinet by Tony Benn.

20 As Professor Godley pointed out in a letter on 27 September, cuts intended to reduce the PSBR by £5 billion would have to be substantially larger. If the consequence was a fall in employment, more would have to be spent in unemployment benefit and less would be obtained in tax revenue. Moreover, cuts would take time to come into effect and immediate results could be obtained only from higher taxes and lower subsidies. These would raise prices still more and would do nothing to cause inflation to decelerate. On his calculations, output would suffer by about 10 per cent and unemployment would be raised by 1 million in 1978. To compensate for the rise (and prospective rise) in prices, union leaders would feel justified in asking for a 20 per cent increase in wages even if unemployment rose above 2 million. No one offered a rebuttal of these arguments.

21 *The Economist*, 2 October 1976, p. 11.

22 *Ibid.*, 17 July 1976, p. 95.

23 *Ibid.*, 18 December 1976, p. 10. In its more unbridled moments it even contemplated a cut of £10 billion to bring public expenditure down from an alleged 60 per cent of GNP to 50 per cent.

24 *Ibid.*

25 W. Keegan, *Mrs Thatcher's Economic Experiment* (London: Allen Lane, 1984), pp. 90–1.

Chapter 6: The Loss of Control: The Balance of Payments

1 Sir Douglas Wass, 'The Changing Problems of Economic Management', Lecture to the Johnian Society, St John's College, Cambridge, 15 February 1978, para. 9.

2 In November 1973 the Conservative government limited increases in pay to 7 per cent with an extra 40p a week for every additional rise in retail prices of 1 per cent. This 'threshold' was crossed many times in 1974 after the first oil shock.

3 The 'effective' exchange rate is the rate measured against a basket of currencies weighted in accordance with the volume of trade in each currency.

4 National Institute, *Economic Review* (November 1975), 17.

5 The only official forecasts published were at constant prices. For the Chancellor's reactions see Denis Healey, *The Time of My Life* (London: Michael Joseph, 1989), p. 381.

6 The big improvement in the November 1976 forecast was not due to North Sea oil but to an 'expected slowing in world commodity price rises' resulting in a 7 per cent improvement in the terms of trade in 1977. (National Institute, *Economic Review*, November 1976, pp. 3, 11).

Chapter 7: The Loss of Control: Domestic Economic Policy

1 Keynes would have liked a separate capital Budget that could meet expenditure out of borrowing and a revenue Budget that was in balance or in surplus. He argued for higher public investment when the economy was slack but feared that financing consumption through revenue deficits financed by borrowing would engender spendthrift habits.

2 C.V. Downton, 'The Trend in National Debt in Relation to National Income', Bank of England, *Quarterly Bulletin* (September 1977), pp. 320–4.

3 Denis Healey, *The Time of My Life* (London: Michael Joseph, 1989), p. 380.

4 *Ibid.*, p. 393.

5 See below, pp. 215–16.

6 Second Report from the Expenditure Committee (Session 1977–78): *The Government's Expenditure Plans 1978–79 to 1981–82 (Cmnd 7049*, H.C.257, 1978), p. xi.

7 Leo Pliatzky, *Getting and Spending* (Oxford: Basil Blackwell, 1984), p. 147.

8 *Ibid.*, p. 154.

9 National Institute, *Economic Review*, February 1977, p. 23 n. For 1977–78, however, the National Institute's forecast in November 1976 was £8.25 billion, or about £7 billion with expenditure cuts of £2 billion.

10 Edmund Dell, *A Hard Pounding: Politics and Economic Crisis 1974–76* (Oxford: Oxford University Press, 1991), p. 274.

11 It must be admitted that the *financial deficit* was still travelling above the corresponding figure for the previous year in the first three quarters of 1976 and that the financial deficit, unlike the PSBR, was higher in the calendar year 1976 than in 1975.

12 Sir Leo Pliatzky at the ICBH Seminar on the IMF Crisis, 20 April 1989, reprinted in *Contemporary Record*, November 1989. Harold Copeman, another ex-Treasury official, has provided a fuller note (unpublished) in which he writes of suspicions that 'public servants weren't trying hard enough to limit price increases and that pay in the public sector was featherbedded'. With rapid inflation, cost increases were both difficult to predict and hard to assess as they occurred. For the health programme, for example, you had 'to know the cash expenditure on the health programme and to find the right cost indices to deflate it by. But both these elements were defective. The indices were crude and uncertain, and cash expenditure wasn't known until several months had passed . . .'.

13 We are grateful to Sir Leo Pliatzky for elucidating the changes that took place in the mid-1970s in the control of public expenditure.

14 P.M. Jackson, 'Public Expenditure', in Michael Artis and David Cobham (eds.), *Labour's Economic Policies 1974–79* (Manchester: Manchester University Press, 1991), p. 84. Instead of rising by 2.5 per cent as planned, public expenditure fell by 2 per cent.

15 M. Wright (ed.), *Public Spending Decisions: Growth and Restraint in the 1970s* (London: Allen & Unwin, 1980), pp.

104–5; Pliatzky, *Getting and Spending*, p. 155.

16 Healey, *Time of My Life*, p. 401.

17 *The Financing of Public Expenditure*, First Report from the Expenditure Committee (Session 1975–76), Vol. II, Minutes of Evidence and Appendix, H.C. 69–II, 11 December 1975.

18 *Ibid.*, pp. 212 ff.

19 *Ibid.*, Evidence of F. Jones *et al.*, pp. 225 ff. Shortfalls were a common occurrence and averaged 3.5 per cent in 1972–73 compared with 3.1 per cent in 1976–77. (*The Government's Expenditure Plans 1978–79 to 1981–82*, Second Report from the Expenditure Committee H.C. 257, 1978, p. 137).

20 *Ibid.*, Q. 852.

21 *Ibid.*, Qq. 854, 862.

22 *The Financing of Public Expenditure*, First Report from the Expenditure Committee (Session 1975–76), Vol. 1 H.C. 69–I, 1975, pp. vi–vii.

23 Healey, *Time of My Life*, p. 401.

24 Using the figures for general government expenditure at 1988–89 prices in *The Government's Expenditure Plans 1990–91 to 1992–93*, Cm 1021, 1990.

25 *Public Expenditure to 1979–80*, Cmnd 6393, February 1976, pp. 132–3. The statement in the text is true only if debt interest and contingency reserve are omitted from the total. They have also been omitted from the figures on which other statements in this paragraph are based.

26 Pliatzky, *Getting and Spending*, p. 218.

27 *Public Expenditure to 1978–79*, Cmnd 5879, January 1975, paras 16 and 58.

28 *Public Expenditure to 1979–80*, Cmnd 6393, February 1976.

29 In June 1976 the Chancellor was forecasting economic growth at 5 per cent per annum and expected North Sea oil to reach £1 billion in 1976.

30 Christopher Allsopp in his contribution to Artis and Cobham (eds.), *Labour's Economic Policies 1974–79* p. 26 gives indicators of fiscal stance in the form of percentages of GDP (about £100 billion in 1976). These show a reduction in what he calls the 'structural balance' (i.e. the PSBR adjusted to assume constancy of employment) from 3.6 per cent in 1973 to 3.2 per cent in 1975 and 1.7 per cent in 1977.

31 Artis and Bladen-Hovell in Artis and Cobham (eds.), *Labour's Economic Policies 1974–79*, p. 93.

32 The difference results from a 7 per cent deterioration in the terms of trade (i.e. the ratio of export prices to import prices) of which no account is taken in figures of imports and exports at constant prices. Once this deterioration is taken into account the fall in the other items becomes correspondingly greater.

33 A.A. Walters, *Britain's Economic Renaissance: Margaret Thatcher's Reforms, 1979–84* (New York and Oxford: Oxford University Press, 1986), p. 114.

34 G.D.N. Worswick in M.D. Intriligator (ed.), *Frontiers of Quantitative Economics* (Amsterdam, New York and Oxford: North Holland, 1977), p. 829. Wynne Godley, however, can take credit for forecasting the sharp adverse movement in the terms of trade in 1972–74.

35 W. Rees-Mogg, 'How a 9.4 Per Cent Excess Money Supply Gave Britain 9.4 Per Cent Inflation', *The Times*, 14 July 1976.

36 J.R.C. Dow and Ian Saville, *A Critique of Monetary Policy*, 2nd edn (Oxford: Oxford University Press, 1990).

37 Between October 1972 and May 1978 Bank Rate was referred to as the Bank's minimum lending rate and was 'normally set ½ per cent higher than the average rate for Treasury bills established at the weekly tender, rounded to the nearest ¼ per cent above that rate.' Bank of England, *Quarterly Bulletin* (December 1978), Statistical Annex. Notes to Table 9.

38 The Fed was advised by its staff in mid-November that the money supply (£M3) had grown in the first half of the fiscal year at a seasonally adjusted annual rate of 18 per cent and that only a very tight monetary policy would allow the official target of 12 per cent to be met by April 1977.

39 Bank of England, *Quarterly Bulletin* (December 1976), p. 412.

40 Domestic credit expansion differed from the growth in £M3 chiefly by net borrowing abroad. Thus it was higher when the balance of payments was in deficit.

41 Statement by the Chancellor on 22 July 1976.

42 N. Kaldor, 'The New Monetarism', *Lloyds Bank Review*, July 1970.

43 M.J. Artis, 'Monetary Policy', in F.T. Blackaby (ed.), *British Economic Policy 1960–74* (Cambridge: Cambridge University Press for NIESR, 1978), p. 278.

44 Statement by the Chancellor on the stand-by, 7 June 1976, in Hansard, Vol. 912, col. 914.
45 R.S. Sayers, *The Bank of England 1891–1944*, quoted by W. Keegan, *Mrs Thatcher's Economic Experiment* (London: Allen Lane, 1984), p. 17.
46 For a fuller discussion, see Chapter 5.
47 David H. Howard, 'Monetary Policy in the United Kingdom', 22 November 1976, Box 113, File UK General No. 1976–1977, Arthur Burns Papers, Ford Presidential Library, Ann Arbor, Michigan.
48 National Institute, *Economic Review*, May 1974, p. 17.
49 William Brown 'Industrial Relations', in Artis and Cobham (eds.), *Labour's Economic Policies 1974–79* p. 216.
50 A.J.H. Dean, 'Earnings in the Public and Private Sectors 1950–75', National Institute, *Economic Review*, November 1974, p. 63.
51 Paul Ormerod, 'Incomes Policy', in Artis and Cobham (eds.), *Labour's Economic Policies 1974–79*, p. 62.
52 For an account of part of the negotiations see Donald MacDougall, *Don and Mandarin* (London: John Murray, 1987), pp. 218–21.

Chapter 8: Comparisons and Conclusions

1 *Hansard*, 6 April 1976, Vol. 909, col. 232.
2 *Ibid.*, cols 235–6.
3 Comparing the six winter months of 1975–76 and 1976–77, the rise is estimated to have been 3.4 per cent.
4 Because of a sharp rise in food prices in the final quarter, the retail price index appeared to register an acceleration of inflation which is not evident in the broader index covering consumer goods and services.
5 The rise in consumers' expenditure is estimated to have been 0.3 per cent.
6 Leo Pliatzky, *Getting and Spending* (Oxford: Basil Blackwell, 1982), Appendix Table A1 and A2.
7 That is, as now recorded. The figures issued at the time showed a peak in the third quarter of 1975. In the three subsequent quarters it remained flat, averaging under £10 billion per annum.
8 Excluding the month of December, sales in 1975 were probably slightly ahead of 1976.
9 When bond prices were falling between July and October 1976, sales of gilts were low and intermittent, but the sequel in the fourth quarter, once bond prices had fallen heavily, was a record volume of sales.
10 National Institute, *Economic Review*, February 1975, p. 72.
11 *Ibid.*, p. 42.
12 As usual, it is necessary to add that these were not the figures available at the time. They are taken from the OECD *Economic Outlook* for June 1990, p. 181. In May 1975 the increase in GDP in 1973 in the United Kingdom was put at 5.3 per cent and the fall in 1974 at 0.1 per cent (National Institute, *Economic Review*, May 1975, p. 59).
13 National Institute, *Economic Review*, February 1975, p. 72.
14 *Ibid.*, p. 80.
15 *Ibid.*, p. 78.
16 *Ibid.*, p. 80.
17 All estimates of GDP should be taken with a pinch of salt. According as it is measured from the side of expenditure, income or output, GDP in the United Kingdom in 1976 was either up on 1973 by 1.9 per cent or down by 1.1 or 2.9 per cent. Such divergences are not, of course, confined to the United Kingdom.
18 Sir Peter Middleton, for example, tells us that in the United Kingdom 'public expenditure went out of control for a decade and a half after the Plowden Report in 1961' (NIESR Jubilee Lecture, 28 November 1988, reprinted in National Institute, *Economic Review*, February 1989.
19 Denis Healey, *The Time of My Life* (London: Michael Joseph, 1989), pp. 432–3.

BIBLIOGRAPHY

Manuscript Sources

Anthony Wedgwood Benn Papers, Benn Archive, London.
Arthur Burns Papers, Ford Presidential Library, Ann Arbor, Michigan.
Bank of England Papers, Bank of England, London.
Gerald Ford White House Papers, Ford Presidential Library, Ann Arbor, Michigan.

Official Papers

Bank for International Settlements, *Thirty-Ninth Annual Report: 1 April 1968–31 March 1969* (Basle: BIS, 9 June 1969).
Bank for International Settlements, *Forty-Seventh Annual Report: 1 April 1976–31 March 1977* (Basle: BIS, 13 June 1977).
OECD, *Economic Outlook* (Paris, June 1990).
OECD, *National Accounts of OECD Countries*, Vol. 2, 1950–78 and 1972–82.
Employment Policy, Cmd 6527, 1944.
The Control of Public Expenditure (Plowden Report), Cmnd 1432, 1961.
The Attack on Inflation, Cmnd 6151, 1975.
The Working of the Monetary System, Radcliffe Committee Report, Cmnd 827, 1959.
Public Expenditure to 1977–78. Cmnd 5519, January 1974.
Public Expenditure to 1978–79. Cmnd 5879, January 1975.
Public Expenditure to 1979–80. Cmnd 6393, February 1976.
The Government's Expenditure Plans. Cmnd 6721, February 1977.
The Government's Expenditure Plans 1978–79 to 1981–82. Cmnd 7049, January 1978.
The Government's Expenditure Plans 1979–80 to 1982–83. Cmnd 7439, January 1979.
The Government's Expenditure Plans 1990–91 to 1992–93. Cmnd 1021, 1990.

Public Expenditure, Inflation and the Balance of Payments, Ninth Report from the Expenditure Committee. H.C. 328, July 1974.

The Financing of Public Expenditure. First Report of the Expenditure Committee. Session 1975–1976. Vol. 1: Report H.C. 69–I, 1975. Vol. II: Minutes of Evidence and Appendix. H.C. 69–II, December 1975.

The Government's Expenditure Plans 1978–79 to 1981–82, Second Report of the Expenditure Committee. H.C. 257, 1978.

United States Senate, 95th Congress, 1st Session, Subcommittee on Foreign Economic Policy of the Committee on Foreign Relations, *U.S. Foreign Economic Policy Issues: The United Kingdom, France, and West Germany* (Washington, D.C.: United States Government Printing Office, March 1977).

Hansard, *Parliamentary Debates*, 5th Series.

Secondary Sources

Allsopp, Christopher, 'Macroeconomic Policy: Design and Performance', in Michael Artis and David Cobham (eds), *Labour's Economic Policies 1974–79* (Manchester: Manchester University Press, 1991).

Armstrong, William, 'Some Practical Problems in Demand Management' (Stamp Memorial Lecture. London: Athlone Press, 1969).

Artis, Michael, 'Monetary Policy', in F.T. Blackaby (ed.), *British Economic Policy 1960–74*.

Artis, Michael and Cobham, David (eds.), *Labour's Economic Policies 1974–79* (Manchester: Manchester University Press, 1991).

Bacon, Robert and Eltis, Walter, *Britain's Economic Problem: Two Few Producers* (London: Macmillan, 1976).

Bank of England, *The Development and Operation of Monetary Policy 1960–1983* (Oxford: Clarendon Press, 1986).

Barnett, Joel, *Inside the Treasury* (London: André Deutsch, 1982).

Beckerman, W. (ed.), *Slow Growth in Britain* (Oxford: Oxford University Press, 1979).

Benn, Tony, *Against the Tide: Diaries 1973–76* (London: Hutchinson, 1989).

Benn, Tony, *Conflicts of Interest: Diaries 1977–80* (London: Hutchinson, 1990).

Bernstein, Karen, 'The International Monetary Fund and Deficit Countries: the Case of Britain 1974–77', Stanford University Ph.D. thesis, 1983.

Bispham, J.A., 'The New Cambridge and 'Monetarist' Criticisms of Conventional Economic Policy Making', National Institute, *Economic Review* (November 1975), pp. 39–55.

Blackaby, F.T., 'British Economic Policy 1960–74: a General Appraisal', in National Institute *Economic Review* (May 1977).

Blackaby, F.T., (ed.), *British Economic Policy 1960–74* (Cambridge: Cambridge University Press for NIESR, 1978).

Block, Fred L., *The Origins of International Economic Disorder* (Berkeley: University of California Press, 1977).

Brooks, John, *Business Adventures* (Harmondsworth: Penguin Books, 1971).

Brown, A.J., *World Inflation since 1950: An International Comparative Study* (Oxford: Oxford University Press, 1985).

Brown, William, 'Industrial relations' in Artis and Cobham (eds.) *Labour's Economic Policies, 1974–79* (Manchester: Manchester University Press, 1991).

Burk, Kathleen, *Britain, America and the Sinews of War 1914–1918* (London: Allen & Unwin, 1985).

Burk, Kathleen, *Morgan Grenfell 1838–1988: the Biography of a Merchant Bank* (Oxford: Oxford University Press, 1989).

Burk, Kathleen, 'Money and Power: The Shift from Great Britain to the United States', in Y. Cassis (ed.), *Finance and Financiers in European History, 1880–1960* (Cambridge: Cambridge University Press, 1991), pp. 360–69.

Burk, Kathleen, *et al.*, 'The 1967 Devaluation', *Contemporary Record*, Vol. 1, no. 4 (1988), pp. 44–53.

Burk, Kathleen, *et al.*, 'Symposium: 1976 IMF Crisis', *Contemporary Record*, Vol. 3, no. 2 (November 1989), 39–45.

Cairncross, Alec and Eichengreen, Barry, *Sterling in Decline: the Devaluations of 1931, 1949 and 1967* (Oxford: Basil Blackwell, 1983).

Cairncross, F. (ed.), *Changing Perceptions of Economic Policy* (London: Methuen, 1981).

Callaghan, James, *Time and Chance* (London: Collins, 1987).

Castle, Barbara, *The Castle Diaries 1974–76* (London: Weidenfeld & Nicolson, 1980).

Congdon, T., 'The Futility of Deficit Financing as a Cure for Recession', *The Times*, 23 October 1975.

Cooper, R.N., 'External Constraints on European Growth', in Lawrence, R.Z. and Schultz, C.L. (eds.), *Barriers to European Growth* (Washington: The Brookings Institution, 1987).

Cripps, F. and Godley, W.A.H., 'Control of Imports as a Means to Full Employment and the Expansion of World Trade', *Cambridge Journal of Economics*, No. 2 (1978), pp. 327–334.

Cripps, F., Fetherston, M., and Godley, W., 'What is Left of "New Cambridge"?', *Cambridge Economic Policy Review*, No. 2 (1976), pp. 46–49.

Crosland, Susan, *Tony Crosland* (London: Jonathan Cape, 1982).

Currie, L., *The Supply and Control of Money in the United States* (Cambridge, Mass.: Harvard University Press, 1934).

Dean, A.J.H., 'Earnings in the Public and Private Sectors, 1960–75', National Institute, *Economic Review*, November 1975, pp. 60–70.

Dean, A.J.H., 'Public and Private Sector Manual Workers' Pay, 1970–1977', National Institute, *Economic Review*, November 1977, pp. 62–66.

Dell, Edmund, *A Hard Pounding: Politics and Economic Crisis 1974–76* (Oxford: Oxford University Press, 1991).

Dell, Sidney, 'On Being Grandmotherly: The Evolution of IMF Conditionality', *Princeton Essays in International Finance*, No. 144 (October 1981).

Donoughue, B., *Prime Minister: The Conduct of Policy under Harold Wilson and James Callaghan* (London: Jonathan Cape, 1987).

Dow, J.R.C. and Saville, Ian, *A Critique of Monetary Policy*, 2nd edn (Oxford: Oxford University Press, 1990).

Downton, C.V., 'The Trend in National Debt in Relation to National Income', in Bank of England, *Quarterly Bulletin* (September 1977), pp. 320–4.

Fay, S. and Young, H., 'The Day the £ Nearly Died', *The Sunday Times*, 14, 21 and 28 May 1978.

Flemming, J., *Inflation* (Oxford: Oxford University Press, 1976).

Friedman, M., 'The Role of Monetary Policy', *American Economic Review* (March 1968), pp. 1–17.

Friedman, M., 'Taxes, Money and Stabilisation' in 'The Money Supply Debate', *The Banker* (December 1968), pp. 1096–1101.

Gardner, N., *Decade of Discontent* (Oxford: Basil Blackwell, 1987).

Garritsen de Vries, M., *The International Monetary Fund 1966–1971: The System under Stress*, 2 vols (Washington: IMF, 1976).

Garritsen de Vries, M., *The International Monetary Fund 1972–1978: Cooperation on Trial*, 3 vols (Washington: IMF, 1985).

Gold, Joseph, *The Stand-By Arrangements of the International Monetary Fund* (Washington: IMF, 1970).

Hall, M., *Monetary Policy since 1971* (London: Macmillan, 1983).

Healey, Denis, *The Time of My Life* (London: Michael Joseph, 1989).

Heclo, Hugh and Wildavsky, Aaron, *The Private Government of Public Money*, 2nd edition (London: Macmillan, 1981).

Henry, S.G.B. and Ormerod, P.A., 'Incomes Policy and Wage Inflation: Empirical Evidence for the UK, 1961–1977', National Institute, *Economic Review*, August 1978, pp. 31–39.

Hicks, J.R., *A Market Theory of Money* (Oxford: Clarendon Press, 1990).

Higonnet, R.F., 'Bank Deposits in the United Kingdom 1870–1914', *Quarterly Journal of Economics* (August 1957), pp. 329–367.

Holmes, M. *The Labour Government 1974–79: Political Aims and Economic Reality* (London: Macmillan, 1985).

'Inflation', *Oxford Review of Economic Policy*, Vol. 6, no. 1 (1990).

Jackson, P.M., 'Public Expenditure', in Artis and Cobham (eds.), *Labour's Economic Policies 1974–79*.

Jones, Jack, *Union Man: The Autobiography of Jack Jones* (London: Collins, 1986).

Kaldor, N., 'The New Monetarism' *Lloyds Bank Review* (July 1970), pp. 1–19.

Kaldor, N., *The Scourge of Monetarism* (Oxford: Oxford University Press, 1982).

Kavanagh, N.J. and Walters, A.A., 'The Demand for Money in the United Kingdom, 1877–1961', *Bulletin of the Oxford Institute of Economics and Statistics* (May 1966), pp. 93–106.

Keegan, W., *Mrs Thatcher's Economic Experiment* (London: Allen Lane, 1984).

Keegan, W. and Pennant-Rea, R., *Who Runs the Economy?* (London: Maurice Temple Smith, 1979).

Kennedy, Ellen, *The Bundesbank: Germany's Central Bank in the International Monetary System* (London: Pinter Publishers/Royal Institute of International Affairs, 1991).

Keohane, Robert O. and Nye, Joseph S., *Power and Interdependence*, 2nd edn. (Glenview, Ill.: Scott, Foresman, 1989).

Keynes, J.M., *The General Theory of Employment, Interest and Money* (London: Macmillan, 1936).

Laidler, D., 'Monetarism: An Interpretation and an Assessment', *Economic Journal*, Vol. 91 (March 1981), pp. 1–29.

MacDougall, Donald, *Don and Mandarin* (London: John Murray, 1987).

Matthews, R.C.O.M., 'Why Has Britain Had Full Employment Since the War?', *Economic Journal*, Vol. 78 (1968), pp. 555–69.

Maunder, P. (ed.), *The British Economy in the 1970s* (London: Heinemann, 1980).

Middleton, P., 'Economic Policy Formulation in the Treasury in the Post-War Period', National Institute, *Economic Review* (February 1989), pp. 45–51.

Ormerod, P., 'Incomes Policy', in Artis and Cobham (eds.), *Labour's Economic Policies 1974–79*.

Parsons, D. Wayne, *The Power of the Financial Press* (Aldershot: Edward Elgar, 1989).

Pliatzky, L., *Getting and Spending*, revised edn (Oxford: Basil Blackwell, 1982 and 1984).

Poensgen, A., 'Britain and West Germany since 1973 – Bilateral Relations within a Multilateral Framework', Oxford University M. Phil. thesis, 1985.

Rees-Mogg, W., 'How a 9.4 Per Cent Excess Money Supply Gave Britain 9.4 Per Cent Inflation', *The Times*, 14 July 1976.

Reid, M., *The Secondary Banking Crisis 1973–75* (London: Macmillan, 1982).

Simon, W.E., *A Time for Truth* (New York: Reader's Digest Press/McGraw-Hill, 1978).

Solomon, R., *The International Monetary System 1945–81* (New York: Harper & Row, 1982).

Strange, Susan, *International Monetary Relations* (London: Oxford University Press, 1976).

Strange, Susan, *Sterling and British Policy: A Political Study of an International Currency in Decline* (London: Oxford University Press, 1971).

Tew, J.H.B., *The Evolution of the International Monetary System 1945–1989* (London: Hutchinson, 1985).

Thompson, Kenneth W. (ed.), *The Ford Presidency: Twenty-two Intimate Perspectives of Gerald R. Ford* (Lanhan: University Press of America, 1988).

Tooby, F.W., 'Too Much Liquidity' in 'The Money Supply Debate', *The Banker* (December 1968), pp. 1106–1115.

Walters, A.A., *Britain's Economic Renaissance: Margaret Thatcher's Reforms 1979–84* (New York and Oxford: Oxford University Press, 1986).

Wass, Douglas, 'The Changing Problems of Economic Management', Lecture to the Johnian Society, Cambridge, 15 February 1978.

Whitehead, P., *The Writing on the Wall* (London: Michael Joseph, 1985).

Wilson, J.H., *Final Term: The Labour Government 1974–76* (London: Weidenfeld & Nicolson and Michael Joseph, 1979).

Wincott, H., 'L'Impasse in Britain', in 'The Money Supply Debate', *The Banker* (December 1968), pp. 1101–1106.

Worswick, G.D.N., 'Note on Professor A.A. Walter's Paper' in M.D. Intriligator (ed.), *Frontiers of Quantitative Economics: Papers Presented to the Third World Congress of the Econometric Society*, Vol. III B (Amsterdam, New York and Oxford: North Holland, 1977), pp. 827–29.

Wright, M. (ed.), *Public Spending Decisions: Growth and Restraint in the 1970s* (London: Allen & Unwin, 1980).

Newspapers and Periodicals

Annual Abstracts of Statistics
Annual Register
Autumn Statement, Annual
The Banker
Banker's Magazine
Economic Trends
Economic Trends Annual Supplement 1981 and *1990*
The Economist
Financial Statement and Budget Report, Annual
Financial Statistics
The Financial Times
Main Economic Indicators (OECD)
The Sunday Times
The Times
The Wall Street Journal

Interviews

Stephen Axilrod
Fred Bergsten
David Finch
Andrew Graham
Lord Lever
Sir Christopher (Kit) McMahon
Sir Derek Mitchell
Scott Pardee
Sir Leo Pliatzky
Dr Karl-Otto Pöhl
Dr Wolfgang Rieke
Sir William Ryrie
Sir Alan Whittome
Jeremy Wormell

INDEX